£14.99

A schooling in 'Eng

Critical episodes in the struggle to shape
literary and cultural studies

JOHN DIXON

Open University Press
Milton Keynes • Philadelphia

Open University Press
Celtic Court
22 Ballmoor
Buckingham
MK18 1XW

and
1900 Frost Road, Suite 101
Bristol, PA 19007, US

First Published 1991

Copyright © John Dixon 1991

All rights reserved. No part of this publication may be
reproduced, stored in a retrieval system or transmitted in
any form or by any means, without written permission from the
publisher.

British Library Cataloguing-in-Publication Data

Dixon, John
   A schooling in English: Critical episodes in the
   struggle to shape literary and cultural studies.
   I. Title
   820.71

   ISBN 0-335-09322-1
   ISBN 0-335-09321-3 pbk

Library of Congress Cataloging-in-Publication Data

Dixon, John, 1928–
   A schooling in English : critical episodes in the struggle to
  shape literary and cultural studies / John Dixon.
     p. cm.
   Includes index.
   ISBN 0-335-09322-1 (hb) . – – ISBN 0-335-09321-3 (pb)
     1. English philology–Study and teaching (Higher)–Great Britain–
History–19th century. 2. English philology–Study and teaching
(Higher)–Great Britain–History–20th century. I. Title.
PE68.G5D58   1991
820.71'141'0904–dc20   91-14737
                                                                CIP

Typeset by Stanford Desktop Publishing Services, Milton Keynes
Printed in Great Britain by Biddles Limited, Guildford and Kings Lynn

To my mother and father
Janet Crosby and Leslie Dixon

Contents

Acknowledgements		ix
Foreword	**Placing academic subjects, culturally and historically**	1
	A goal for theory	1
	The need to analyse institutional structures	3
	A study of conflict, contradiction and difference	4
	Oppositional networks and relations across classes	6
	Constructing subjects through teaching and learning practices	7
	Aims for a book of this kind	8
Part I	**The University Extension 1867–92**	11
Chapter 1	**The democratic movement for a peripatetic university**	13
	The agitation for radical reform	13
	Women learn to combine – and men join them	14
	The breaking down of intellectual caste	17
	Liverpool: pioneer work by city professors	20
	Loyalty to the commonwealth of workers, men and women	22
Chapter 2	**Programmes and practices for a new subject**	27
	Subjects beyond university structures	27
	Studying textual annotations or the dramatic poem?	29
	Constraints and scope in the definition of 'Literature' courses	32
	An evolutionary study of Literature	35

vi *A schooling in 'English'*

Chapter 3	**Efforts to theorise teaching and learning**	37
	Theoretical questions raised by dramatic readings	37
	Imagining the effect of every scene	39
	Focus on the poem, or on the reflective product?	42
	Studying a concrete struggle, not a moral theory	44
	Making the whole intelligible and significant	46
Chapter 4	**Inventing discourses for a new project**	48
	Evidence for new discursive strategies	48
	Actors (and directors) studying the parts	49
	Vivid, gigantic images and the unconscious mind	53
	Discursive strategies, social constraints – and achievements in retrospect	56
Chapter 5	**Change at the centre of academic power**	60
	Archaic structures face competitive pressures	60
	The new institutional framing	62
	Maintaining the old standards: the exam papers	64
	English Language and philological notes	64
	Set 'Texts' and 'English Authors' (1896 titles)	65
	A knowledge of History, the Literature fitting into it?	67
Inter-chapter 6	**Literature and society: a different view**	69
Part II	**Cambridge 1919–29**	77
Chapter 7	**A space – and demand – for reconstruction**	79
	A deluge that would sweep away many landmarks	79
	Resistance and ideological conflict in Cambridge	80
	Improvising a new 'English' course	82
	Contributions of the teacher recruits	83
	Forces structuring innovation	85
Chapter 8	**New directions of theoretical interest**	88
	Opening up options for research	88
	The challenge of a new approach to language – in use	91
	Signs and their interpreters	92
	Limits and potentials in their modelling	95
	Adapting the model for Criticism	97
	A dynamic model of reading	100

Contents vii

Chapter 9	**Experimental investigations in an English course**	103
	Teaching, investigating and learning	103
	The signs and their potential	106
	The character of various misinterpretations	108
	Criticism and ideological field-work	111
	Discriminating among poems	117

Chapter 10	**New discursive options and theories**	119
	Discourse, knowledge and institutional forms	119
	A context for discovery	120
	Didactic or collaborative investigation?	122
	Scope for 'original composition'?	123
	Theorising functions of critical discourse	125

Chapter 11	**A brake on innovation, despite new demands**	129
	Changing structures of degrees and power	129
	Retrospect and new questions	131

Inter-chapter 12	**A revolutionary theoretical alternative**	135
	Language, psychology and culture	135
	From modelling monologue to modelling dialogue	136
	Dialogue, inner speech and active response	139
	Experience, consciousness and social evaluations	141
	Reading, culture and evaluation	143

Part III	**Restructuring an elite system 1960–79**	145

Chapter 13	**Pressures for radical change in education**	147
	The Space Race, telecommunications and curricular reform	147
	Rejecting a system biased towards exclusion	149
	Schoolteachers undertaking the reform of English	150
	The initial challenges for teaching and learning	154

Chapter 14	**Theoretical guidance for new approaches**	158
	Setting directions for research	158
	An international seminar on English	159
	Constructing a theory of (student) writing	162
	Social transactions between journalists and readers	166
	Reading for social and historical meaning	168

Chapter 15 A second phase: rebellions, challenges and liberation — 172
Student rebellions — 172
Reshaping the social sciences — 173
Women: a new consciousness of themselves in the world — 176
Academic bases and divided labours — 179
Scope and constraint in teaching experiments — 181
The lack of an institutional centre — 183

Chapter 16 Into dialogue, but against the grain — 185
Theoretical gaps and a shift of focus at CCCS — 185
Making meaning, socially constructing, and interacting — 186
Learning how to mean — 188
How to understand conversations – and reading — 191

Chapter 17 Reading as dialogue in a social context — 194
Readers construct – and texts constrain — 194
A dialogic 'secondary' response — 196
Social reception and production of art — 199
Displacements, contradictions and tensions in reading — 201
Selecting 'texts' and studying readings — 202
Potentials to develop — 206

Afterword Lessons for the future? — 209
Placing the cultural historian — 209
Traditions still to be drawn on — 210
Necessary institutional structures — 212

Bibliography and references — 214
Name index — 223
Subject index — 226

Acknowledgements

Professor Ian Reid of Deakin University was probably the first of several friends who encouraged me to undertake a historical review of 'English'; Dr James Squire was certainly another. The focus was at first on exam questions, then on practices of teaching and learning. The move on into institutional structures was prompted by recent discussions with a lifelong friend, Professor Talal Asad, now at the New School for Social Research, New York. Thus, the invitation from my editor, Ray Cunningham, to write a book on the institutional shaping of 'English', happily drew these various strands together.

Once started, I had useful suggestions on Part I from James Britton, Norman Morris, Ian Roxborough and Henry Parris. Professor Russell Hunt of the University of New Brunswick was an ideal dialogic reader of the early sections of Part III. And at a later stage Ian Reid helped me sort out some pretty confused chapters in the course of a lively interview for his Deakin students.

When I wanted to hear the testimony of actual Cambridge students of the 1920s, Barbara Brenchley offered her help. Thus, I was able not only to see Lionel Knights and Raymond O'Malley individually, but to enjoy reminiscences round the tea-table at Jean Stewart/Pace's, with Barbara, Elsie Duncan-Jones and Terence Barnes joining in. Later, as I studied the papers I'd kept from the early days of the Birmingham Centre for Contemporary Cultural Studies, I had a valuable afternoon's discussion with Professor Stuart Hall.

In addition, many students, past and present, have helped to lay the foundations for this work: at Bretton Hall College, Wakefield (1963–81); in the Bread Loaf Summer Schools at Oxford (1984–8); and in the University of New Brunswick's summer schools (1989 and 1990). Above all, it was the wealth of their ideas for investigating reading, writing and viewing – and the excitement they brought to this work – that convinced me of the value of an experimental component in literary and cultural studies.

I am much indebted to all of these old and new friends. I wish I had learned more from them; I still count on doing so when the book comes out. As a retired teacher I am also especially grateful for the assistance of the librarians at the Bodleian Library, the British Library, Camden Borough Libraries, the English Faculty Library at Oxford, the Library of the London Institute of Education, the Harriet Irving Library at the University of New Brunswick, and the New York Public Library. Allan Tadiello of Balliol College Library kindly provided me with a copy of Bradley's 1891 paper.

Finally, Leslie Stratta read the whole draft, giving the kind of friendly criticism I have come to rely on in all our joint work over the last thirty years. Throughout the months of writing, too, Mollie Dixon has listened acutely and responded to each section as it developed: wherever a voice speaks directly to the reader, this is due to her.

FOREWORD
Placing academic subjects, culturally and historically

A goal for theory

No one told me, when I started reading English Language and Literature at Oxford, that – officially, at least – the subject was only fifty years old there. No one lectured on the struggles to define a course, the forces that actually shaped the new degree, the roads impeded, blocked, or subjected to implacable diversion. It was a 'discipline' without a history, and without a theoretical foundation either, so far as the university lectures went.

Nearly fifty years later, it is harder – I hope – to imagine a course in literary studies, or any similar field, which did not try to place itself, historically and culturally. This has become a primary goal for 'theory'. What's more, after the events of 1990, any historical narrative of a grand progress towards modern (or post-modern) practices should surely be read with scepticism? Perhaps, after all, some of the roads not taken would have been preferable?

Unfortunately, I have still to read a history that would place what five generations of us have now been doing as students and teachers of 'English', in schools and higher education. Even the successive titles we have worked under – 'Modern Literature', 'English Language and Literature' and more recently 'English' – are not always accounted for. In fact, relating what I'll call for short 'English' to cultural and social history seems a much more complex undertaking than I had anticipated.

Simply to illustrate the difficulties, I will take three recent efforts, all from Britain. The first was by Terry Eagleton, in his chapter on 'The Rise of English' (1983). In this sketch, 'English was literally the poor man's Classics', a cheapish alternative 'specifically beamed' by authority into various 'oppressed layers of Victorian society', including women and working men (p.27). 'A convenient sort of non-subject to palm off on

2 A schooling in 'English'

the ladies', its rise in England 'ran parallel to the gradual, grudging admission of women to the institutions of higher education' (p.28).

In keeping with this view, no working-class or women's voices of the time are quoted. They are not social agents. It is others who 'beam', 'grudgingly admit', and presumably set up the alternative institutions that were used – the 'Mechanics' Institutes, working men's colleges and extension lecturing circuits' (p.27). In Eagleton's account, these unnamed others simply determine events. Coming from a professed Marxist, this seems a very unlikely story. A day's reading on the founding of the University Extension movement – and the central role of a group of Northern women – is enough to show up its inadequacy.

Chris Baldick's thesis on *The Social Mission of English Criticism* was published the same year. The same new institutional settings are referred to, including the Extension movement. Nothing is said about its inception, in a lecture series organised by women's groups in four Northern cities: Liverpool, Manchester, Sheffield and Leeds. Nor is the first topic mentioned: the development of the theory of gravitation.

Instead readers are specifically told that 'women [were] almost entirely restricted to English history and literature or modern languages if they were to embark upon any programme of learning' (p.67). ('Restricted' by whom? – I should ask; since they themselves organised the first courses and invited the lecturers.)

This is history from above, it seems, seasoned with a new kind of left-wing fatalism. There is little left for women to do but suffer. 'Ladies' Colleges and Extension lectures for women tended to reproduce on a grander scale the predominance of French conversation and poetry-reading' (p.68). No evidence whatever is offered for this generalisation – and if any exists, I haven't met it.

Besides, the central practices of the Extension lecture series are completely misread. 'The form of the Extension lecture itself (since it was rarely possible to back this up with close reading of a series of agreed texts)' left the lecturer 'to expound the peculiar beauties' in 'a more or less biographical manner' (p.75). Actually, the practice introduced by James Stuart in 1867 was for lectures to be followed by 'classes', where students could raise questions and their weekly written work was handed back with comments (following his Scottish university traditions). As for having texts available, Richard Moulton, one of the earliest and best of the 'English' lecturers, often made a point of printing a selection for his students.

These criticisms, it seemed to me at the time, were not merely quibbles over niceties. Rather, the absence of any detailed analysis of actual practices – in either work – was the result of a certain model of 'culture'. This model gave authoritative weight to selected voices (to Lord Playfair, Canon Browne, or the ageing John Morley, say), without having to justify the choice, or to place them historically. Were they active members of the Extension, or not? Were they speaking as representatives, or not? And, if so, what section(s) did they represent?

The resulting view of cultural – and educational – history is pretty bleak. Yet it seems to hold an ascendancy on the Left. Thus, as recently as 1989, Brian Doyle's thesis on *English and Englishness* called the Extension movement a 'semi-state programme' (p.23) – a pretty odd description of a movement based on voluntary local committees, organising courses for which the state (and Oxbridge) never paid out a penny.

Doyle's history continues what must now count as a tradition; women and working-class students' voices are silent, like those of their lecturers. Instead, an Oxford Vice-Chancellor is given his innings, with fairly predictable results for a VC: the Extension was 'learning what Oxford means' (p.28). He couldn't be expected to say, could he, that these lecturers and students had set out to undermine the whole territory he stood for, and to teach subjects – like Modern Literature – that his university was still determined to exclude? (Yet some of the Extension movement *did* say that, I've found.)

It was a surprise, then, to find cultural historians who counted themselves as radical critics but who still based their work on unanalysed models and working assumptions.

The need to analyse institutional structures

If 'English' did emerge within 'alternative' institutions, it is necessary to study these institutions, in order to understand the forces that shaped how it was defined, and what forms of study were attempted. Moreover, the original teachers in a *'university* extension' were inevitably formed in 'orthodox' institutions: how did they feel about their own formation; why did they choose alternative – and much less prestigious – work; what conflicts did they experience, social and cultural, and where did past orthodoxies impinge on the alternative present?

Equally, what forces stimulated women, working-class men, and – I should add – women and men of the Co-operative Societies to organise, attend and often pay out of their own pockets for extended courses by *university* lecturers? After all, in England and Wales, it was not until the 1870s that universal *elementary* education was set up for the likes of them. These must have been real pioneers. What range of subjects did they choose – besides gravitation – and what seems to have attracted some of them to the new courses in 'English'?

Having raised questions like these, I can see in part why they were pushed aside in the books I have just referred to. First, to answer them demands scope, something much more than a chapter, certainly. Even then, a cultural historian will probably have to focus intensively on an initial decade or so, and not scan half a century, as these writers tend to. Second, the attention of these radical critics was manifestly occupied elsewhere.

Eagleton, for instance, was alert to very much wider changes in the later 19th century, especially 'the failure of religion' (1983: 22). From the point of view of the Victorian ruling class this represented a loss of ideological control, he comments. So for someone sensitive to the needs of this class, like Matthew Arnold, imaginative literature offered an alternative means of integrating social classes and exerting subtle forms of control over the working masses, he claims. Thus, to be brief, the Rise of English.

Baldick, while agreeing about Arnold's project, related the rise of English to three narrower factors: the movements in adult and specifically women's education, and the demands of the imperial Civil Service, with its new competitive exams. But Doyle returned to broader themes: the attempt 'to colonise' the working class 'by its cultural superiors', as he saw it, and to fit 'respectable' members for a limited role in government. The aim was to 'develop a new collective sense of Englishness' (1989: 19).

So the invention of 'English' courses, on this view, occurred in a society producing cultural institutions that were national (or imperial), and these courses got degree status – ultimately – because the society was beginning to professionalise. The latter trend affected not only public administration (with its entry exams) but also 'welfare, journalism, publicity and the arts'. The new subject, as Doyle put it, represented just part of a 'schedule for organising the nation' (p.20).

A study of conflict, contradiction and difference

There must be elements of truth in all these theses, it seems to me. But again, the tendency is to define the small-scale cultural movement – the formation of 'English' studies – entirely in terms of ruling-class ideological goals, or of institutional pressures on a national scale. Was there really no ideological conflict – as 'alternatives' to orthodox universities and their subjects were set up? Did the new institutions owe nothing, in their structures, to the social classes that supported and jointly organised them?

What these three cultural historians were pointing to may be important, then, but needs to be transformed, in my view. The possibilities of opposition, or even of subverting dominant power, should be taken into account. (Whatever Arnold wrote at the time, the wave of agitation in 1867 achieved a reform of the franchise beyond anything Parliament had feared and anticipated – giving an ideal springboard for the Extension movement.) The coexistence of contrary – even contradictory – traditions and movements in the society has to be recognised.

That said, it is certainly important to look for evidence of wider social forces impinging on the new subjects – of which 'English' was only one. There is little doubt, for instance, that the new competitive exams for entry to the imperial Civil Service had long-term effects, even in Oxbridge, and especially on their new Exams Delegacies for schools. The immediate consequences for Literature courses (at various levels) were pretty devastating. Yet the Extension lecturers hung out against the model: this is part of their significance. It's a difference that cries out for investigation.

Similarly, the 'failure of religion', with all that it entailed, does help to account for the decline of clerical hegemony at Oxbridge, the slow secularising of university courses – the end of an era when Jowett could have his professorial salary withheld (and his career ominously threatened) because his position on the Thirty-nine Articles was suspect. But at Oxbridge, after dramatic struggles, it also produced a dangerous new breed – the married don.

With the first married dons, like Mandell Creighton (1871), did come a new professionalism, an effort to make personal research a foundation for teaching the new subjects like 'Modern History'. This implied the rejection of an honours degree course based – like the Classics – on a very short list of 'set books' (Hume, Lingard, Hallam, with chapters from Gibbon and Guizot!). He had to set to and teach himself the history of the Medieval Papacy. But that wasn't enough: Creighton was one of the first in Oxford to teach Extension courses, at the invitation of Ladies' Committees in Birmingham, Bristol and Falmouth (1870). His first subjects were Dante, inspired I take it by Rossetti's *The Early Italian Poets* (1861), and The Renaissance, a joint interest with his friends the Paters. And fifteen years later, for all the labours on his specialism, he was founding the *English Historical Review*.

Meanwhile, the woman who married him, Louise von Glehn, joined a Ladies' Committee for Lectures in 1873 – the majority being wives of recently married dons. Yet when this group of Oxford 'ladies' organised a lecture course, they had the solidarity to invite in, as 'friends', women teachers and pupil-teachers from the new elementary schools. Both the Creightons, in fact, made lifelong friendships in the Extension and Co-operative movements.

These two people, I would claim, are representative of certain key changes and oppositional movements in Oxbridge. Without alliances like theirs, an Extension movement might never have got off the ground. Their lives embody and relate some of the key tendencies that social and cultural historians should be interested to study – in action, not just in abstraction.

Oppositional networks and relations across classes

If this is so, what more can be learnt from such representative figures about modelling a cultural history? First, that within the broad structures of the Victorian class system there were networks, drawn together by various projects – some of them oppositional. Take a small-scale network like the group of Modern History dons: together they set up the first intercollegiate *lectures* in Oxford (1869), a key institutional break from teaching dominated by college *tutorials* – and a new form of collaborative effort. This little group had many links or cross-membership in other networks, for instance the 'Committee for Lectures' that included Louise Creighton, Mary Arnold (Mrs Humphry Ward), Clara Pater, Bertha Johnson and Charlotte Green. Through Tom Green, the philosopher (and the first don ever to stand for election to the town council), many of these same people also became active in projects well beyond the tense, discordant circles of Oxford University in the 1870s.

Thus, in 1878–9, when the women decided that their only hope was to set up an 'alternative university' of their own (over a baker's shop), they were able to call on a rebel group of dons to help them. Tom Green became provisional secretary of the new Association for Higher Education, pending the election of a joint committee of women and men. And when a list of initial subjects was canvassed, it was an ardent student of Tom's, a teacher of Philosophy at Balliol College, who agreed to run a course on English Literature: Andrew Bradley.

All this typifies what was going on within Oxbridge. More critical, of course, are the social relations set up when such networks cross the sharp class boundaries of the time. Do the professionals inevitably colonise with their 'superior' culture? How do networks mediate, or resist, established relations of power and solidarity? This ought to be a critical question, as we read their accounts.

What was the significance, for example, of Frances and Mark Pattison inviting a group of working women to the Rector's lodge at Lincoln College, Oxford, so that they could form a trade union? (Try imagining it happening today, and then add in Victorian stock responses to unions!) To my mind, the critical fact in Bertha Johnson's first-hand account is that Mark Pattison – that withered old reformer – poured the tea. And a later event seems equally significant: Frances attended the Trades Union Congress, speaking on behalf of women workers.

Unless cultural historians understand people in face-to-face networks, where conflicting values are sifted, reinforced and challenged in everyday encounters, it is difficult to see how they can make sense of the great flux of changes history confronts us with. Certainly, with a subject like 'English', unless they reconstruct groups in action, they will inevitably exclude any analysis of culture being *made* through practical activity – whether of lecturers, or students, or both together.

Constructing subjects through teaching and learning practices

What's more, once historians do reconstruct groups in action, a further level of analysis may become possible – of the greatest interest to teachers and students of 'English'. What in fact *is* 'English'? It is primarily constituted, I would claim, in the activities jointly carried through by teachers and students – in the oral and written dialogues they engage in.

This is the gravest omission in the three cultural histories I have been discussing. What happened in the Extension movement? An alternative method of teaching literature was invented. Why? After all, every public-school product of the time already knew how to teach it: that was what happened in Classics lessons. It simply meant the 'catechetical' approach: you prepared your 'lesson' on Vergil; the teacher asked one of you to read it aloud, and translate; then, one or other of you was asked to construe the verbs, the adverbs, the nouns, the adjectives, and so on; then to explain the reference in line 3... That was Classics; that was teaching classical literature. And, unfortunately, the model fitted the new competitive exams only too well. Indeed, it could be extended to any required level of difficulty, and was, in the final papers for honours degrees.

This was teaching literature, then, and it was 'universal' – essentially the same in Harvard or Yale's version of Classics, as Gerald Graff has recently illustrated (1987). In 1870, so far as Oxbridge was concerned, 'lecturing' by comparison was an occasional matter, not the concern of college tutors. The odd celebrity was brought in, perhaps, or a Professor of Poetry appointed – as Arnold had been – to give his five or six lectures in the course of a year. Sometimes students went, sometimes not. In fact, when the Liberal government appointed a professor like Stubbs, to bring a bit of scholarship into Modern History, nobody attended his well-prepared lecture course, he complained. (It was no help in the final exams, apparently. But his course for the Ladies' Committee got a different reception.)

8 *A schooling in 'English'*

So what did the Extension 'lecturers' on Literature do – instead of catechising? How did they organise their courses? What evidence is left of their lecturing and their students' questions and written work in response? And how did they explain – to themselves and maybe their students – what they were trying to do? If we cannot find any answers to such questions, we don't know what they made of these code words 'Literature' and 'English' anyway.

What's more, to take Terry Eagleton more seriously than he did himself, the new teaching of literature probably did aim to shape subjectivities, at times. Maybe he is right to claim that, with 'the failure of religion', lecturers – some lecturers – felt 'morality' was 'no longer to be grasped as a formulated code' and people must learn to reflect on 'the oblique, nuanced particulars of human experience' (1983: 27). Perhaps this would serve the purposes of the ruling classes, perhaps not. But the question is: what happened in practice – were these goals and unseen purposes actually carried through? Only a very detailed analysis of teaching and learning practices could test this kind of hypothesis, surely?

Aims for a book of this kind

To sum up: all these criticisms of fellow historians have become self-critical definitions for the work I am attempting. These are the lessons I am trying to teach myself, you might say:

(a) *To focus on a period of a decade or two*
I have selected three such periods and movements, which I hope to show are crucial to the potential development of 'English':

(i) The University Extension work from 1867 on.
(ii) The teaching of (Section A) English, at Cambridge, from 1919 to 1929.
(iii) The wider movement in English and Cultural Studies from 1960 to 1979.

This book is therefore planned as a series of 'case studies', not a connected history. It will not cover every interesting development – there will be gaps. Some continuities, however, will become obvious.

(b) *To study networks and representative members of them*
This is one way to get at the complex impact and interrelation of wider social forces on 'English'. It will also demonstrate the way 19th century notions of 'modern subjects' – such as 'English Language and Literature' – not only cover up shot-gun marriages

but are also inevitably in conflict with demands and interests that cut across 'disciplines'.
(c) *To analyse institutional structures*
Studying what these constrain and enable, for people who jointly make and/or work within them, should help to explain how 'English' comes to be constructed, defended, attacked and changed in various ways.

More specifically, the conditions and strategies of teaching and learning finally produce the activities we can call 'English'. Or I could put it this way: they constrain and enable a particular set of possibilities for understanding selves, groups and societies. And in order to do so, they must include an analysis of specific types of dialogue, which mediate and construct the way people act and relate.
(d) *To study the production of literary studies (and more)*
I am explicitly looking for courses where students and teachers are not simply followers of a tradition – for cultural breaks, if you like, and the potentials they release.

As 20th century media emerge alongside print, I want to study and assess how these new forms of cultural production are taken into account, or marginalised, in developing 'literacies'.

I realise, of course, that many readers would have wished me to cover the 1930s, the 1950s, or the 1980s. There are two reasons behind the decision not to do so. First, in the three periods I have selected literary (and cultural) studies were swept forward by creative energies from below – from students and their aspirations. I wanted that to be central to this book. Second, a connected history would have demanded a book at least twice as long, to accommodate the social context and the necessary critical perspectives. That is beyond what I felt I could expect of my publishers, let alone potential readers.

Besides, it is already clear that at times the effort to assemble evidence and analyse its ramifications has outfaced me. This book has to be a sketch for a much longer – and perhaps a collaborative – effort. That is why for the moment I have restricted myself to England for the mainstream, trying occasionally to indicate a convergent or conflicting flow elsewhere (as in Interchapter 12).

However, like all unfinished work of its kind, it includes the goal of persuading readers that the overall project is worth continuing – and improving.

PART I
The University Extension 1867–92

CHAPTER 1

The democratic movement for a peripatetic university

The agitation for radical reform

From 1866 a great surge of democratic agitation linked London with the manufacturing cities of the Midlands and the North. Its first achievement was a reform of the House of Commons that outstripped anything anticipated by the press or by leading Tories and Liberals, and staggered London society. (Next time, radicals began to say, the target would be the Lords and the end of aristocratic rule.) But the movement swept on: now there must be a national system of education, free, non-sectarian, compulsory – and open equally to girls and boys. Women would win equality in this system. And it would be organised, not by central government, but by local School Boards (of women as well as men), democratically elected. After that? – municipal ownership and control of gas, street lighting, the water supply, sewage disposal... with slum clearance and new housing for the working classes. And who could say: as the working-class co-ops – retail and wholesale – annually increased their financial strength, a coming shift into industrial, productive co-ops might change the face of capitalism.

Feelings and hopes like these were alive in every town and city: among skilled workers, now with the vote; members of the co-operative movement; women, but especially middle-class women, struggling to gain recognition as equals in work; the rebellious and non-conformists among a growing class of professionals; a small but active minority of reformists in the ancient universities...

In 1867–9 what might have seemed at the time a historical accident brought representatives of these groups together. What emerged was a national campaign over the next two decades to extend, not elementary, but university education to every city and major centre in the country. And within the institutions produced by that movement, new 'disciplines' of study and new 'subjects' – among them, Modern Literature – were going to be formed.

Women learn to combine – and men join them

What kinds of institutions were set up by this movement? What seem to be the most significant decisions and outcomes in those two decades of University 'Extension'? I want to start with the voices, plans and hopes of the original participants, and to trace their actions. It is a story worth remembering, and not without its relevance today.

Early in 1866 a famous group of women, based in Langham Place, organised the London Society of Schoolmistresses. A Commission of Inquiry into the run-down state of endowed (secondary) schools was in progress, and these women were determined not to let slip their opportunity. It was a time when girls had very restricted access to any kind of education and none to the universities. One of the group, Annie Clough, went back to Liverpool to set up a parallel association in her home town; by March 1867 she was speaking to another new assocation, in Manchester. Through these societies, she wrote, women teachers 'learned to combine; they were no longer alone... they were now part of a system and were gathering new strength and dignity' (Clough 1897: 110).

In her Manchester paper she made a far-reaching proposal: that groups of schools combine to invite university lecturers to give courses in their town. The response was a decision 'to draw up a scheme for a council to be elected by Schoolmistresses' or Educational Associations already existing ' in Liverpool, Manchester, Leeds and Sheffield.

Meanwhile, James Stuart, a young Cambridge Fellow, was approached to give a series of lectures and 'classes' that autumn in all four towns. Invited to speak on teaching methods, he replied that it was better to demonstrate the teaching of something specific, rather than tackle such an abstract subject head-on. So it was agreed that he would hold a series of eight weekly sessions in each centre, on the subject of Physical Astronomy – 'elucidating the discovery and meaning of gravitation' (Stuart 1912: 155). From the start, then, the movement expected to deal with fundamentals.

It is vital, though, to appreciate some of the difficulties that faced these pioneers. 'I spent many weeks in August and September of 1867 in Liverpool', wrote Annie Clough,'trying to make the coming lectures known. Many friends helped me... and together we visited schoolmistresses and families, doing our best to persuade them to look favourably on our plan, but it was very uphill work, and there was plenty of discouragement' (1869: 128). One reason was plain enough to the Schools Inquiry Commissioners: 'a long established and inveterate prejudice, though it may not often be distinctly expressed, that girls are less capable of mental cultivation, and in less need of it, than boys' (Taunton Commission Report 1868, Vol. I).

Nevertheless, the courses succeeded, beyond all expectations. Not only was there strong support, with an average attendance of 80, 160, 100 and 200 respectively in the four towns above; more significantly, when Stuart distributed three or four questions, offering to read and comment on any answers that were sent to him by post, roughly 300 arrived in the first week. Over half the audience wanted to respond. And this response radically changed the form of his women's 'classes' from then on – leading him to invite questions as well as answers, and to use this 'most valuable assistance' in a special half-hour session at the conclusion of each succeeding lecture. It was the beginning of a dialogue, 'conversational teaching' as he later called it. What is more, as he commented in his contribution to *Women's Work and Women's Culture* (Butler 1869), some of those papers were 'pre-eminently good, and the average... showed a thorough appreciation of the subject' (p.129).

Stengthened by this work, representatives from the original four towns, plus Newcastle-upon-Tyne, met in Leeds on 1 November 1867 to form the Northern Council for the Promotion of Higher Education for Women. It was to be the first of many such ventures. Appropriately, Josephine Butler was elected president and Annie Clough secretary. The nomination at that meeting of James Bryce (Commissioner for the Schools Inquiry), Thomas Markby (Cambridge Local Exams Board) and Joshua Fitch (HMI) indicates the kind of backing these women were rightly learning to expect. By 1868, courses had already spread beyond these five towns to include Bowden, Birkenhead, Bradford and York, while the lecturers included men from Oxford for the first time. The following year there would be courses in twenty-three centres. A 'university' with over 2000 students, set up in three years.

In fact, a revolution in women's education was under way. But they were not alone, even at this stage. Again, a kind of accident appeared to start the process: 'Mr Moorson, a college friend of mine', says James Stuart, 'who was one of the junior managers at the Crewe Railway works, wrote [in autumn 1867] urging me to come and give a lecture to the workmen there in their Mechanics' Institute which had been newly built. He was aware of my lectures for ladies, and wanted something done for men' (1889: 24). In replying to a hearty vote of thanks from an audience of 1500 (there happened to have been a great meteor shower the night before!), 'it struck me that this was an opening for a further move in connection with my notion of a peripatetic university' (1912: 159). So Stuart agreed to return next summer for a course – published the same year as *Six Lectures to Workmen at Crewe* (1868).

Next came an invitation from the Equitable Pioneers' Society of Rochdale, the original Co-operative. When Stuart arrived rather early for his second lecture, 'It's one of the best things you ever did', said the door-keeper. It turned out that a group of co-op members had been discussing the diagrams he left, had raised a number of questions, and were coming along beforehand, hoping to put them. 'I found it so useful a half hour that during the remainder of the course I always had such a meeting' (Stuart 1912: 163). The 'lecturer' was willing to adapt his teaching to new demands from his students.

It was part of an explicit ideological position that broadened the whole campaign. Thus, in 1871, Stuart (a Scot by birth and education) had this to say to the Leeds Ladies' Educational Association:

> One of the great dangers and difficulties in this country of England at this present time is the grievous class distinctions which there are in it... It seems to me that nothing could more tend to perpetuate that distinction than a system of class education, such as now too largely exists. It seems to me, on the contrary, that nothing could more tend to work against that class distinction than any efforts which we make towards a system in which our rich and poor, our men and women, should be taught by the same individuals.
>
> (Jepson 1973: 24)

And he included himself, a Fellow of Trinity, among such 'individuals'.

So here were new institutional structures and relations being set up; and they lasted for much of the next two decades.

(a) The courses were arranged for and organised by local committees, who learned to 'combine', on occasion electing members to represent their group in a regional council. In doing so they stood to gather 'new strength and dignity' by co-operating to achieve a long-term goal – higher education for themselves and others.

(b) The lecturer depended on an invitation from the committee, sometimes after consultation with people they had specially appointed for that purpose (among them, from 1868 on, Thomas Green, of Balliol College, Oxford, Albert Rutson, secretary at the Home Office, and Dr Hodgson of London University).

(c) The course ran for six weeks or more. (For comparison, the Oxbridge term lasted eight weeks, and there intercollegiate lectures were just about to be introduced – after the experience of Extension courses.)

(d) Both 'lectures' and 'classes' formed part of the normal course, with opportunity for students to raise questions and comment in speech or writing, and to answer weekly questions in writing, if they wished.

This structure left a significant degree of power with the local group, representing the students, rather than with the teachers (as in a college). In well-attended courses – and the average stayed around 100 for two decades – active students who wanted it had special access to the teacher through the 'classes', through individual comments on their written work, and through general comments as the work was returned. 'Lecturers', as they were called, had to show their ability to hold an audience and to respond to a class, in 'conversational' teaching; otherwise, they were unlikely to succeed.

A Democratic University of peripatetic teachers and active, self-organising students: this is what was proposed, in effect. The decades 1870–89 were to prove its testing ground – and its most triumphant moment. During that time it must have reached in the order of 150,000–200,000 new students, at a conservative estimate. Is there still something to be learnt from this model?

The breaking down of intellectual caste

After careful lobbying, the established English universities began to give cautious but formal recognition to this movement. The appeal to Cambridge was supported by the North of England Women's Council, the Crewe Mechanics' Institute, the Rochdale Pioneers, the Mayor and Inhabitants of Leeds, D. J. Vaughan of Leicester Working Men's College, Richard Enfield of the Nottingham Mechanics' Institute and Dr J. B. Paton of the Nottingham Congregational Institute (1871).

After negotiations, the Cambridge Senate authorised a syndicate, with Stuart as secretary, to organise courses in various centres (1873); in 1876, a London Society for the Extension of University Teaching was formed, to 'co-ordinate work in the Metropolis'; in 1878 an Oxford Committee for (Extension) Lectures was set up with Arthur Acland as secretary. It sounds imposing, but so far as the movement in the country was concerned, these formal structures were of relatively minor importance, I would argue. Institutionally, power remained with a local centre. There was no monopoly: a joint committee for Cambridge, London and Oxford was unable to stop continued competition among lecturers outside the capital. Equally, some freelances – among them the famous lecturer on Literature, John Churton Collins – later worked for more than one committee. What then did the central syndicate or committee offer? For the voluntary lecturer in its ranks, status, a secretary, and, in a few favourable cases, college support; for the very small minority of Extension students who wanted them, recognised exams and certificates.

From a historiographical point of view, though, there was one more lasting result: from this period on, it was organising secretaries in Cambridge and Oxford who produced *the* history – and the central propaganda – for the movement. First, James Stuart, Richard Moulton and Robert Roberts (for Cambridge); later, Michael Sadler and Halford Mackinder (for Oxford); it is their voices we still hear. Currently, I know of no contemporary group of women, co-operators, trade unionists, (pupil) teachers or other students and committee members who tried to trace the movement as a whole, or even regionally. So it is the organised contribution from the old university centres that takes the foreground in the standard histories.

There are characteristic limitations to this perspective, which we will come to in a moment. But in some respects, it is persuasive, of course. 'The original purpose... of University Extension was to create students, and to create them out of a new class', Robert Roberts asserted. 'Both these ideas were new in education and were a direct outcome of the growth of democratic feeling... [It] meant the breaking down of intellectual caste and the universal extension of the intellectual franchise' (1893).

To 'create' such a possibility both sides had to actively change their practices and ideology. Men from an Oxbridge 'caste' had to learn to treat ordinary people in new ways; the 'new class' had to learn to see 'intellectual franchise' as within their grasp (though over half of them hadn't the right to vote). Each side was dependent on the other. The minority in Oxbridge and elsewhere who responded to that appeal had to convince women and working-class people that – at a time when universal *elementary* education was still the obvious target – they the students were capable of setting up and undertaking a higher education course.

And a small group at Oxbridge actually made consistent efforts to do so. As early as 1871 Stuart wrote to the *Co-operative News* suggesting a 'complete peripatetic university scheme for the Co-operative Societies'. Understandably, at the time, that was not the obvious priority for their education funds. Over a decade later, however, Sadler, the new Oxford secretary, made an enthusiastic tour of northern co-ops, attending their annual conference, and by 1886 could report that 'the lectures [at Manchester, Ashton, Bolton, Rochdale, Marlborough and Doncaster, held in association with local co-ops] are in the main well attended [and] entirely managed and paid for by artisans' (1886 Report in Sadleir 1949). As for the Fustian workers at Hebden Bridge, a manufacturers' co-op, they started to organise courses the same year and continued practically every session till 1900.

In the Midlands the Cambridge syndicate made an excellent start in attracting working men: the first twelve-week courses at Nottingham, Leicester and Derby (autumn 1873) each ran an afternoon on English Literature, 'at a time convenient for ladies', together with an evening choice between 'Force and Motion', for 'young men engaged in business', or 'Political Economy' 'specially for the working classes'.

Attendances averaged 100, and the following year there was backing from Nottingham trade unions and the Sheffield trades council. By 1875 the Syndicate was suggesting to local groups that 'both [General and Executive] Committees should include ladies, young men and working men'. But there were deep-rooted problems, especially as economic conditions worsened in the later 1870s.

One notable silence in the Oxbridge reports was the question of costs. That, after all, was left to the local committee. To pay a middle-class lecturer for twelve sessions (lectures, classes and comments on papers) the going rate was roughly £35–40. Travel, meals, overnight stay, advertising, printing the syllabus, hire of rooms and so on, raised this to at least £80, often more (Jepson 1973: 184). But as Hudson Shaw, one of the favourite lecturers on the co-op circuit, pointed out: 'you are dealing with men whose wages are not more than 18 or 19 shillings a week on average. Is it not absurd to expect an average working man [or woman] to pay five shillings, two shillings and sixpence, or one shilling for a little course of Extension lectures?' (Oxford Lecturers' Conference 1892) Subsidies from co-ops or unions were vital, then. Inevitably, though, there were many other priorities for these organisations.

Nevertheless, better-off, skilled workers did respond in their thousands. When Roberts was appointed assistant secretary at Cambridge in 1881, he immediately set about recruiting more working-class students, particularly in the North-East. Here, in the Northumberland and Durham coalfield, he had outstanding success. By 1884 'of the five morning centres, Mr Small (of Christ's College) and I took four, and the fifth was supplied by Professor Lebour of the Newcastle College of Science. The aggregate attendance at these five centres was about six hundred, the audience being, except in one centre, Blyth, almost exclusively working men', he reported.

A regional committee of pitmen was set up and S. Neil, their secretary, wrote: 'I believe this system of calling the [Local] Committees together is one of the real causes of the success of the Lectures among the miners... The meeting of so many men from widely separated districts, all studying under common difficulties, affords a fine outlet for the repressed feelings which these struggles engender' (Moulton 1885: 188). It was this committee that raised funds and negotiated courses in Political Economy, History, Mining and Geology, for example. 'A great awakening of the intellectual life of the working classes is taking place', wrote Roberts in the *Cambrian News*, Aberystwyth, in 1887; he proudly estimated that in twelve Northumbrian mining centres one in seventeen of the population had been attending.

What's more, this was one of the key areas for Richard Moulton's immense success in Literature courses, as we shall see later. When a successful self-help reading circle was set up in the mining village of

Backworth, he published a book recording their work (in London and Boston, USA, 1895).

So the Cambridge and Oxford secretaries, and a handful of talented and enthusiastic lecturers with them, did indeed make a difference to the whole movement. But how about this Professor Lebour – and his colleagues at Newcastle College (significantly founded in 1871)? And what about the Owens College, Manchester (home of Roscoe's 'Science Lectures for the People'), and the Extension College for Women it also set up as early as 1871? And, as successive local colleges were founded at Bristol (1876), Leeds (1877), Sheffield (1879), Birmingham (1880), Liverpool and Nottingham (1881), didn't they, too, make characteristic contributions to the Extension movement – venturing out, for example, into applied and industrial science, a field beyond the competence of Oxbridge?

To begin to answer such questions, I want to look closely at the development of the Extension movement in the town that helped to start it: Liverpool. Here, as it happened, Andrew Bradley was to become their first Professor of Modern Literature.

Liverpool: pioneer work by city professors

When Josephine Butler moved to Liverpool in 1866 she found it an international city, its twelve miles of docks lined with warehouses. Its population was immense, second only to London's, 'with a large intermingling of foreign elements'. She noted 'its varieties in the way of creeds and places of worship, its great wealth and abject poverty, the perpetual movement... and the clash of interests in its midst'. In her husband George's school, Liverpool College, among 800–900 pupils there were Greeks, Armenians, Jews, Africans and Americans. So – well ahead of its time – no religious compulsion was exercised (1892).

Josephine was president of the Northern Council from 1867 till it dissolved in 1874, 'having finished its pioneer work'. For in January of that year, after addresses by James Stuart, Emily Davies, and William Rathbone, the town's Liberal MP, a public meeting in the town hall raised £1000 on the spot to clear Girton in Cambridge, the new women's college, of its debts and went on to establish a joint Association for the Promotion of Higher Education (APHE) in Liverpool.

As a first step, the Association raised a guarantee fund of £2000: by the autumn of 1874, two resident Extension lecturers were appointed to organise full-time courses in Liverpool, its suburbs, and (with the help of committees) local towns. Thus, a proposal of Annie Clough's, made six years earlier, was actually implemented:

It might be very valuable, for the improvement of an even higher class of school than those before mentioned, to establish professorships on subjects of general interest... In the large towns some 20 or 25 lectures might be delivered by one professor in the course of three months... Professors might also be appointed to a district of several small towns, taking three or four, according to size and locality.

(Taunton Commission Report: II, 86–7)

Jethro Teall (later Director of the Geological Survey) and William Cunningham (later Professor at the LSE) were the two men selected. Earlier that year, Cunningham had already given successful courses in Leeds and Bradford on Political Economy; on that first evening, wrote the *Leeds Mercury*, he had 're-delivered his lecture in the [Philosophical Hall, Leeds] to a still fuller audience of working men' (9 January 1874). The experience in Liverpool, he told his daughter, 'convinced him that for awakening the interest of students in a subject and directing their first efforts to pursue it seriously, [Stuart's] plan of study had no rival'. And, a further advantage in his eyes, it 'freed teachers from the tyranny of the examination system' (Cunningham 1950: 30).

His impressions take us a step closer to the actual work, and its effects on both sides – on teacher as well as students. 'It was gratifying that his classes usually increased during a course of lectures, and he enjoyed the work of organisation... Lists of books likely to be found in free libraries were supplied, as far as possible low in price, and members of the class were invited to send in difficulties in writing, which formed the basis for later discussion' (p.31). In some terms Cunningham had upwards of 600 students altogether, which meant 'correcting' about 200 papers weekly. 'I noticed his unwearied patience in reading numbers of papers', wrote his mother during a visit, 'and the pointed yet kindly and candid manner in which he made general remarks on [them], after his lectures' (p.33).

'Many of the students of those days were of the artisan class.' To make this possible, differential fees were agreed. In the wealthier parts of Birkenhead, Waterloo and Everton, and for some of the Ladies' courses on Political Economy and Deductive Logic, a guinea was charged; more appropriately, given its title, the People's Course on the Production and Distribution of Wealth cost as little as 2/6*d*, or 4/- for those who joined the classes as well.

The work brought Cunningham into contact 'with men of all classes, and face to face with the actual conditions of industrial life. [It] left an indelible impression on me, and gave a new reality to economic studies' (p.34). He attended the Co-operative Congress in Halifax (1874), representing it when the Leeds Co-operators made their first industrial investment, buying a colliery the same year. In 1877 he attended the Trades Union Congress in Liverpool, and in 1879 the Edinburgh Congress. It was a new life for a young Scottish intellectual, whose main interest was, as he said, philosophy.

Through such people, then, Liverpool APHE alone had organised 40 courses between 1874 and 1880, many in literature or history, but also in geology, biology, heat and light, and astronomy. Cunningham added Sunday Lectures for the People, on Progress and on Socialism.

In 1877, however, came a change of direction. Under pressure from the School of Medicine, Charles Beard, chair of the APHE, called a meeting between representatives of the School and the Extension lecturers. The upshot was a proposal for a university college, for day and evening students, in 'all branches of a liberal education... to qualify for degrees in Arts and Science, and at the same time... technical instruction in Physics, Engineering, Navigation, Chemistry and allied subjects [such] as would be of immediate service in professional and commercial life' (Brown 1892: 17).

In spite of a recession in trade and an appeal for the new cathedral, by 1880 the College Committee had raised £90,000 from Liverpool's wealthy merchants, shipowners and provision trades. Not a penny came from government funds. Beard was especially influential locally as minister of the strong Unitarian church: he had spent a year at Berlin with Ranke, as a young man, and – said Andrew Bradley – 'was one of those who felt most strongly that a city like Liverpool, wanting the appliances of university education within itself, lacks a necessary element of human life in the full sense of those words' (Obituary, *Liverpool College Magazine* 1888).

Will Rathbone, a member of his congregation, had already given support to trade union leaders over a Bill to safeguard their funds, and founded a centre for training nurses (1905). He was a shrewd handler of local Conservatives, telling them among other things that 'it would never do to have us "radicals and Infidels", as they chose to call us, have the credit of raising all the money'. This ensured that five foundation chairs would be endowed: in Classics, Experimental Physics and Mathematics, Natural History, Philosophy and Political Economy, and Modern History and Literature. Together with the four part-time chairs in Medicine, these formed the basic curriculum in 1881, when the University College opened.

Within the decade, further chairs were added in Modern History and in Latin (1884), Engineering (1885), Inorganic, Physical and Industrial Chemistry (1885), Organic Chemistry (1886), and Political Economy and Commercial Education (1888) [Kelly 1981].

Loyalty to the commonwealth of workers, men and women

But who was to benefit? From the start women were admitted; there was no maximum age; and there was no religious test. The College offered full-time courses at three levels: Cambridge Local Exams and Higher Locals (the pre-university exams recently instituted), leading to a London B.A. or B.Sc., taken externally. More important, as we shall see, it did not insist on students going in for any exams at all. 'We are ready to take any who wish to work, on the most elastic principles that we can', said the Principal, Gerald Rendall (Fellow of Trinity, Cambridge). It was not the plan, then, to exclude all but a tiny social or intellectual elite – on the Oxbridge model. What's more, for the full-time Arts and Science courses, women and men joined in roughly equal numbers by the second year.

Oliver Lodge, Lyons Professor of Experimental Physics and Mathematics, seems to have thoroughly enjoyed his inaugural lecture. No movement would be more lasting, he said, than the revival and revolution in the whole system and plan of education. One was led to rejoice in the system of local self-government, untrammelled by excessive and paralysing central control, which rendered such results possible. Think of the loyalty to the commonwealth of workers, men and women, that had been called out. A college was not a building, but a society. Passing an exam was one thing, the training necessary to understand a subject something far higher.

> Languages, literature and history are coming to be taught in schools now by methods incomparably more enlightened than... in my own boyhood; and elementary science is urging its claims... . Considering [Electricity] as a pure science we seem to be on the verge of some great and epoch-making discovery as to its intimate nature and its relation to ordinary matter... on the eve of a revolution in our methods of obtaining Power and Light. I foresee a time when the large towns... will be really as healthy and pleasant places to live in as the country.
>
> (3 October 1881)

Ironical as his conclusion may sound to some citizens of Liverpool today, it indicates the breadth – and unacademic directness – of the appeal this democratic movement was making a century ago.

So the five new Professors began work, with roughly a hundred day students (each taking three courses on average); special day courses; a great variety of evening courses and classes for 400–500 students; day and evening extension courses for the Ladies' Educational Association that Annie Clough had founded; and gradually, further Extension courses in Waterloo, Bootle, St Helens and Birkenhead. As Rendall remarked in 1883, 'In almost every department the College is now working at high pressure, higher probably than could be maintained for any length of time... The temporary indisposition of a single Professor would involve the collapse of all [his] teaching' (July 1883 in Kelly 1981: 59). Fortunately, according to the ebullient Lodge, 'we four set to work to make a college, and certainly it was difficult to imagine a more brilliant team'.

Degrees were not the main target in the first decade. Even when day students rose above 200, less than 20 took the degree exams (independently available through the Victoria University, linking Liverpool with Manchester). In part the fees (£1.10s. a session) must have put many off. But equally our current assumption that students enter university to get a specialist paper qualification just didn't hold. In contemporary Oxbridge, let's recall, the majority of the national elite were not thinking of an honours degree, nor studying a specialist 'subject'.

Thus, in some respects, the evening classes were still the natural focus initially. For them, after the 1/- entrance fee, the charge was 5/- a course. 'We put in a good deal of time and energy', said William Herdman (Natural History). And 'the work was worth doing', said John MacCunn, who lectured on Political Economy and History: 'The classes were large and responsive, and the men and women who sat on the benches – ranging from 18 to 30 years of age, or thereabouts – were in many cases of the kind that read steadily and thought for themselves, and were quite capable of assimilating good material... These evening classes rallied round the college many friends of the right sort, and won for it much permanent good will.' 'Several of the assistant masters [in schools]... came as senior students to my evening courses', Lodge remembered, and were 'not above sitting on the same benches with such of their more advanced pupils as they brought along with them' (1901: 4).

Herdman takes us further:

> They attracted students – sometimes of a mature age – who knew something about the subject, who really cared for it, and who were willing to make some sacrifice to study it further. I don't think it is too much to say that the Biology Society, the Liverpool Marine Biology Committee, the Port Erin Biological Station, and the Scientific Department of the Lancashire Sea-Fisheries have grown out of the evening classes in Zoology... in the early Eighties.
>
> (1907)

So – regardless of paper qualifications – there were practical outcomes of real importance. An active group of citizens were beginning to study the environment; to introduce the next generation to scientific investigations at the frontiers of knowledge; to think seriously about the economic basis for their history...

It was in this context, then, that Andrew Bradley gave 'consistently popular' evening classes, and began his Saturday lectures on

Shakespeare for the Ladies' Educational Association. The latter was not a soft option for women: there were further series by his colleagues MacCunn, on Philosophy; Herdman, on Biology; and Rendall, on Language. Besides, it was in this setting Bradley made his first efforts to theorise a new subject, as we shall see.

What made such work possible? Lodge had come straight from Queen's College, London, the first women's college. Bradley had been lecturing for the previous two years to women, in the alternative university set up in Oxford by the local APHE. MacCunn was a Scottish graduate with experience of a more democratic system. As he said later:

> Democracy had won. The franchise had been twice extended in 1832 and 1867. It was shortly to be still further widened in 1884. New and virile classes and interests had been admitted to power. Municipal self-government had been inaugurated... . Religious disabilities... done away. The poor law had been reformed. Free trade had been carried. Social amelioration had begun in Factory legislation. National education was, at last, coming to the front. In a word, democratic citizenship had become a fact.
>
> (1907)

Well, it had for an energetic minority, let us say. Nevertheless, that was certainly a driving force, the basis for a programme and for new practices.

But with a College came new constraints. True, those evening classes, and the Extension lectures in other centres, preserved a direct relation between the new professors and their potential students. But in Liverpool, at least, the local committee had been replaced; no seats were kept on the University Court for women and working men. The institutional pressure was now from a wealthy merchant class, with a balance to be kept between their radical and conservative interests. It was a different distribution of power. And, within the city, it stood in the way of those direct alliances with the women's movement, the unions and the co-operatives.

However, it did not stop men like Lodge getting full support for their electrical experimental plant, despite writing for the Liverpool Fabians. Bradley's political interests were 'keen and real', too, MacCunn reports. And there was plenty of plain speaking by his colleagues, too: addressing Elementary Teachers in 1888, Professor Mackay condemned the 'plutocratic monopoly of learning' at Oxford. 'The erudition of our century has been above all the work of Germany... . The truth is that this whole movement of thought, the greatest revolution since the Renaissance and the Reformation... among us is working in the dark' (1914: 341, 349). As for MacCunn, 'the workshop, the friendly society, the trades union, the co-operative association, the political committee [produces political intelligence] not less surely than in middle class business life', he told the Liverpool Society of Social Science and Social Work (1911). 'In the exercise of your own self-government ... you have a politics of your own.'

CHAPTER 2

Programmes and practices for a new subject

Subjects beyond university structures

The Extension movement, backed up by local colleges, was under way and innovators on both sides intended to teach Modern Subjects. But how could new academic subjects be invented? Where would their founding ideas be discussed? At Oxbridge and the nine great public schools – the dominant institutions of the upper classes and wealthier Anglican clergy – there was little interest. Classics was still the mainstay of college tutors; in the late 1860s, 'modern' subjects were still struggling for recognition of any kind.

Yet to outside observers, as well as internal critics, there was little to be said for current teaching of 'classical' studies. 'Far too many boys emerged from the public schools with little knowledge of the classics, with less of modern subjects, and with no mental cultivation or interest in study' (Clarendon Commission 1864). As for Oxford, Mark Pattison's sardonic comment of 1868 is not altogether unjust:

> Certainly the Oxford BA ought to be the most finished specimen of education in the world, if the cost of production is the measure of value. £120,000 a-year [is] applied as prize money or bonus distributable among scholars, and another £50,000 a-year spent on teachers and masters out of endowments, besides nearly another £50,000 levied in fees by tutors private and public...
>
> [Yet] the honour-students are the only students who are undergoing any educational process which it can be considered as a function of a university either to impart or exact... The remaining 70 per cent not only furnish from among them all the idleness and extravagance which is become a byeword throughout the country, but cannot be considered to be even nominally pursuing any course of university studies at all.
>
> (pp.230–1)

Outside these institutional structures, though, things were intellectually alive. In fact, this was the heyday of periodical journalism. In the two decades from 1867 you could pick up a monthly or weekly and expect to read pioneering articles by men like Huxley, Bagehot, Mill, Maine, J. R. Green, Freeman, Ruskin, Bright, Gladstone, Harrison, Leslie Stephen, Arnold, Pater, on the one side, and on the other, poems and serial stories by Morris, Rossetti, Swinburne, Meredith, Thackeray, Trollope, Hardy, Henry James... And, significantly, among the contributors were an increasing number of leading women: George Eliot, Elizabeth Gaskell, Harriet Martineau, Mary Humphry Ward, Octavia Hill, Louisa Twining, Beatrice Potter, Millicent Fawcett, Edith Simcox, Annie Besant...

The journals attracted editors like Leslie Stephen (after he resigned his Cambridge fellowship) and young John Morley (a campaigning radical, cut off by his father for his religious doubts). What's more, their work was increasingly available to readers of all classes in the new Municipal Libraries, the Co-op Reading Rooms, and the Mechanics' Institutes – where audiences of thousands also gathered to hear Charles Dickens, in his last years, reading his own work.

It was an era when original thinking – and the discussion of it – found a home outside archaic educational structures. As a result, it aimed to attract, not a cloistered and male elite, but a national circle of readers. And its coverage was comprehensive.

These journals were one part of the critical context, then, in which 'modern' subjects were formed and disseminated to a wide public. A second part, for those who could afford it, was the annual conference of the British Association for the Advancement of Science or the Social Science Association. In the longer term, of course, these were increasingly fed by specialist societies, with their own journals; but for a period, the desire for a general audience prevailed.

For literary studies there was no comparable focus or centre. This made the journals all the more influential – in a period when Matthew Arnold, Pater, Symonds, Harrison, Stephen, Gosse, Lang, Churton Collins, Saintsbury and many others were active contributors. As Richard Moulton put it:

> The grand literary phenomenon of modern times is journalism, the huge apparatus of floating literature of which one leading object is to review literature itself. The vast increase of [literary] production consequent upon the progress of printing has made production itself a phenomenon worthy of study...
>
> (1885: 5)

Though not taken up immediately, it was a seminal idea to put forward.

But there were limits to periodical models, thought Moulton. True, their characteristic, 'judicial' form of criticism often resulted in 'a wise economy', anticipating 'natural selection and universal experience'. However, as he shrewdly pointed out, this was not the foundation needed either for literary teaching or for more permanent forms of criticism. Here, an 'investigative' form of criticism was needed, an analysis of literary works that brought 'a closer acquaintance with their phenomena'.

I believe Moulton owed this discovery – still not altogether recognised? – to the innovating experiences of Extension courses.

Studying textual annotations or the dramatic poem?

Extension lectures and classes offered a new context for criticism. What did Moulton, Collins, Bradley and the rest stand to learn in so far as they tried 'to create students, and to create them out of a new class'? As expert products of the prevailing 'classical' system, what did they have to unlearn, reject, or transform for the sake of their new students? And what discursive strategies could they invent, beyond periodical criticism, given a spoken medium, not print, and an opportunity for 'conversational teaching', not one-way address?

First, they were united about what to get rid of: the traditions of editorial commentary – and teachers' cross-questioning – handed down with classical texts. 'It would be a bitter disappointment', said Bradley, 'to those who hope most from the study of English if it should turn out in twenty years' time that the story of classical education had been repeated, that notes upon the double negative and the derivation of monstrosities had hidden the characters of Shakespeare...' (1884: 24).

The danger was present and real enough. 'As an educational manual... the annotated editions of [Shakespeare's] works give the student little assistance except in the explanation of language and allusions' (Moulton 1885: vi). Thus, 'When the average pupil and the average [school] teacher find a play treated by the editor merely as a *text* for verbal interpretation and discussion, a hundred pages in length, they are tempted to forget that the *play* is anything beside this and they rise from the study of it without ever having studied it as the thing it is – a dramatic poem' (Bradley 1889, my emphasis). 'It is possible to be very learned in Shakespeareana and to know nothing of Shakespeare.'

The silence about dramatic effect, the absence of the play as dramatic poem, pointed to teaching practices which many lecturers in the Extension movement were determined to reject. 'For heaven's sake, don't let us murder Shakespeare, etc., by treating them as we treat Aeschylus and Sophocles [in Oxford]', wrote his friend Nettleship, in 1886. But deep-rooted classical traditions had already been transplanted into Modern Literature – with institutional force behind them.

The Extension lecturers were not entirely first in the field. Through London Matriculation exams and the Cambridge and Oxford 'Locals', a version of literary studies was already being enforced. English Literature had indeed been established in the 1860s. According to Oxbridge, it was a minor examination subject, suitable for secondary schools and Pass men. At London University you could get a degree from the 1860s on by answering the same type of banal factual questions. These exam provisions gave the universities two forms of power: first, through the textbooks they produced, second through the questions they set. The one fed the other. 'Instead of regarding a great poem or a great drama as the expression of genius and art', wrote Collins, '[Clarendon Press editions] regard it merely as a monument of language' (1891: 57). At University College, London, English Language and Literature questions, if anything, hit a new low, as the Annual Calendars show.

Consequently, in elevated university circles 'the idea prevails that anything like the discussion of literary characteristics and dramatic effect is out of place in an educational work – as, indeed, too "indefinite" to be "examined on"', wrote Moulton (1885: vi).

The slogan of 'definite knowledge' had certainly been used to give a characteristic naivety to honours exams in Modern History. It called up positivist ideology in the service of in-grown classical practices, leaving little room for any form of cultural study to develop.

We shall be returning to the impact of 19th century exams on modern literary studies; for the moment, what is noticeable is the united opposition of key Extension lecturers. The masterpieces of English Literature, said Collins in 1891, 'have been resolved into exercises in grammar, syntax and etymology. Its history has been resolved into a barren catalogue of names, works, and dates.' And as an experienced exam 'coach' before he joined the Extension, he knew what he was talking about. So literature must be rescued from the disastrous effects that had resulted 'from the refusal of the universities to distinguish between a literary and a philological study'. 'Its boundaries must be enlarged' (p.5).

Central to that rescue was the actual enjoyment of reading. Significantly, as the veteran reformer, Mark Pattison, was reading the Antigone at 70, 'with greater pleasure than I ever did before', he took time off to write a note of encouragement to Collins, still in his early days as a lecturer. 'I sincerely hope you may never forfeit that happy gift [of enjoying poetry], but that you may lay up for age, a store of joyous associations, with all the great classics of the world...' (1883). Collins not only did so, he communicated that enjoyment as an integral part of his work. As one of his students wrote, looking back, 'To some of us parts of the Greek plays, passages from Shakespeare, and many poems of Tennyson and of Browning will always recall his reading of them, and be for ever associated with the deliberate cadence, the sonorous music, the wealth of restrained feeling that fell on our ears... as we listened to his voice' (Luce 1908).

A characteristic Extension 'lecture', then, was a blend of recital and comment. 'He has shown that it is possible to read extracts from a play better than they are given on the stage... at the same time [commenting] on them with penetrating criticism': this was the first reaction in Philadelphia, when Moulton went out to help launch the US Extension movement in 1891 (Moulton 1926). It was not accidental that at Cambridge, Moulton had been secretary of the Music Society, an organist, and a friend of the young composer, Hubert Parry; nor that he was a lifelong singer. 'He considered with wise care every detail of gesture and voice management', a colleague remembered, 'winning an interested and eager audience for the masterpieces of Greek tragedy and comedy, and for the books of the Bible [Job and Isaiah especially], as well as for the more popular works of dramatic literature' (A. J. Grant in Moulton 1926). ('It's as good as the theatre!', they said in places like Newcastle-on-Tyne, where 700 turned up for his courses year after year.)

Bradley drew a further lesson from this practice, of profound importance for his students:

> For reading which has as its object not poetical education but to get the good of poetry *at once*, the best rule is – read what you enjoy. It may not be as good as something else, but that is no reason against enjoying it; it is only a reason for abstaining from foolish assertions that it is better than something else. *Evangeline* is not as good as *Hamlet*: but *Evangeline* enjoyed is worth fifty *Hamlets* unenjoyed.
>
> (1884: 21)

The reminder is still salutary, and raises crucial questions for 'poetical education' in any form. At the time, though, it was heretical.

In a sense, of course, the stress on enjoyment and social recital was an obvious response to popular experience outside academe: reading aloud in the family circle, or wider, was a well-established Victorian practice. The serial novels – and other extracts from the journals – were habitually read aloud. This was the 'floating literature' of the time. People like Collins even committed long passages to memory, ready in store for the moment when, for instance, his host's 16-year-old son asked him 'where to find a really good description of a great battle'. ('Whereupon he reeled off fifteen pages of Napier without a pause... to the great delight of Basil and all of us' (F. B. Miles in Collins 1912: 138).)

And right across class barriers, people already enjoyed oratory, recitations, dramatic renderings. Typically, the same northern cities that set up the Extension were just setting up their great choral societies, too. To such students, it must have been encouraging when academics recognised the 'obvious' in everyday life.

Constraints and scope in the definition of 'Literature' courses

Reading literature socially and sharing its enjoyment: here was a prime focus for the Extension lecturer. But what literature? It is important to consider what the institutional structures of the Extension tended to promote or exclude during this formative period.

The basic unit was a 6–12-week course. These units were organised in the autumn or the spring term, running up to Easter, but not in the summer – when students must have preferred to get outside! The maximum contact, then, was two 12-week courses a year. This was roughly the same as the Oxbridge provision, actually: three terms each of 8 weeks. At first sight, then, from a lecturer's point of view, this seems a strong foundation for a year's course in Literature. But what about the students, and the organising committees: what were their priorities?

So far as the committee were concerned, if they were to balance the budget – without special subsidies – they had to plan a course that would attract roughly 100 students, sustain their interest for 6–12 weeks, and justify the money students must spend (on the fee, on books or equipment, on travelling to the centre). In the smaller towns and the suburbs, where most of the courses were run, this was never easy. The Cambridge reports show many 'centres' that lasted only one year or two. In these circumstances, a run of courses on a single subject, like English Poetry and Drama, might be a bad gamble. Thus, lecturers like Collins, who worked in a hundred Extension centres overall, could usually not plan more than single-unit courses.

Besides, this was an age, it must be recalled, when academic 'specialism' was just beginning. Most of the school teachers and pupil teachers who came in their thousands – at a rough estimate – would be covering the whole curriculum, or a fair part of it. Few of the remaining students would want nothing but imaginative literature either.

Nor was this very different from current practices at Oxbridge, where the majority of the national elite were studying – or failing to study – for Pass degrees in a broad range of subjects. Even the dominant old model, Classics, consisted after all in a medley of things – biographies, campaign memoirs, dramas, histories, maths treatises, lectures on logic, political and forensic speeches, philosophical dialogues, poems (didactic as well as lyric), and early bits of social anthropology. As for the coming subject, 'Natural Science', the Royal Commission of 1875 did not divide it into sub-specialisms, when they recommended that it should count for one-fifth of the secondary curriculum.

Not that the lecturers themselves were necessarily specialists, either. Bradley applied for two posts at Liverpool: Philosophy and Political Economy, or Modern History and Literature. (The reason why he didn't get the former – for he was already a distinguished teacher of philosophy – was that certain council members were afraid of his 'theological unorthodoxy', said his friend Lodge.) One of the men who took his place in the Oxford APHE for women, the ebullient Frederick York Powell, produced a translation of the Icelandic sagas, wrote textbooks for Modern History, and tutored in French Literature – inviting to Oxford poets like Verlaine (1891) and Mallarmé (1894). Such all-rounders would become exceptional by 1900, but meanwhile they were often precisely the people to be attracted to the Extension. 'Here [in Oxford]', Powell wrote in 1889, 'one is well-paid to teach people who don't want to learn, and thereby enabled to teach people who do want to, pretty cheaply' (Elton 1906).

What does all this add up to? First, any expectations today based on a three-year specialist degree – the typical form of mid-20th-century 'English' in England and Wales – have to be set aside. In 1870, what are to be expected are one- or two-unit courses, running for anything from 6 to 24 weeks.

Faced by this constraint, the choices in 'Modern Literature' begin to appear less reductive than Terry Eagleton, for instance, thought. Actually, the broad definition of 'Literature' which he assigns to the 18th century (1983: 17) continued at least through to 1900. For example, George Saintsbury's *Nineteenth Century Literature* (1896) includes: The Development of Periodicals, The Historians of the Century, Philosophy and Theology, Later Journalism and Criticism in Arts and Letters, Scholarship and Science – as well as Poetry, Drama and the Novel. But, given 6–12 lectures and classes, normally without any certainty of another Literature unit to follow, what were students and lecturers to choose?

The first criterion, as already indicated, was to choose the kind of text that was enjoyable both to read and listen to, and usually not beyond the scope of say one or two lectures – allowing for interwoven commentary. That helps to explain the choice of plays and poetry, and the exclusion of novels (with other longer works). So much for 'imaginative' Literature. As for Science, Philosophy, History, Political Economy – plus a good deal more that Saintsbury did not mention – these could be picked up in further courses, and no doubt were. What's more, apart from the drama, a similar mix was being catered for in the journals of the time, available to students in reading rooms and public libraries. Poetry jostled in many of those pages with the latest science and technology.

Unfortunately, though, there are no records – to the best of my knowledge – of the sequence of units pursued by those ardent students who kept going from year to year. In fact, as yet, there is not even an annual list of the courses on offer across the shifting range of centres. What individual students picked from the range of Extension courses can only be guessed – despite Baldick's confident assertion.

Drama and poetry units, then, were components in a much wider scheme. What about the choices within those units? Do they indicate a formation in 'Englishness', for example, as Brian Doyle would expect? In some respects, the answer is Yes. The one unfailing favourite is Shakespeare. Let's remember, though, that his plays were not selected by authority, or even by lecturers; unless they satisfied the organising committees and students the course wouldn't run. Among lyric poets, the recurring favourites (given the current restricted evidence) seem to be Victorian – Tennyson and Browning especially. In other words, the popular poets of the age.

But the repertory did not stop there. Greek drama was among the great successes of Collins and Moulton: in fact, during the 1880s Moulton gave courses on Ancient Drama in 20 centres, 'representing all classes of society' (Moulton 1926: 36). In the early 1890s he also went on to organise a course on The Bible as Literature – independently at this point, as the Cambridge Syndicate would still not support a layman speaking on such a subject! In fact, a list of formative books that resulted from many years teaching in the movement has to include:

World Literature and its Place in General Culture (1911): Moulton
A Literary Study of the Bible (1891): Moulton
The Ancient Classical Drama (1890): Moulton
Shakespeare as a Dramatic Artist (1885): Moulton
Studies in Shakespeare (1903): Collins
Shakespearean Tragedy (1904): Bradley
Illustrations of Tennyson (1891): Collins
A Commentary on Tennyson's 'In Memoriam' (1901): Bradley

Significantly, perhaps, Moulton is the only lecturer, so far as I know, to discuss in detail a possible Extension curriculum in drama, poetry and prose. I am not suggesting that his ideas are necessarily typical of the movement, but as he spent 25 years in full-time work to found it – probably the biggest single contribution by any lecturer of the time – they are worth considering, by way of concluding this chapter.

An evolutionary study of Literature

Moulton's earliest version of a sequence of Literature units appeared in 1887, in 'The University Extension Movement' – (the first book on the subject – with an introduction by Professor Stuart, now an MP). Here he gives 'specimens of three years' plans' for Literature, Modern History, Natural Science, and Political Economy – the last, I note, including Owen, Marx and Lassalle. The Literature proposals run as follows:

Year One: Survey of English Literary Development
Literature of the Elizabethan Age
Year Two: Shakespeare and the Romantic Drama
The Ancient Classical Drama
Year Three: Modern Great Masters – Goethe, Tennyson, Browning
The Art of Prose Composition

English poetry and drama certainly dominate, but the focus was clearly not exclusive. Besides, Shakespeare was not there simply as a national idol: using the Prologue to Goethe's *Faust*, Moulton was currently interpreting 'the antagonism between High Art and Popular Taste: the reconciliation of which (as notably in the Shakespearean Drama) makes the Highest Art'. Thus, he went on, in Romantic Drama the 'popular playwrights, in the teeth of Criticism, created a new departure in Art' – an art where 'the appeal is, not to Criticism, but to human sympathy' (lecture at Sheffield 1884). The choice was explicitly ideological, then, and oppositional.

The 1891 syllabus for 'Literary Study of the Bible' carries the idea of 'development' a step further. 'The Bible is a whole literature... universally recognised... [ranging] from the earliest literary efforts of the world to a period in touch with modern thought', and thus lending itself to an *'evolutionary study of literature'* (my emphasis). In terms of 'literary morphology', Ballad Dance had differentiated into Epic, Lyric and Drama, and these again into Oratory, Idyll, Prophecy, Wisdom or the Gnomic, and Parables.

In his Chicago retrospect, reissued in 1915, there is a final summing up (Moulton 1911). The current conception of Literature, due to the renaissance, was 'almost an accident of history'. First, the rising literatures of Europe had confronted the mature literatures of Greece and Rome. Then a 'departmental scheme' isolated Greek, Latin, Oriental, Romance, German and English literatures, each studied 'by different students in different classrooms'. Such work could not rise above the provincial.

'An evolutionary attitude' was necessary. The first literature was oral. 'Writing and books and authors make a particular stage of literature.' 'Originality had to be invented', just as the very notion of 'individuality'

36 The University Extension 1867-92

was a 'late product, evolved slowly out of the social ideals' of 18th century thinkers. The following ought to be 'many terms in a process that interprets them all':

the ballad dance, where 'bodily movements serve for a long time as a sort of scaffolding, assisting rhythm'
narrative, with a narrator speaking throughout, and the incidents conceived as past
drama, with the speakers dramatised and the incidents 'presented' as happening
'lyric' as reflection, with music predominating...

His first chart then relates: Drama and Oratory; Epic and History; and Lyric and Philosophy. The second cuts a section across time to give three great stages:

A. Floating, oral literature.
B. Fixed, book literature.
C. Floating, periodical literature (the present currency).

Finally, he turns to the notion of 'World Literature': this was a different thing, not simply for the Englishman, the Japanese and the Frenchman, but also for 'different individuals of the same nation'. Each social or ethnic group, he seems to be saying, would construct its own literary 'World'. The British Empire might be the greatest fact in the history of Britain, but 'even that is narrow compared with English-speaking civilization... perpetually being enriched by what it can absorb of national cultures other than its own'. National 'cultures', on this view, are seen as inevitably – and rightly – plural, then. Thus the past pedigree of 'English-speaking civilization' included Babylonian, Arabic, Hebraic, Hellenic, Indian, Persian, Norse, Celtic and Germanic ancestors. And Chinese or Japanese literatures would have their own, distinct pedigrees.

To take a world view in 1915, in the middle of the 'Great War', was already to make a political statement. I am not claiming, naturally, that this final outline was fully implemented, even at Chicago, never mind the Extension in England. But the long-term stance behind these schemes does testify, it seems to me, to projects beyond the narrowly 'national' and 'English'. They were in clear opposition to existing practices – the list of isolated literatures in different classrooms, for instance, referred to the University of London's degrees from the 1860s on. Given the constraints of the Extension, of course, Moulton's projects were severely limited. By 1918 they were largely rejected in the established 'English' degrees: nationalism did prevail, as Doyle rightly emphasises. But today, I see no reason to relegate such schemes to silence.

CHAPTER 3

Efforts to theorise teaching and learning

Theoretical questions raised by dramatic readings

We have seen the names of the key authors and some of the texts: the question is: What became of them in the course of lectures and classes? The titles tell us nothing about that. To define 'literary studies' within the Extension we would need to know what actually happened – and, so far as I know, almost all that evidence is lost. What is actually left? First, very detailed 'syllabus outlines' for a range of courses; second, occasional lectures that were printed, at the time or later; third, what were essentially by-products, the books which lecturers constructed from their experience of teaching, sometimes with the aim of clarifying their purposes. I have chosen to focus here on the most radical change of all: the challenge to invent a new form of discourse.

A tradition of dramatic reading with commentary inevitably called on new discursive forms. Whereas the reader of a contemporary review article started with text on the page (and often very brief extracts at that), students in the lecture hall felt 'the response of the spectator' (in Moulton's words), as body and voice enacted imaginary events in front of their eyes. Things changed for the lecturer too: there were serious challenges as he commented and reflected on that shared experience. New uses of his language were demanded – for which the discourse of reviews and periodicals offered little help, at the time.

Behind this, of course, lay deeper problems about what constituted a 'literary work', how a specific rendering of it could be justified, and what active 'spectators' might expect to be doing. Several of these theoretical difficulties were only partially met, if that. Yet some fundamental questions *were* asked.

'Production must always be far ahead of criticism and analysis... [carrying] its conquering invention into fresh regions', wrote Moulton (1885: 37–8). And, incidentally, he pointed out, 'the revolution' that

Shakespeare created in world drama, carried it 'at a bound so far beyond Dramatic Criticism that the appreciation of [his] plays was left to the uninstructed public' (p.v) – a fact that his new class of student could relish, no doubt.

Inevitably, then, because 'poets are pioneers in beauty, passages [may have] to be read over and over again... effect compared with kindred effect... To train is to make receptive.' And in this process 'sympathy is the grand interpreter'.

However, there is a stumbling block: 'the details of literature and art are open to the most diverse interpretation. They leave conflicting impressions on different observers, impressions both subjective and variable in themselves, and open to all manner of distracting influences, not excepting that of criticism itself.' (Thus the effects of the 18th century critics who had condemned Shakespeare's grave 'errors'!)

What was needed was a psychology 'not yet systematized, that deals with the distribution [of various elements of the human mind] amongst different individuals'. This would allow us to understand why readers differ, how 'the will and consciousness act as disturbing forces, refracting what may be called natural effects into innumerable effects on individual students'.

In general, then, students had to recognise that 'it is not the objective details [i.e. the 'text' – J. D.] but the subjective impressions they produce that make literary effect'. Nevertheless, 'the objective details are the *limit* on the variability of the subjective impressions' (p.24).

So what must the students learn to do? 'The inductive critic simply puts together all the sayings and doings of Macbeth himself, all that others say and appear to feel about him, and whatever view of the character is consistent with these and similar facts of the play, that view he selects' (p.25). Thus, 'interpretation of literature is of the nature of a scientific hypothesis, the truth of which is tested by the degree of completeness with which it explains details of the literary work as they actually stand... which most nearly explains the words as they are'.

This is a first step in explaining the gap between printed text and dramatic enactment – a problem still not too well theorised today. The current Cambridge philosophy of science took Moulton so far: he could use the underlying model of induction, hypothesis, objective details, refracting forces and mathematical 'limits' as a useful first approximation to get at some of the underlying difficulties. (It is clear, incidentally, who he was trying to impress!) Nevertheless, there are signals that he is struggling: think of 'simply puts together', 'appear to feel' and 'similar *facts*'.

Behind the model, I might comment today, lay his actual lecturing, where personal meanings were socially acted out and communicated – and somehow based on signs in social use. Quite a bit of this escaped him, no doubt, and was bound to do so, given his philosophical assumptions. But at least he recognised the existence of a gap, and realised it must be theorised. A problematic was being defined.

Besides, because he recognised differences among readers, he was very decent in practice. 'We are met with the difficulty that Shakespeare has drawn the characters [in *Julius Caesar*] with such subtlety, and so delicately balanced the motives, that various impressions are left.' 'Different readers', he confesses, 'find themselves at the close partisans of Caesar or Brutus'! So he decides only to speak 'for myself' (1903: 128). Alternative 'hypotheses' just have to be accepted – provided they fall within the 'limits' on 'variability', presumably.

I believe there are valuable proposals here, as well as unresolved problems. But theoretical difficulties were not easily catered for in a peripatetic university, of course. Indeed, for the subject of Modern Literature, there was no obvious institutional centre, where lecturers like these, pioneering a new 'subject' and determined to make a clean break with established traditions, could meet and discuss. Moulton acknowledges help from his brother (a Cambridge headmaster) and a college friend. Collins tends to formulate his position in public arguments in the periodical press: there are many signs how ill-prepared his Oxford course in the new ('definite') subject of Law and Modern History had left him. His self-confessed leaning to polemic is no help either.

Only Bradley had a solid base for speculative and theoretical work. An outstanding student of Tom Green, drawn by him into original philosophising, with a range of close friends that included Lewis Nettleship, Bernard Bosanquet, Arnold Toynbee, his brother Herbert (F.H.) Bradley and his early Liverpool colleagues, Bradley had a better chance than most to make sense of the emerging practices for a new subject.

Unfortunately, his contribution has recently been written off by Terence Hawkes (1986). According to Hawkes, 'the essence of Bradley's position lies in the notion that the words on the page transparently express character' (p.36). In what follows, I hope to show that this is something less than a half-truth, and that Bradley's notions – in essence or not – have much more to offer the teacher today.

Imagining the effect of every scene

Andrew Bradley went to Liverpool in 1881, with 'a keen interest in modern politics, in popular education, and in the industrial movements now going on in England'. 'Philosophy and Literature [were] not a dilettante luxury to him but a passion.' 'He [had been] invaluable', wrote a brilliant student of his, 'in helping to clear up for us all those difficulties and mystifications which beset the beginner... He made philosophy a real thing for us' (Testimonials: Bodleian Lib.). Bradley knew that, if Modern Literature and the Extension were to succeed, there must be a paradigmatic break with classical education. His early occasional lectures put the case powerfully and with great clarity.

To start with:

> Exert the imagination. It does not matter whether we study a song or a tragedy, but let us take as an instance a play of Shakespeare... We must have continually before the mind's eye the effect of every scene upon the stage, so that the scene and what is uttered and done forms a picture before us.
>
> (1884: 23)

This is the primary act. In this sense, as he later elaborated, an actual poem is 'not a mere number of black marks on a white page'; it is 'the succession of experiences – sounds, images, thoughts, emotions – through which we pass when we are reading as poetically as we can' (Bradley 1904: 4). The distinction is still easy to forget.

What he sees himself fighting, as a teacher, then, is 'the tendency to substitute other studies for the study of the poem as a poem'. By all means, carry out the 'more prosaic task – that of learning to understand the mere words'. But the activity that follows must be imaginative. Without that – he implies – there can be no enjoyment.

At the same time, the act of imagining people in action must be disciplined, too:

> Every moment of our reading [a Shakespearean play] ought to be a moment not of laziness but of tension. We do not know it, we do not understand it, until by a continual comparison of what they do and what they say we have arrived at a distinct idea of the characters; until we know them as friends, so that their words and acts are exactly what we should expect of them; until we see how the collision and the catastrophe arise out of the characters and the circumstances in which they are placed; until we realise the terror or the pathos or the humour or the passion of the highest moments.
>
> (Bradley 1884: 23)

'This vigorous use of the imagination then is what we chiefly need.' The new focus is on 'understanding' characters in action: constructing in the mind's eye what they do and what they say, realising the force of it moment by moment, and 'knowing' them so well that the collision, the struggle, is recognised to be inevitable.

That implies a new kind of teaching: a new dialogue with the 'class' about how to construct a scene from a text, line by line; about how to construct character in action from the particularities of what's said and done; and about the attempt to realise, on reflection, why a collision was inevitable – and how that affects us as spectators. It is a simpler and more concrete model than Moulton's. Yet Bradley is tacitly proposing new kinds of discourse (and new social relations) between lecturers and students. It was a formidable task to take on.

Of course, Bradley continues, it is impossible for the individual reader to do all this perfectly, and vain to expect our imagination will take the place of the theatre, but when we dwell upon the great words in reading, 'the attempt makes a play of Shakespeare's a new thing'.

And here, 'reading' – as so often at the time – implies dramatic 'reading aloud', for:

> lastly we must do our utmost to realise in the great passages the metrical effect which cannot be separated from the total effect, and realise the terrible force of those single lines made up of hurried whispered questions and replies in the murder-scene of Macbeth, and the dying away of Hamlet's voice upon the words 'The rest is silence'.
>
> (1884: 23)

There are still many gaps, of course, in this idealised account. It was not even intended to be systematic, I believe. A crucial distinction had to be made, he felt, and an alternative to philological instruction to be sketched.

Bradley is not addressing an audience of theorists, let's recall; he is offering pragmatic advice to an evening class of Liverpool students (and himself). While outlining readers' activities in a specific kind of realistic drama, he is also indicating to fellow teachers in the audience the kind of joint work they can help to set up.

It was the beginning of a new disciplinary tradition for reading. And within the Extension movement, at least, he was not alone. Thus, back in Oxford, teaching APHE for women and Extension courses, York Powell advised his students: 'If, as is most to be wished, a group of students agree to work together, the Play or Poem... should first be read (aloud) and then discussed at regular meetings'. *Character parts should be allocated and studied beforehand.* 'Great attention should be paid to the actual reading, to the true meaning of the words, the exact force of the phrase, the harmony of the verse, and the rhythm of the prose. Much help can be got from hearing good actors or reciters' (Extension Syllabus 1889). That's the rough sketch for the 'Home Study of Shakespeare'; Bradley seems to me to be filling it out – especially the instruction in italics.

In 1884, then, Bradley focused on the fallacy that confuses a text and a poem. It is still a productive distinction, as Louise Rosenblatt has recently shown (1978 – see Part III).

The key impact was to be on teaching. What were students experiencing in the course of a reading? In effect, that was proposed as the central question. I don't believe the teaching methods of the day were capable of giving an adequate answer – indeed, are they now, at university level? But a direction was given for crucial experiments. So it is not altogether surprising to find an early Liverpool student recalling that:

> Strong, the jovial and humorous professor of Latin, got us, in my first year [1889], to produce the Mobellaria of Plautus... performed for three nights to audiences few of whom could follow a word... We rehearsed for three weeks at a school run by ladies who were very much of the 'college set', and the rehearsals were good fun.
> (Muir in Hodgson1943: 24)

The reformers were carrying their opposition right into the enemy camp – the teaching of Classics.

For anyone with an analytic interest, such experiments must have been immensely stimulating. Acting things out or giving dramatised readings implies realising that the text is a script, I would say. This was bound to raise new problems. Speech is not too well represented by text anyway – and especially the speech of dead languages. Yet the literary exemplars selected by Extension lecturers were normally dramatic or lyric: they were not merely spoken but physically enacted. How might that upset and transform established views of the poetic 'substance'? And, more crucial still, when the performance was over, what remained? What in fact were lecturers talking about, when they turned from a reading to discuss 'it' with the class?

Focus on the poem, or on the reflective product?

Bradley seems to me to have become increasingly sceptical about current practices as he tried to answer the last two questions. First, what do we retain after a reading? Suppose, he says to an imaginary opponent, you feel sure you recall the action and the characters, though you have forgotten the words. Can you reasonably claim you possess, if not the whole poem, the most important part? No: 'for in forgetting the words you must have lost innumerable details of the action and the characters'. The mistake you are making is to assume that action and character can exist 'as ideas, on the one side', with the words as 'certain sounds on the other'. But this is a fallacy: the play is an experience of something in 'which the two are indissolubly fused' (Bradley 1909: 17).

In that case, we might ask, what about 'The Plot' and 'The Characters', those inevitable preliminaries to every current edition of

Efforts to theorise teaching and learning 43

classical or modern drama? In this separated form, they were no part of the play, Bradley is saying, but 'a product of it in your reflective imagination, a faint analogue of one aspect of it, taken in detachment from the whole' (p.18.) In one step Bradley had cast doubt on a central, established convention in the 'critical editions' of his time.

The distinction he was making is fundamental. On the one hand there is a 'play', a dynamic succession of experiences through which you pass. On the other, a 'product' of it formed by 'your reflective imagination'. The two were not to be confused (as they still are, all too often). So what precisely does that imply?

First, Bradley has no wish to question, 'in a wide sense of "poetic"... the poetic value of this product, as you think of it apart from the poem.

> It resembles our recollections of the heroes of history or legend, who move about in our imaginations, 'forms more real than living man', and are worth much to us though we do not remember anything they said. Our ideas and images of the 'substance' of a poem have this poetic value, and more, if they are at all adequate.
>
> (p.18)

This is a fascinating suggestion, it seems to me. Those vivid imaginary creatures and their worlds continue to 'move about', to operate actively and powerfully, but in forms that are somehow acculturated in part to the 'substance' of our own minds, I take it. (Was he thinking of Dickens's childhood experiences, perhaps, in the 'Uncommercial Traveller'?)

At the same time, though, Bradley is raising questions about the 'adequacy' for criticism of the characteristic 'product' of reflection. Might it not equally count as 'the debris of a poem' (p.12), in comparison with the actual shaping experience?

If so, what had the practice of forming of a 'product' by reflective imagination to do with the disciplinary practices of reading?

> Well, I do not dispute, I would even insist, that, in the case of so long a poem as 'Hamlet', it may be necessary from time to time to interrupt the poetic experience, in order to enrich it by forming such a product and dwelling on it.
>
> (p.18)

Again, there seems a lot of potential in this idea, but, rather teasingly, he leaves it there. For the purposes of his lecture the broad distinction had to be enough.

A three-part model was being proposed: first, there was a text; then a dramatic experience; then possibly a period of reflection, imaginatively constructing a product from elements of the experience – but by no means the whole of it. And within this threefold division, it was the disciplining of the reading that was central.

Why be so wary of the 'products' in an age of periodical criticism? Why question their adequacy in general terms? And why be so ready to subordinate them to the reading itself? I suspect such questions were forcibly put to Bradley at the time; if not, they would certainly be put to him in university circles today!

Bradley's line here is unusually sceptical, even for him. But I can see at least two reasons for it. The first arises from an underlying dissatisfaction with much contemporary criticism. The second, from a significant silence in his own analysis here.

Studying a concrete struggle, not a moral theory

About the typical printed 'product' he was quite explicit: critics were characteristically confusing poetry with moral philosophy. They were not thinking about the way a play operates. Thus, tragedy, he told a Glasgow audience in 1889, 'exhibits [the fundamental contradiction in human nature] not in a theory but in the shape of a struggle at which the spectator holds his breath' (Bradley 1889: 11). 'The dramatic point of view is concrete'; by comparison our moral judgement of life is abstract (p.19). Presumably, this ought to affect what we expect to find in drama, the way we watch it, and how we talk about it afterwards.

Thus, '[I do not suppose] that Shakespeare, for instance, was as tedious as his critics; that, like one of them, he invented for each play some central idea and then incorporated it into men and women; that, like another, he considered wellnigh every good or evil fortune that befalls his characters as a reward or punishment; or even that, like others [with a glance at himself – J. D.], he saw in tragedy a picture of the contradiction of man's nature' (p.20).

Again, Bradley is pointing to the obvious. Suppose you watch, or take part in, the acting out of a drama today: it is a concrete experience, people doing things and suffering there in front of your eyes (and internally, if you yourself are taking a part). In a realist tradition of theatre, you recognise the participants in the imaginary world as lifelike persons, in specific but changing social relationships to each other.

Thus, Bradley argued, 'the appropriation of the poet's mind should be... [by] an analysis which never ceases to be also imaginative vision, and a vision which sees in their relations and in their movement the objects of analysis' (p.21). Again, the stress is on the concrete and dynamic.

It did not make sense, then, to talk about such 'imaginative visions' as if an abstract idea had priority – as if they were just a derivative of abstract thinking. Besides, by reducing things to highly general categories, critics stood to miss a lot. Theoretical abstractions necessarily

Efforts to theorise teaching and learning 45

selected certain elements for discussion and relegated others; drama, by contrast, 'does not fear to show every element in the situation'. Because, as you watch, 'the needs of action are removed... art, being purely contemplative, can survey its object on all sides', in Bradley's view (p.19).

So, if 'literary works of imagination are the artistic interpretation of the world or of life by means of language' (p.6), they are characteristically more concrete, many-sided and dynamic 'interpretations' than abstract moral discussion. There is not much doubt what he had in mind. When I read literary essays in journals of the 1880s, one thing is striking: the original discourse – and the visions derived from it – are characteristically marginal, or absent. (Moral) generalisation reigns. And Bradley is demanding a different kind of study and analysis.

At the same time, though, he makes two subtle qualifications. Admittedly, he says, compared with history, drama 'produces its effect by an artificial simplicity... People and circumstances are brought together and manipulated simply with a view to [the given situation that is being imagined]. The poet isolates and simplifies... presenting one aspect of a fact' (p.15). The visions of art are 'idealised'.

This 'simplification' that characterises art, removes it from the full complexity of life, then. There is already a degree of abstraction. And the artist too can have abstract ideas. Only, it is not 'first an abstract idea... then an action, and then characters, and then language and metre; the substance and the form are one thing to [the artist]' (p.21).

A fundamental point is being made, it seems to me, about drama and theory as contrasting poles of discourse. Discussion of poetic drama as an 'experience', Bradley is asserting, must find forms of language that retain – rather than eradicate – its characteristics as a kind of dynamic 'vision'. Only in that way will the actual 'struggle', with its complexity of 'elements', be grappled with adequately. Abstract discourse, by comparison, must lose touch with the characteristic substance of drama, and thus its value. Products of this kind are inadequate to the experience. This contrast of Bradley's is too cut-and-dried, we may agree today, but allowing for that fact, it still seems to me to be relevant.

It is one thing to propose a new species of discourse, however, another to invent it. We shall trace the struggle to do so in the next chapter.

Meanwhile it has to be noted that after 1901, Bradley drew in his horns about 'products'; something about his retirement – and the congenial atmosphere back at Oxford? – seems to have inhibited his earlier radicalism.

Making the whole intelligible and significant

Equally, it has to be pointed out, Bradley left untouched a key issue affecting the scope and the purpose of imaginative reflection after the events. In 1885, as we have seen, Moulton had already acknowledged the basic problem: with a subtle play like *Julius Caesar*, spectators ended up favouring different people. Manifestly, they did not read the same significance into the events.

Moulton hoped for a new psychology, showing how 'the will and consciousness act as disturbing forces'. Bradley, so far as I know, failed to take up the issue. In retrospect, it is a telling silence, I believe.

For there was one text above all, which – so Bradley and his generation had been taught – held the key to the significance of life, society and the universe. But, to their distress, they had learnt that its significance was in dispute throughout the scholarly world. This was the Bible. There is no doubt at all that Bradley, of all people, was fully alive to the contest then going on about the significance of its stories. Thus, in editing Lewis Nettleship's *Remains* (1897), he includes the following extract from their letters to each other:

> To the ordinary English mind, as far as I can see, such ideas as those of the incarnation and the passion have not only never taken shape in pictures or statues, but they have scarcely reached the imaginative stage of poetry, except in the case of a few hymns...
>
> Why doesn't someone take the Christian myth, say the myth of the incarnation, and trace its development in the European imagination?... [perhaps] setting people's mind free from the bondage of the suppose facts of Christianity and the idea of their necessity to religious belief...
> (R. L. N. to A. C. B. September 1877)

The idea that the significance of a story will be contested, so that it changes or develops its significance over historical epochs – and does so as radically as Nettleship suggests here – was not unfamiliar, then. And it must once have been a painful process for young Bradley – son of the minister of the Clapham sect – to recognise this. Thus, only a characteristic form of suppression, it seems to me, can account for a major theoretical perception like this, gained in a religious context, not being applied to Modern Literature.

The result, I believe, is an unresolved confusion, in practice and theory. A social and historical perspective is missing.

Of course, neither Bradley nor his contemporaries were likely to deny their own search for significance – in Shakespeare especially. Their Victorian formation guaranteed that this motivated their very act of reading his plays: they seek for, and expect, certain kinds of significance

Efforts to theorise teaching and learning 47

in the lived-through experience – by comparison, perhaps, with their everyday lives?

> We take the nature and the human life around us for granted. Custom hides from us the meaning of the spectacle. Our own existence and the existence of others seem to go on of themselves... and it is only by an effort that we can sometimes trace in the confused mass of details a central meaning, or see in the succession of events that working of moral forces, of hidden laws, of ennobling ideas and passions, which once seen would make the whole intelligible and significant.
>
> (Bradley 1884: 6–7)

Like many of his contemporaries (Marx included), Bradley still needed to make out 'forces' and 'laws' that related to 'ideas and passions' in ways that could create a more human world. He had, as a matter of fact, reflected philosophically upon the experience of the plays and had earlier offered his own interpretation of their significant moral order (in line with his edition of Green's *Ethics*). Had this kind of 'product' become suspect to him? Or what?

Whatever the answer, as the key theorist thrown up by the Extension movement, he had left the development of discourse on Modern Literature with an unsteady base – at the very heart of his revolutionary proposals for it.

CHAPTER 4

Inventing discourses for a new project

Evidence for new discursive strategies

Bradley's model of reading was meant to steer what teachers like him should be doing. In several ways, I can see, it was well adapted to the conditions and aims of Extension lectures on Literature. But what about the actual practices? What evidence have we that Bradley, or Moulton, or Collins and the rest did use the opportunities on offer as they enacted poems or sections of plays in front of their audience? And what about students' written work and the oral questions they raised in the 'class'? Was a major shift in discourse carried through into their thinking and writing?

Unfortunately, I have so far only uncovered one bit of evidence of students' writing, and that comes not from a course but from an independent 'Classical Novel-Reading Union', set up in the colliery village of Backworth, Northumberland, with John Barrow as secretary. Backworth had an almost unbroken connection with the University Extension, he writes, and the CNRU had its birth in 1890 during a course of a purely literary nature. Meeting in the local Students' Association room, a group of 46 had decided to set up a committee and organise a series of discussions every two months on 'great classical novels'.

'Leading points' for discussion were collected from various 'competent literary authorities', including Moulton, but – in terms of discursive originality – the specimen essays published by Barrow and Moulton (in Moulton 1895) are disappointing. They suggest to me that prepared readings were no part of the meetings: thus the vital stimulus to discursive change was missing.

To date, then, I have no evidence on the students' side. Equally, on the lecturer's side, I have still to find anything approaching a verbatim transcription of an actual Extension lecture. So what evidence is, in fact, available to illustrate the discursive strategies that formed the basis for teaching and learning 'Literature'?

Books with their established written conventions turn out to be a poor guide. Working through those written up by lecturers at the time, I have found only one that comes close to the lecturing mode: Bradley's *Shakespearean Tragedy* (1904). Here, at any rate, a serious transformation of current written conventions was attempted. Significantly, the book was subtitled 'Lectures on...' and the contents listed as ten 'lectures', in keeping with their origin as 'a selection from materials used in teaching at Liverpool, Glasgow, and Oxford' (p.vii). In other words, a spoken voice should be constructed from the printed text. We'll be returning to that.

In the opening lecture, Bradley set himself two problems (p.2):

(a) how to read the play 'more or less as if [we] were actors who had to study all the parts... [wanting] to realise fully and exactly the inner movements which produced those words and no other, these deeds and no other, at each particular moment';
(b) how, while not setting imagination aside, 'to compare, to analyse, to dissect... [with the aim of] a reading now enriched by the products of analysis' and a 'true conception of the whole'.

These seem to be fairly representative goals for the movement. I shall select two extracts, then, to elucidate what his own solutions were like in practice. This method will indicate a range of typical and interlocking strategies, as I have called them (Dixon 1989). So I am asking the reader and myself two further questions: do any of Bradley's discursive strategies have longer-term value, and isn't an analysis of such strategies – in some form or other – a necessary foundation today for literary studies?

Actors (and directors) studying the parts

We can usefully think of these Shakespeare 'lectures' as a production for a group of voices. Sometimes the voice is that of a character. Sometimes it is that of a running commentator, emotionally involved in the drama going on in front of his eyes. Then there may be a shift to the voice of a more detached narrator, looking out (or back) over events on a larger scale, perhaps.

What happens as the original dialogue of the play is turned into narrative? The narrator will be extending and transforming the 'action', of course: even the 'events' and the 'conflict' may be his construction, rather than the characters'. However, as the narrator or running commentator imaginatively constructs an 'inner struggle', the voice too is likely to shift, taking on contours of the character's voice (Ruthrof 1981 – see Part III).

All this is pretty familiar, you may feel. Discursive shifts like these are part of everyday story-telling, at home or at work. But the conventions of prose essays tend to cut them out – especially in eras like the Victorian age, when so much prose was built upon the model of dead languages, and 'correctness' of composition was much taught. These practices favoured a significantly more impersonal voice, that of the lecturer as authoritative interpreter, I would say. Well, within Bradley's lectures, too, there is the voice of more detached generalisation. The question is: how is it related to those other voices?

It is not so much the existence of various voices, then, as their dynamic relationships that I want to analyse. Shifts from one to another should serve some purpose, should be cues to the listener/reader that new ways of making and organising meaning have been selected.

Within this chapter I have to be content with parts – with extracts – rather than the whole lecture. Let me begin then, by inviting the reader to construct a shifting set of voices from the following script, laid out to cue in some of the changes. Think of potentials in rhythm, tempo, and pauses, too. Better still, read aloud.

A   (Generalising about Macbeth's behaviour)
'What appals him is always the image of his own guilty heart or bloody deed, or some image which derives from them its terror or gloom. These, when they arise, hold him spell-bound and possess him wholly, like the hypnotic trance which is at the same time the ecstasy of a poet.

B   (Moving into narrating)
As the first 'horrid image' of Duncan's murder – of himself murdering Duncan – rises from unconsciousness and confronts him, his hair stands on end and the outward scene vanishes from his eyes.

C   (Intervening with a general argument)
Why? For fear of consequences? The idea is ridiculous. Or because the deed is bloody?... [Omission here]

B   (Returning to the narrative)
It is the same when the murder is done. He is well-nigh mad with horror, but it is not the horror of detection. It is not he who thinks of washing his hands or getting his nightgown on. He has brought away the daggers he should have left on the pillows of the grooms, but what does he care for that? What *he* thinks of is that, when he heard one of the men awaked from sleep say 'God bless us', he could not say 'Amen'; for his imagination presents to him the parching of his throat as an immediate judgement from heaven. His

Inventing discourses for a new project 51

wife heard the owl scream and the crickets cry; but what *he* heard was the voice that first cried 'Macbeth doth murder sleep', and then, a minute later, with a change of tense, denounced on him, as if his three names gave him three personalities to suffer in, the doom of sleeplessness:

D   (Enacting Macbeth's inner thoughts)
Glamis hath murdered sleep, and therefore Cawdor
Shall sleep no more, Macbeth shall sleep no more.

E   (Moving into running commentary)
There comes a sound of knocking. It should be perfectly familiar to him; but he knows not whence, or from what world, it comes. He looks down at his hands, and starts violently: 'What hands are here?' For they seem alive, they move, they mean to pluck out his eyes. He looks at one of them again; it does not move; but the blood upon it is enough to dye the whole ocean red.

C2   (Returning to the argumentative voice)
What has all this to do with fear of 'consequences'?

A2   (Closing with the generalising voice)
It is his soul speaking in the only shape in which it can speak freely, that of imagination.

What is going on here? Bradley characteristically begins with general tendencies in 'the character'. 'What appals him is always the image.' Voice A offers a product of reflection, looking back over the play as a whole. It asserts the power, but also – as it claims earlier – the limits of Macbeth's imagination, and does so in general terms ('is always').

The word 'appals' – deliberately brought forward for emphasis – cues us not to read this voice as detached; 'hold him spell-bound' and 'possess him wholly' reinforce this feeling, while (the classical) poetic 'ecstasy' gives the listener the merest hint of an alternative evaluation.

With voice B a narrator takes over: 'As the first "horrid image"... rises from unconsciousness and confronts him.' We are a step closer to the 'experience'. The scene is almost present now, half sketched in a phrase and the concreteness of 'his hair... on end'. This seems sufficient to prompt a significant revision by the narrator – changing the image from 'Duncan's murder' (static and external) to the full weight of 'himself murdering Duncan' (active and inner).

Voice C intervenes, as it were, dismissing a line of argument about the source of this image. It is the most detached position so far.

After the paragraph I have omitted, the narrative is resumed, but subtly transformed. It begins not with events, but with a state of affairs. 'He is well-nigh mad with horror.' This state is presented through a series of contrasts. Without her being named, we hear the insistent voice of Lady Macbeth in the background (grammatically subordinated).

Actually, the argument is continuing, in a new form. The form 'What *he* thinks of is ...' frames the evidence for a continuing state of mind. Within that frame, the narrator moves more concretely, from 'His wife heard the owl scream' to 'the voice that... cried'. These are inevitably evocative of the scene. But the narrator intervenes to interpret the force of the cry (adding a teacherly note on the tense in an aside), before introducing the 'denunciation' itself. As his voice changes to D, we are back in the 'experience' – and within the mind of Macbeth.

While the sound of 'Macbeth shall sleep no more' is fading, a new narrator – more like a running commentator – breaks in: 'There comes a sound of knocking'. He enacts each movement or glance, now, almost in Macbeth's role. The force of these urgent, broken lines leads up to 'but the blood upon it is enough to dye the whole ocean red'.

Then, surely, a pause. Then, a flicker of the argument, leading back to the spectator's general reflections – with a difference. When the extract opened, Macbeth was construed as suffering some external power: it holds him spell-bound, *it* possesses *him* (like a trance, like an ecstasy). When this voice returns, there has been a significant shift of meaning: Macbeth's unconscious 'is his soul speaking... freely' – the reflective voice places and recognises him as the agent now.

At this moment, we understand Macbeth better than he does himself. And thus, on our next reading, the experience is potentially 'enriched'.

I think it is fair to claim success for Bradley, within his own terms, on this occasion. To generalise: it seems that the success of this strategy depends on keeping a dynamic relationship going between general tendencies and particular scenes, speeches, or moments. Discursive shifts that move us closer – or right back into – the experience should then suggest new potentials for reflective discovery – as they do in this instance.

This discursive strategy is typical of Bradley when he is working with 'character' as his organising principle. It permits him to integrate several strands of perception, feeling and thought:

- moving closer to inner feelings, thoughts and attitudes,
- evoking memories of them through a (transforming and interpreting) narrative,
- relating spoken words to imagined movements and actions, to suggest – on occasion
- patterns of contrasting action and feeling between two protagonists,
- re-awakening the experience through snatches of the spoken words...

In effect, this prevents 'characters' from becoming sets of disembodied traits, as they continued to be in all the textbooks. Instead, at such moments, perceptions are actively *generalised* from more concrete materials, or actively *realised* in particulars.

However, one central limitation does become obvious, I believe, after reading successive examples of this strategy. You can see it at work in the brief reference (above) to the scene after Duncan's murder. The narrator's focus is on Macbeth; Lady Macbeth is peripheral for the moment. True, she will later be given focal sympathy and attention. But the play itself doesn't work like that: the two of them are presented in interaction.

Bradley is not incapable of taking in both protagonists: with Cordelia and Lear, or with Banquo and Macbeth, for example, it is the interaction that becomes focal at times. With the central figures, though, he chooses to focus on the individual. This arises from his ideological assumptions about 'character', I believe. Victorian notions of the individual and character were very much part of his Evangelical formation, of course, though his friend Nettleship was already resisting them. Bradley does not quite escape them, it seems to me.

Thus, what might have been only a temporary device, a first simplification, well suited to working with an 'actor' and studying the 'part', became an engrained narrative strategy – inculcated unconsciously in the next generation of teachers. Something essential in drama was habitually excluded, in the narratives and thus in the generalised reflections. And yet there were still manifest gains.

Vivid, gigantic images and the unconscious mind

For several generations of students, Bradley's strategies for studying characters in action were a merciful release, as we shall be seeing in the next chapter. However, it is important to remember that he did more than study characters – central as that was to his major work. Thus, the two lectures on *Macbeth* explicitly open not with 'the characters and the action' but with the 'special tone or atmosphere' of the play. In a surprisingly modern way, Bradley sees the need, first, to explore the imagery of the drama, to construct a 'general effect':

> Darkness, we may even say blackness, broods over this tragedy. It is remarkable that almost all the scenes which at once recur to memory take place either at night or in some dark spot. The vision of the dagger, the murder of Duncan, the murder of Banquo, the sleep-walking of Lady Macbeth, all come in night-scenes.
>
> (p.333)

This characteristic discursive movement, from a generalised state of affairs ('Darkness... broods over the tragedy') to specifics, continues with gathering force. 'The Witches dance in the thick air of a storm... The faint glimmerings of the western sky at twilight are here menacing... The moon is down and no stars shine when Banquo, dreading the dreams of the coming night, goes unwillingly to bed...' The voice is not just accumulating evidence, but evoking the quality of varied moments for the audience, as the images are aroused from memory. Then, darkness is 'broken by flashes of light and colour'. This too is explored. Then 'the image of blood is forced upon us continually...' So that finally, looking back over the imaginative product, 'it is as if the poet saw the whole story through an ensanguined mist, and as if this stained the very blackness of the night'.

Prevailing imagery, then, is not so much inspected or listed as gathered and evoked. A 'general effect' is indeed constructed, by a kind of synoptic method – well suited to the Extension lecture. Thus, within the general headings, the particularising voice has scope for powerful effects. This strategy allows both the characters' and the spectators' feelings to be vocally expressed, as new qualities in the imagery are foregrounded.

These groups of images are the initial themes of Lecture IX. But suddenly a curious change in strategy occurs, worth looking at closely. I want first to present it schematically, drawing attention to key shifts in his thinking.

Initially, a generalising voice is looking back over the 'atmospheric' images, seeing them as agencies now:

A1 'Now all *these agencies* – darkness, the lights and colours that illuminate it, the storm that rushes through it, the violent and gigantic images – *conspire* with the appearance of the Witches and the Ghost to awaken horror, and in some degree also a supernatural dread. And to this effect other influences contribute. The pictures called up by the mere words of the Witches stir the same feelings...

A2 In Nature, again, *something is felt to be at work*, sympathetic with human guilt and supernatural malice. She labours with portents...

A3 Then, as if to deepen these impressions, Shakespeare has concentrated attention on *the obscurer regions of man's being*, on phenomena which make it seem that he is in *the power of secret forces lurking below, and independent of his consciousness and will...*

A4 To these are added other, and constant, allusions to sleep, *man's strange half-conscious life...*

A5 All this has one effect, to excite supernatural alarm and, even more, a dread of the presence of evil not only in its recognised seat but *all through and around our mysterious nature.*

Inventing discourses for a new project 55

It seems to me that, almost unconsciously (!), Bradley stumbles on a new, thematic interest here. To begin with, atmospheric 'agencies' are manifestly having their 'effect', awakening horror and dread. Then, more obscurely, something is felt 'to be at work' in Nature. Then comes a shift: it is not external agencies alone, but 'the power of secret forces lurking below', within 'man's being', that we spectators watch with horror.

Are these forces the same as the agencies, or not? The ambiguity is partly resolved with 'man's strange half-conscious life' and more fully – I believe – with 'our mysterious nature'. For that telling 'our' suggests that all this has implications for us, the audience, not just the protagonists.

Bradley, I suggest, has gradually accomplished a fundamental change in his perspective, and ours, as we contemplate the imaginative product. You will say that this goes a long way beyond evoking 'atmosphere'. It certainly does; and I'm not at all sure he realised exactly where he was heading as he worked on these later images.

His new theme is pretty clear, despite the way he subordinates it: it is our 'strange half-conscious life' and what may be present 'all through... our mysterious nature'. This is a thematic interest well worth pursuing through the murderous events of *Macbeth*.

Bradley, however, holds back from that kind of treatment; consciously or not, he grudges it a primary focus. How does he stumble into it, then? It is actually the flexible movement of his 'voices' that permit this to happen. To show this I have to fill in some of the details omitted above.

The key transition comes after A2:

> In Nature, again, something is felt to be at work, sympathetic with human guilt and supernatural malice. She labours with portents.
> [Enacting Macbeth's inner voice]:
> > Lamentings heard in the air, strange screams of death
> > And prophesyings with accents terrible,
>
> [Breaking into running commentary]
> > burst from her. The owl clamours all through the night; Duncan's horses devour one another in frenzy; the dawn comes, but no light with it.
>
> [Shifting to embedded narrative]:
> > Common sights and sounds, the crying of crickets, the croak of the raven, the light thickening after sunset, the home-coming of the rooks, are all ominous.

Inevitably, the enacting of 'accents terrible', lamentings and screams, brings new evocative power into the voice. Bradley's own language has to rise to match the force of the original. So that the natural signs become 'ominous' to the narrator. He feels their impact. And, together with him, we the audience are experiencing events now, ambiguously recovering the feelings of spectators and participants. Thus, when the reflective voice re-emerged, not surprisingly, it had something more to acknowledge – even though Bradley hedged!

Of course, the final code word 'evil' (A5) – rather than 'secret forces' – indicates Bradley's reluctance to take the analysis further. And after all, if he had pursued it, what might have become of the notion of 'character'? So he hovers on the brink. It was not as easy for Bradley's generation as it would become after 1918 – alas – to recognise the murderer in us. Nor was human nature so obviously impelled by mysterious forces. Bradley deserves some credit, then, for moving the frame so far – or rather, perhaps, for betraying a split in his whole view of things?

Discursive strategies, social constraints – and achievements in retrospect

I have looked at just two kinds of discursive strategy that Extension lecturing opened the way for – given the desire to bring speaker and audience into new relations with a 'poetic experience'. These two rely on powerful and subtle shifts in the spoken voice as it takes up new discursive options. The context of the lecture and the expectations of the students, I believe, would foster such strategies, once they had become conceivable.

Now let us turn to consider what the context might have inhibited, and seemingly did. We have to imagine those Literary and Philosophical Halls, Co-op Reading Rooms, Mechanics' Institutes; the men and women assembling there – up to a hundred, and for the lecture itself maybe more; what they had just come from, and what a range of social expectations they brought.

So there they sat down; but did they have any texts with them? As it happens, we know they sometimes did (Moulton 1884). Nevertheless, the books that came to be written up by Bradley or Moulton or Collins do not assume that, discursively. I can think of no section where these lecturer-authors take a piece of text and work forwards and back over it, for instance, as I have just been doing. In fact, offhand, I can remember only two places where they pause to consider a phrase or word in detail – Moulton showing the effect of ambiguity, Bradley that of prosodic form.

The lecturers themselves demonstrate the movement from text to experience. They recite. But – in their books at least – they don't use new discursive strategies to make any of that complex, transforming activity explicit. Was this an unconscious use of the teacher's power? In part, perhaps, but more seriously it was a gap in their whole formation. The 'close reading' that Chris Baldick expected had yet to be invented.

The same omission is true even of 'reading a part'. The size of the audience, and perhaps inadequacy of their own experience, seems to have ruled out any practice of actually working with a group to enact a lyric or a speech – as I might do in teaching today. Certainly, if it happened, it was not taken up into their discursive strategies. Bradley talks of reading 'as if they were actors', but for him it is only a kind of thought experiment, roughly characterised, not the real thing. (Yet, as student drama clubs actually were beginning again, it would be interesting to know if their background presence was felt at times, however obscurely.)

So the constraints of size of audience, of assumed equipment, and of physical context could well have affected the discursive options that were selected, invented, or explored. But in the Victorian 1870s and early 1880s there were hidden constraints of a different kind, with any mixed audience. These were not inescapable, but they were socially conditioned.

They affected, of course, the novel, the drama, and the poem just as much as the lecture. Thus, when Gissing writes about Dickens in 1898, 'in the England of *our times*', he says, '... we must needs treat Dickens as, in many respects, antiquated... To write a novel in the spirit of antagonism to all but a very few of his countrymen would have seemed to him a sort of practical bull; is not the law of novel-writing, first and foremost, that one should aim at pleasing as many people as possible?' (pp.63, 67, my emphasis).

Pleasing and not giving offence: in the founding years of the Extension, these must have seemed obvious enough criteria for selecting and discussing literary works. The lectures, as Moulton put it, had to be 'a safe meeting ground for all parties' – for that reason, 'without religious or political bias' (1887: 15). What's more, when Bradley summed up 'the essential tendencies' of recent literature for his Glasgow students (*c.* 1890), he put the great increase in production – and 'the change in the character of the reading public' – first; the 'decided advance... of decency and refinement' second; and 'the greatly increased share taken by women in literary production' third.

The stress on decency and refinement – seen often as a specific woman's contribution – was pretty typical of his generation. Both words were given their full weight, we must remember: the cultural heroine to bear in mind is probably George Eliot. (Collins was remembered as the 'Ladislaw' of his group at Balliol; Frances Pattison was a young protégé of hers; the Creightons called their first house 'Middlemarch'; Green quoted her in his *Ethics*.) Nevertheless, by the turn of the century, the silences were obvious.

Equally important, I suspect, were the constraints in discussing religious issues (and thus, often, the deeper ideological conflicts they represented). Bradley's list of tendencies did include 'the interest in social problems' and 'the growth of the historical and critical spirit'. But the very wording of the latter is a kind of code. What he implied – in an inoffensive formula – included the destruction and radical transformation of ways of reading biblical texts. This was still a painful, disputed and polarising conflict for many individuals who attended the Extension lectures, no doubt (as Mary Ward's international best-seller showed, in 1888).

However, in one direction, the lecturers were less constrained than we might expect. For the popular subject of Political Economy, Arnold Toynbee taught young Oxford radicals a historical approach to the Industrial 'Revolution' – as he called it: a revolution in 'the relations between employers and workmen', which had left workers half-way between 'serf and citizen' (1884). To overcome the terrible effects in the new cities – the destitution, misery and vice – two great forces would realise a socialist programme: the voluntary agencies and the action of the state. And more in this vein.

In Toynbee's lectures in the North, Ricardo was heavily criticised, while Marx and Lasalle were spoken of with respect, though their programme was held to face 'overwhelming difficulties' in England, at least.

Thus, on social and economic issues, there was a strand of plain speaking. If it was not taken up by the lecturers on Modern Literature, this seems likely to be the result of personal formation, or maybe disciplinary choices, rather than broader social conventions.

Certainly, the work of these rebels was itself socially channelled and contained. Nevertheless, the break they made is still relevant. To sum up, in their own terms:

(a) They restored the social enjoyment of poetry and drama as the main goal for studying it. They entirely rejected the exam traditions of the day – and in the next chapter we shall see why.
(b) They recognised that in reading poetry and drama, students must live through an experience, and lecturers must in part begin to enact it before their eyes.
(c) By dwelling on parts of a text, putting together the sayings and doings of a character, for example, they showed how imaginatively active students could enrich the experience itself. As each scene became vivid to the mind's eye, they showed how conflict and catastrophe were understandable, at times even inevitable.
(d) They favoured poetry and drama where the point of view was realistic and concrete: hence, moral issues were many-sided and

dynamic, not simplified and idealised, as they might be in allegory. This was perhaps in answer to their own search – and their students' – for the working out of complex moral forces and hidden laws in social life around them.

(e) While blending recital and comment, they invented new discursive forms, in which voices moved flexibly between enactment, running commentary, interpretative narrative, and generalisations. They explored the discursive potential of lecturing, its ability to create a closer acquaintance with the phenomena of literature than the criticism of contemporary journals attempted. (Bradley in particular could be very sceptical of these retrospective products, or debris, of the actual experience.)

(f) Their tradition welcomed students' questions and aimed to build up a pattern of conversational teaching in the classes that followed the lectures, basing this in part on students' written work. 'It constitutes the training ground for the teacher', said Moulton.

(g) Moulton in particular progressively aimed for a wider panorama of world literature. He suggested an evolutionary study, starting from ballad-dance, moving on to narrative, drama and lyric, and then to further, differentiated morphologies...

Different individuals and nations, he recognised, would construct their own literary genealogies – but he emphasised the enriching of national cultures by what they could absorb from others, not a narrow focus on Englishness.

For him, the historical epoch of a fixed, book literature with individual authorship might be passing, giving way to a floating periodical literature in his own time (as it has in ours to radio, television and computerised access).

There were problems unsolved in theory and practice – some explicitly recognised, others not – but, within their institutional frame, some key directions for literary studies in a democratic university had already been piloted.

CHAPTER 5
Change at the centre of academic power

Archaic structures face competitive pressures

It is time to turn now to the main centres of academic power. What was going on during this same period? In Oxford and Cambridge, Modern Literature – and much more – faced a long period of exclusion. The essential requirements for entry remained classical Greek and Latin. Women were not admitted. In fact, in 1867 the official teachers were still celibate; marriage was prohibited to all but heads of colleges. All fellows of colleges had to publicly accept the Thirty-nine Articles of the Church of England; many went on to take holy orders.

The minimum cost for students was £200 a year: effectively, sons of the aristocracy, the gentry and the wealthier clergy were the main beneficiaries. Over a third came from the nine 'public schools', which were intimately tied into the system. Students arrived around the age of 19; not all stayed to take degrees, and of those who did over two-thirds did not take Honours. None stayed for postgraduate work: formally, none existed. The largest single group studied Classics, including some classical history and philosophy. This was taught, not by university professors or lecturers, but by a college 'tutor', who often had to be supplemented – when it came to the exams – by an expensive 'coach'. Aristocratic students had only recently stopped wearing their distinctive dress.

For the majority, then, whether students or fellows, not much appeared to have changed since the previous century. And in 1867 the majority of fellows intended to keep things that way. There was much dismay, anger, scorn and derision, therefore, as step by step over the next fifty years these institutional structures were transformed. Not surprisingly, it took almost thirty years for Modern Literature to get recognition at Oxford, and even then the Honours course was deliberately subverted. It was a good fifty years before Cambridge succumbed.

In the decade after 1867, though, active minorities raised one question after another: the fellow's right to marry; abolition of the remaining religious tests; opening more fellowships to competition; the college's responsibilities for teaching; intercollegiate planning of lectures; provision for 'poor' students; extension beyond Oxford and Cambridge; the admission of women; new degree subjects, backed by a new professoriate...

All these issues and more came in a flood in the early 1870s. Inexorable social forces saw to this. A key factor was Gladstone's decision in 1868 to throw open the whole Civil Service to competitive entry (organised by Oxbridge interests). It was symptomatic of the new demand for 'qualification' as a prerequisite for the expanding professions. Even commissions in the Army and Navy could no longer be bought.

Thus, within a decade many ambitious Oxbridge students had two goals: a (high-ranked) First in finals and a place at the top of the order in the national Civil Service exams. Results such as these gave access to plum jobs in academic, professional, or political life. And they shed distinction on the college, in turn.

Competition did not replace 'interest', naturally, but it raised the threshold for access. It was the sign of a new order; the schools and universities had to adapt – and fast. Men with Firsts faced intensified competition in the fellowship exams, based on the same system. Those successful had a *métier* to hand on: indeed, a little handbook on 'Pass and Class' (1860) was the sole claim to fame of the professor who inaugurated the History Honour School at Oxford. Colleges like Balliol began to sweep the board in fellowship exams and, later, in the Civil Service entry, simply because a liberal group of fellows (headed by Jowett and Green) were determined to change the quality of teaching. And other colleges, inevitably drawn into the competition, had to put their resources into training men for a special kind of success.

The competitive Honours exam became punitive – in ways we will investigate – and was intended to be so. It called for six months' unremitting preparation for a highly distorted performance. A peculiar kind of positivism and fragmented learning were fostered, as we shall see – of packaging and scoring by 'facts' assimilated. Original thinkers like Green and Pattison condemned it, but had no option but to submit, for their students' sake.

However, from the 1870s on, the absence of any alternative standards, and especially any organised form of postgraduate studies, opened up divisions in the 'liberal' camp. A new, research-oriented professoriate was being introduced – after helpful pressure from their allies in a government commission. But who would listen to the professor? Only the Oxford women's group seemed to want Stubbs to lecture to them. (His books got a reception in Germany, not in Oxford, he grumbled.) But without 'research' and the 'seminar' (both alien, continental terms), what foundations could there be for new directions in long-established subjects – let alone the new subjects knocking at the gates?

As the 1880s progressed the issue became more insistent. Men were going to Germany for the doctoral work, and that meant research by thesis. Couldn't 'research' papers be made a substitute for exams? How about practical work in the new science labs? And what was to happen to graduates from the Dominions, the Empire, and – in increasing numbers – the United States, who looked forward to postgraduate study in Europe. Could Oxbridge afford to offer them simply the first degree? Would most of them transfer to Germany instead?

Within the context of these struggles, literary studies were small fry. Until 1919, their obscure story in Oxbridge had two faces: the rearguard action fought at each stage, and the successive projects launched, only to end in defeat, or abject compromise. These events left their mark on the subject that emerged – and still do, to this day.

The new institutional framing

During 1894–5, a new Oxford degree in *Literis Anglicis* – a title that tells its own story – was finally organised within the Faculty of Arts. Thus, the Board of Studies set up to administer it was elected by outsiders: 109 teachers of *Literae Humaniores* and 50 of Modern History. They had already ensured that no student would be eligible for the new Honours degree unless he had secured first, 'at least an elementary knowledge of Greek and Latin language and literature', and second, 'a competent knowledge of history, the literature, as documentary evidence, supporting or fitting into it' (Palmer 1965).

This was an exclusion device – with a Catch 22. Until 1914 the only sensible option for a student was either to start his degree by specialising in Classics (for 'Honour Moderations' – Part I) and switch to English (for Finals – Part II), or to start English after completing finals in another subject. The Faculty was not exactly giving encouragement to the upstart crow.

The most distinguished members of the Board were Sir Frederick Pollock, an eminent authority on Jurisprudence, and Charles Firth, whose work on English History in the 17th Century later earned him a professorship. D. B. Monro, who chaired the Board, was a Homeric scholar. Thus, as Firth candidly observed, 'almost two-thirds of the Board had no experience of teaching either English Language or Literature and general principles could not supply the lack of expert knowledge' (1909: 35). As a result, they 'imposed, as is usually the case with new schools, far too much work on the candidates'.

As for the course itself: 'the representatives of language knew exactly what they wanted and never varied in their demands, the representatives of literature were less consistent and less harmonious' (Firth 1909: 33). The scheme that resulted 'had many defects' (p.34).

To teach the new course the Faculty had two professors – A. S. Napier and J. Earle – both of them specialists in Old and Middle English Language. A modest budget (£50 initially) added such part-time lecturers as the Board could recruit and appoint.

In terms of power and institutional practices, therefore, the outcomes were entirely without surprises. The authorised model for teaching and examining (dead) languages was well represented. The editing of texts on historical lines was equally available. Thus, there was no further need for authorising discourses to spell out the goals of a *schola literarum anglicarum*. And none appeared.

Lectures began on 14 October 1895, as follows:

Professor Napier:	Historical English Grammar
	Specimens of Old English Dialects
	Old English Authors
	Middle English
Professor Earle:	The Salient Passages of Beowulf
G. N. Richardson MA:	The Elizabethan Drama
E. de Selincourt BA:	English Literature from 1789

Richardson and de Selincourt (both part-time lecturers, not fellows) had eight weeks to cover their respective periods. Next term, de Selincourt switched to specific poets, two weeks each for Coleridge, Byron, Keats and Shelley. T. C. Snow lectured on The History of Literary Criticism; and Professors Earle and Napier moved on to more 'Old English Authors', English Literature from 1066 to 1400, and Middle English (including *Sir Gawain*).

In the event, two men entered for the exams in June 1896, Alfredus B. Gough and Arturus J. Sargent; 'one scratched before the paper work began and the other as soon as it ended' (p.34). The Calendar listed the classified results in the Arts: 133 successful in *Lit. Hum.*; 105 in Modern History; 2 in Oriental Languages; and 0 in *Lit. Anglicis*. The Faculty seems to have exceeded expectations in keeping the new subject in its place.

After all, in the wider sphere the years from 1896 were the peak of British imperialism. A newly appointed Professor of Poetry (though not involved in student teaching) had just given a clarion call to 'treat poetry as the expression of the imagination, not just of the individual poet, but of the English people'; to 'keep before our eyes the true genius of the nation'; 'to trace the growth of imaginative life in the English nation through its poetry'; never to impede 'the march of the Anglo-Saxon race'; indeed, to 'multiply through the British Empire, the study of our best classical authors' (Courthope 1895: xiii, xxii).

Without the study of 'writers who have embodied their thoughts in the most beautiful and enduring form' there was 'a grave danger that the language of England will yield to [the very heat and fervour of democratic competition]... the desire of writers to say some new thing or invent some new style, the ceaseless immigration [sic] of foreign sentiments, words, and idioms', all contributing 'to eat away the old standards of literary English' (p.xiii). These desires for innovation, this democratic fervour, this immigration of sentiments – all needed the discipline of the new degree, presumably. But the Faculty did not listen.

Maintaining the old standards: the exam papers

The Oxbridge exam papers of the time did indeed impose a specific set of discursive disciplines. There were two papers a day and, for those aiming at a First or Second in *Literis Anglicis*, ten papers in all. Each paper contained about 10 to 12 'questions' and students (like applicants for fellowships) were allowed three hours. Here the hidden rules of competition entered. The aim was to out-match the best of the 'opposition' in terms of the adequacy of each answer, and the number of answers completed. Some papers of the 1880s actually instruct students not to attempt more than nine questions; in 1896 there was no limiting rubric for the English papers. From other evidence, I believe the examiners might have expected six as par for the course, nine as exceptional (Slee 1986).

On average, therefore, candidates had from 20 to 30 minutes per question. Over five days or so they were expected to produce 60 to 90 'answers'. It seems an odd way of setting standards.

Indeed, what kinds of disciplinary practices can be assessed in such a context? Or consider the converse: knowing beforehand the constraints on time and scope that would be imposed, what were lecturers, tutors and coaches likely to be doing? The exam papers give a very clear idea, in this case, of the 'content' of the course they imposed. I will analyse three major strands: the treatment of 'language', of 'texts' or 'authors', and of 'periods'.

English Language and philological notes

'Language' is treated as sets of positive facts: the dialects of Old Germanic; the derivation of Old English vowels; changes in the declension of substantives (or in the relative pronouns); contrasts in the accentuation of Romance words (or the comparison of adjectives); the present tense endings of OE verbs; the unaccented 'e' in classes of substantives... All these were evidently answered by 'book work', by memorising textbook or lecture notes.

Conventionally, there were also supposed to be 'problems'. What phonetic processes are illustrated by ABC? Discuss the syntax of XYZ. Explain the forms; explain the endings; explain the pronunciation; explain the constructions (in the following passages). Write philological notes. The last instruction sums up this set. 'Problems' they might have been, to an editor struggling with scribal forms; now they were reproducible 'facts' from his footnotes, or at best applications of the professor's general rules.

Such questions seem trivial, perhaps, but nevertheless are immensely formative. Consider the conception of studying 'language' that emerges. Dialects, for instance, are tacitly defined: sets of vowels (and consonants); sets of words with specified grammatical functions; sets of endings according to syntax – concepts of this form.

Actually, in the everyday world, dialects exist wherever people from a speech community are doing things, severally or together – in cultural interaction, in social conflict, in efforts to organise socially... We trace them later in 'documents', each drawn from a specific historical context. From this evidence we struggle to reconstruct the participants, the speech community, and what was going on, on this occasion.

The discipline of 'philological notes', then, taught students to be blind to such sociolinguistic practices (even those going on all around them). Language was no longer part of doing things, in history. Rather, it was about being parts of a system in some kind of academic outer space.

Inevitably, it was dissociated from reading, from the act of making meaning. There are no questions in 1896 that ask how the form affects the significance, for someone engaged in reading a 'document'. There are actually no documents, only 'passages' and 'words' for translation, or comment on forms.

Set 'Texts' and 'English Authors' (1896 titles)

The model of philological notes was well suited to the exam context: fragmented units of positive knowledge that could be reproduced in 20–30-minute bursts. But what about 'texts', starting from *Beowulf*, or 'authors', from the *Gawain* poet (sic) on. How could they be treated?

It turned out the method was ready to hand: 'Shakespeareana' – as Bradley put it. There were numerous privileged facts that could be known about writers and their work. Thus:

The part of England where it was composed and date of composition	*Gawain*
'Anything known of the author', or Mullenhoff's theory of its origin	*Gawain* *Beowulf*
Sources, models, 'debts', 'obligations'	OE Literature, the Knight's and Monk's Tales, early Shakespeare, *Romeo and Juliet, Richard II*, Milton, Pope, Burns
The metre: Siever's theory or special characteristics	OE verse *King Horn*, Miltonic blank verse
Differences between first and later editions	*Paradise Lost, The Ancient Mariner*
Analysis of the plot, construction, substance or contents	*Love's Labour's Lost, Twelfth Night*, two Bacon essays, *Lyrical Ballads*
References to peoples and old sagas, to medieval romances, to ecclesiastical controversies, to French and English critics, or to Napoleon	*Beowulf* Chaucer Milton Dryden Wordsworth and Byron
Johnson's criticisms of	*Essay on Man, Tale of a Tub*

Questions of this type had three advantages. First, they could be covered by reference to standard editions, if there was no time in lectures. Second, they relieved students of the immense burden of reading all those texts or authors. Third, they lent themselves precisely to neat summary.

Together with the philological notes, this 'editorial apparatus', as we might call it, formed the staple of the exam. But what about texts in their own right, you may be thinking – 'texts' as 'poems', for instance. What actually could be done with them in the time allowed?

Occasionally, the examiners themselves betrayed an awareness of the difficulty:

Write a short account of the works of Marlow.
Write a short criticism of the poetry of Burns...
Give some account of Hazlitt's critical writings.

Some account indeed, in 300–500 words. These were the kinds of questions conveniently provided for in Austin Dobson's *Handbook of English Literature* (revised edition, 1897), where each entry ran to a page or so on average.

Even to the well-intentioned examiner, the problem of scope was insurmountable. But, having said that, a serious question of focus still remains. What kinds of reading – if any – were being authorised? I can find only three indications:

Write an essay on the character of Henry IV, as represented by Shakespeare in different plays.
Has the term 'Poetical Justice' any meaning applicable to the tragedy of *King Lear*?
Show by an examination of one of Miss Austen's novels in what qualities her originality as a novelist consisted.

Despite their clumsy formality (itself a sign of insecurity, perhaps?), I suppose that these three do evince an interest in Shakespearean characters, and in qualities of vision in *Lear* or Jane Austen. Something was struggling to escape – but in such a system, what hope had it?

A knowledge of History, the Literature fitting into it?

If the new school had no room for basic work on the act of reading, it had at least plentiful advice on hand from Modern History. What was initially made of this? Amazingly little. The papers covered by the two Professors reveal no interest in history. Language 'undergoes changes' or 'development', is 'influenced', and ends up with 'differences'. The lack of human interest is deep-rooted. Consider the presuppositions underlying a typical question or two:

Give an account of the influence of French on English from the Norman Conquest to the end of the fourteenth century.
Enumerate a few of the important changes which English has undergone since Chaucer's time.

It is as if a 'language' was an independent entity. Thus, one language can have effects on another. Or, in a passive way, a language can submit to being changed. There is no concept of people doing things – of Normans who conquer (from one decade to another), or Chaucer who travels Europe and writes throughout an 'age'. The history of dominance, struggle and negotiation between social groups – using and forging language as they do so – is verbally excluded from our imaginations.

But the 'period' papers covered by the lecturers seem little better:

> Describe the principal types of Elizabethan prose.
> Trace the development of political satire in the seventeenth century.

These arbitrary markers – a reign, a century – suggest a naive sort of political history, somewhere in the background. In fact, the student is not required to refer to it, though.

Indeed, only three questions might claim to take history seriously:

> Trace the history of legal restrictions which limited the freedom of literature during the seventeenth century.
> Compare Swift and Burke, showing how each may be taken to represent the intellectual and literary tendencies of his time.
> Account for the popularity of Cobbett as a political writer.

'Legal restrictions', 'popularity' and 'representative tendencies' are not altogether unconnected. Yet I doubt if even the candidates who answered these questions had any clear view of the social context for literature – had asked consistently who was restricted and who enabled; which social tendencies were represented and which repressed or marginalised; which production agents and reading publics made selected writers popular, for what reasons... Of course, supposing they had, such questions would have been more than usually ironic, given the candidates' own restricted context as writers.

Historical imagination and analysis, it seems to me, were bound to be killed by the lack of scope. There was no room for discursive strategies that moved flexibly between the 'documents' and their historical context (at the time of publication, or even in 1896).

'Enumerate' is the telling word. And it leads inexorably to 'Describe the principal types'. This listing of typifications – in an ordered 'development', no doubt – was the best that students could hope to achieve. They were being formed to assert abstract generalities, whatever the discursive demands of the drama, narrative and discussion they were reading.

If they read them! There was no incentive to read literature, it seems to me, in the language of the examiners or the conditions of the exam. The disjunction between the main purposes of the Extension lecturers and the new School could hardly be more complete. Enjoyment? Where was the room to express it? An uneasy giant lay buried beneath this new institution: what chance would it get to escape? Is it free yet, I wonder.

INTERCHAPTER 6

Literature and society: a different view

Historical investigation was one of the great intellectual achievements of the 19th century. Applied to two of the central texts – the Old and the New Testament – it had revolutionary effects. What authors – what origins, in oral or written discourse – what generic forms – with what editing and re-editing – at what periods – in what cultural milieu – under what social and political conditions – with what audiences (and opponents) in mind...? Questions such as these became the subject of intense discussion, with constant refinements in methodology, and the source of ever-ramifying enquiries, especially in the great German centres of learning.

For the new study of Modern Literature there was nothing really comparable in Britain. Histories of English Literature – broadly including poetry and prose fiction, historical writing and political oratory, philosophy and controversial theology, outstanding works on law, political economy, science and the like – were indeed produced throughout the century. But almost without exception these followed an earlier version of historical narrative, and the exceptions – like Taine's famous work – made some very dubious assumptions.

Thus, when John Churton Collins tried to introduce historical studies of literature into the Extension movement, in 1888, he must have half-realised he was asking for the impossible. The characteristics of literature, he declared, were determined by historical conditions. This called for an analysis of 'the conditions, political, social, moral, intellectual, under which [a given work] developed, and out of which it sprang' (1888: 4).

Though he boldly threw down a list of 50–100 contemporary texts for his 'map' of the 16th century, there is no further evidence how those 'conditions' were going to be elicited, supplied, or structured.

In general, I believe, there were clear enough institutional constraints on any attempt to set up historical studies of that kind – whether in the

Extension, or at Oxford. In fact, the task was left to an outsider, another of those remarkable Victorian rebels who spent their lives in self-education. This one in his younger days had resigned his fellowship, unable to subscribe to the Articles; joined John Stuart Mill, Henry Fawcett, John Morley and others in founding the Radical Club (1870); edited one of the popular journals; and finally ended up organising the *Dictionary of National Biography*.

In the year he was dying, 1903, Leslie Stephen was invited to Oxford – through his nephew, Herbert Fisher – to lecture on 'Literature and Society in the Eighteenth Century'. The results could have made a difference to English Studies from then on, for anyone who listened critically. (Perhaps one or two did? – Phoebe Sheavyn, for example; but she left Oxford not long afterwards.)

'[Every writer] is, of course, an individual, and the critic may endeavour to give a psychological analysis of him', he began. But every man was also an organ of the society in which he had been brought up. He was 'dependent upon what in modern phrase we call his "environment" – *the social structures of which he forms a part*, and which give a special direction to his *passions and aspirations*. That suggests problems for the historian of *political and social institutions*' (1927: 8, my emphasis).

Suppose the historian goes beyond dates, statistics and 'objective' phenomena seen from the outside:

> If we allow ourselves to contemplate a philosophical history, which shall deal with the causes of events and aim at exhibiting the evolution of human society – and perhaps I ought to apologise for even suggesting such an ideal could ever be realised – we should also see that the history of literature would be a subordinate element of the whole structure. The political, social, ecclesiastical, and economical factors, would all have to be taken into account.
>
> (p.13)

And, despite the apology, he proceeds to sketch what he means. Starting around the end of Queen Anne's reign, he looks for 'essential parts of the system'. First, 'the supremacy of the class which really controlled parliament', the aristocrats [squires and landed gentry, led by the peers] and the "moneyed") men ['representing the rising commercial and maufacturing interests']. Then, the unusually close relation between this political class and the literary, and their exclusive focus on London. Thus, the institutional base for their close relation: 3000 coffee-houses, by 1708, each with its habitual circle.

Take a list of twenty or thirty literary names, including the chief authors of the time: all received public appointments. But the offices were rarely bestowed as rewards for literary distinction; the system worked the other way. Promising university students, like Prior and Addison, were brought out under the wing of a statesman. 'He could reward personal dependants at the cost of the public; which was convenient for both parties' (p.41). The rapid development of a press with political power did the rest: literary merit was manifestly useful.

This was no ordinary ruling class, either. The town had superseded the court:

> The parliamentary statesman, no longer dependent upon court favour, had a more independent spirit and personal self-respect. He was fully aware of the fact that he represented a distinct step in political progress. His class had won a great struggle against arbitrary power and bigotry. England had become the land of free speech, of religious toleration, impartial justice, and constitutional order. It had shown its power by taking its place among the leading European nations [even humbling the great Monarchy, the French]... These successes, too, had been won in the name of 'liberty' – a vague if magical word.
>
> (p.45)

What's more, 'the most intelligent Frenchmen of the coming generation admitted the claim; they looked upon England as the land both of liberty and philosophy' (p.45). Thus, the cultivated classes could regard 'themselves and their own opinions with that complacency in which we [English] are happily never deficient' (p.46).

The coffee-house clubs, then, represented critical tribunals, which included the rewarders as well as the judges of literary merit. Generosity could be stimulated by flattery, but usually these political patrons did not find it necessary to exact the personal subservience of the past. 'The aristocrat was no doubt conscious of his inherent dignity, but he was ready on occasion to hail Swift as "Jonathan", and, in the case of so highly cultivated a specimen as Addison, to accept an author's marriage to a countess' (p.43).

How could all this affect what was written? Politically, the answer was obvious. But, socially (and directly affecting the passions), Stephen saw evidence of a crucial 'absence' (or 'transformation') and an ever-present 'rational' tone.

As compared with the contemporary French salon, the coffee-house was marked by the absence of any feminine element. So what became, for instance, of the Elizabethan or Restoration love lyric? Clubs were the last place to offer an appreciative audience. 'It is necessary to smuggle in poetry and passion in disguise, and conciliate possible laughter by stating plainly that you anticipate the ridicule yourself. In other words, you write society verses like Prior, temper sentiment with wit... turn out elegant verses, salted by an irony which is a tacit apology perhaps...' (pp.82–3). Where the passions are concerned, you become a Wit.

As for the prevailing tone, writers had to talk the language their hearers understood, and adopt 'the traditions, conventions, and symbols with which they were already more or less familiar' (p.23). Instead of the old concrete imagery, there was a system of abstract reasoning. 'Diagrams take the place of concrete pictures' (p.75).

The effects were best seen in Locke, whose philosophy blended spontaneously with the ordinary language of these circles. Locke ruled the thought of his own and the coming period because he interpreted so completely the fundamental beliefs (the creed, philosophical, religious and political) which had been worked out at his time. But he ruled by obeying – by his adaptation to this audience. Like the theologian of the age, Tillotson, he was no longer a member of a learned corporation condescending to instruct the laity:

> It was taken for granted that the appeal must be to reason, and to the reason which has not gone through any special professional training... The writer, that is, has to suit himself to the new audience... He has to throw aside all the panoply of scholastic logic, the vast apparatus of professional learning, and the complex Latinised constructions, which, however admirable some of the effects produced, shows that the writer is thinking of well-read scholars, not the ordinary man of the world.
> (p.50)

So the 'tacit confederation of clubs... are conscious that in them is concentrated the enlightenment of the period. The class to whom they belong is socially and politically dominant – the advance guard of national progress... It believes in what it calls the Religion of Nature – the plain demonstrable truths obvious to every intelligent person' – from the right circle, we should add (p.54).

Just as Religion and Political Theory must be based on the Law of Nature, so must Art. The critics' rules, as Pope expressed the general doctrine, were 'Nature methodis'd'. That was to say, the set of instincts and prejudices of the Wit were taken as normal. 'He wishes, in the familiar phrase, to be "correct"; to avoid the gross faults of taste which disfigured the old Gothic barbarism of his forefathers... [and which were] still attractive to the vulgar' (p.83). There was no option for the critic, then: he should have before him the great classical models, 'and regard the English literature of the seventeenth century as a collection of all possible errors of taste' (p.53). (Like its revolutions? – J. D.)

To sum up so far: this was the kind of 'system' that Stephen thought might be theoretically constructed, criticised and developed. In this version he related writers to audiences, within specific conditions of publication, discussion and criticism. And he related both to the interests – and active participation – of a dominant social class with a conscious, innovating social project. The 'economical' factor is rather simplified; that might well be significant, but it is certainly not excluded by the method.

The opening phase I have summarised here is a sketch, no more: it must have occupied two lectures, at most. But Stephen had more to offer. His model was potentially dynamic, allowing for historical change.

There is a taste of this in the opening lecture. Here he briefly considers what was temporarily being marginalised around 1710: the Elizabethan achievement. From the year of the Armada, 'the class which supported the stage also represented the strongest aspirations of the period, and a marked national sentiment'. A great intellectual shock was stimulating parallel, though independent, outbursts of activity. The inadequacy of the old forms made itself felt, and their successors had to be worked out by a series of tentative experiments. This was work beyond 'the power of any individual': the dramatists learnt together to embody these new things.

Nevertheless, the national spirit 'which took the great Queen for its representative' was singularly brief in its impulse. Under James, the strongest current of political sentiment was increasingly opposed to the court. The most vigorous and progressive classes were becoming alienated. The unity was broken; but the players still adhered to their patron. Thus:

> The drama comes to represent a tone of thought, a social stratum, which, instead of leading, is getting more and more opposed to the great bulk of the most vigorous elements of the society.
>
> (p.30)

This is a significant addition to the model, I believe. 'The growth of new [literary] forms is obviously connected not only with the intellectual development but with the social and political state of the nation' (p.24). Equally, as the case of the stage illustrates, 'special social developments radically alter the relation of any particular literary genus to the general national movement' (p.31). The literature of a ruling class may represent, or fail to represent, the main national movement.

A similar argument is used to account for the change after the death of Anne, the failure of the Jacobite rebellion, and the rise of Walpole.

> The speedy decay of the system followed for obvious reasons. As party government became organised [and dominated by the Whigs – J. D.], the patronage was used in a different spirit. Offices had to be given to gratify members of parliament and their constituents, not to scholars who could write odes on victories or epistles to secretaries of state. It was the machinery for controlling votes [in the ascendant House of Commons].
>
> (p.42)

74 The University Extension 1867–92

There Walpole had to reconcile the interests of the aristocratic 'ruling class' and 'the moneyed men'.

> The old club and coffee-house society broke up with remarkable rapidity. While Oxford was sent to the Tower, and Bolingbroke escaped to France, Swift retired to Dublin, and Prior, after being imprisoned, spent the remainder of his life in retirement. Pope settled down to translating Homer, and took up his abode in Twickenham... [Addison] ceased to preside at Buttons'. Steele held on for a time, but in declining prosperity and diminished literary activity... No one appeared to fill the gaps.
> (pp.100–1)

> The institution, in modern slang, differentiated... The more aristocratic clubs became exclusive societies, occupying their own houses, more devoted to gambling than literature; while the older type, represented by Johnson's famous club, were composed of literary and professional classes.
> (p.39)

So, we could say, most writers lost their social relation with power and its institutional base. The literary class itself became differentiated, adds Stephens. 'Pope represents mainly the aristocratic movement' from this point on. 'He had become [financially] independent – a fact of which he was a little too proud – and moved on the most familiar terms with the great men of his age' (p.109). The upper circle, for which he stood as interpreter, took itself to embody the highest cultivation of the nation. (For the most explicit summary of 'the general tone of their class-morality' Stephen analyses Chesterfield's *Letters* (pp.110ff).)

It followed that, for Pope, 'the only kind of poetry that was congenial to his environment was satire' (p.116). This turned to account 'the growing sense that there was something wrong about the political system' (p.119).

For most writers, though, the bookseller had to replace the political patron. 'Tonson and Lintot were making fortunes; the first Longman was founding the famous firm... the disreputable and piratical Curll shows at least the [growing] demand for miscellaneous literature' (p.102). 'Inferior scribes' did the drudgery of the active political press. 'Journalists' no doubt were often in a degrading position. But the 'author by profession' was beginning to be recognised – Thomson and Mallett from Scotland, Ralph from New England, Johnson from the country, attracted by Cave's new *Gentleman's Magazine* – 'an event that marked a new development in periodical literature' (p.103).

Stephen does not deal in any detail with the book trade of the 1720s and 1730s and its search for new markets: his eye is rather on the professional authors and the movements in religious and social life (outside London) currently affecting them. But he concludes this lecture with a characteristic claim:

For us the interest is the development of a new class of readers, who won't bother about canons of taste or care for skill in working upon the old conventional methods, but can be profoundly interested in a straightforward narrative adapted to the simplest understandings... Defoe was showing in a new sense of the word the advantage of an appeal to Nature; for the true life and vigour of the nation was coming to be embodied in the class which was spontaneously developing its own ideals and beginning to regard the culture of the upper circle as artificial in the objectionable sense.

(p.136)

Quite why middle-class ideals should develop 'spontaneously' here I cannot guess; elsewhere, they are obviously much indebted to Defoe (and his like), who created a type of the 'English class to which he belonged'. 'Crusoe is the very incarnation of individualism... This exemplary person not only embodies the type of middle class Briton but represents his most romantic aspirations' (p.135). The adventurous Briton was beginning to 'push his way into strange native confines' and to 'oust the wretched foreigner, Dutch, French, Spanish, and Portuguese'. This was 'the voice of the race which was... to lay the foundation of the Empire' (p.136). Yes, indeed! – but surely the practices hinted at in those last phrases – the pushing and ousting – were also formative of 'ideals' of the race, in their own way?

There is a degree of historical abstraction, then, in the model. Characteristic practices are hinted at, but not spelt out. More could have been made of the specific production and marketing of printed material. As for 18th century manufacture, commerce, colonising and enslaving – these are not directly in evidence, we could object today. Still, half consciously, isn't Stephen indicating another kind of story, waiting to be acknowledged.

A start had been made. In fact, Stephen had a clear message for the next generation. Begin with the class(es) whose social and economic power gives them political dominance. Are they unified in their project, or divided? Has one class perhaps the energy and confidence of recent success in achieving power? Is one already becoming alienated from the existing ruling class? What do they see themselves as standing for?

What are the relations of the dominant classes with writers, and with literary production (journalism as well as books)? What institutions link the two, perhaps? What genres are the dominant classes fostering or making available? With what potential for transforming existing conventions of form? What new (ideological) problems are being tackled, in philosophical, religious, and political discussion, for instance? What dominant ways of thinking are becoming taken for granted? What shaping is being given to passions and aspirations?

As and when publishers gain a leading role, what class and what projects do they represent? How are they related to the politically dominant classes? What (new or established) markets are they aiming at? What (new) interests are they seeking to express or typify in their products? How does this affect the authors (women or men, of what social origins?) whom they choose, relegate, or marginalise?

'Our descendants', he told his audience, 'will be able to see the general characteristics of the Victorian age better than we, who unconsciously accept our own peculiarities' (p.9).

> The philosophy of a period is often treated as though it were the product of impartial and abstract investigation... [To my mind, it is] itself determined to a very great extent by the social position. It gives the solution to problems forced upon the reasoner by the practical conditions of his time.
>
> (p.3)

As for art and genius, 'Nobody doubts that all authors are in some degree echoes, and that a vast majority are never anything else'. The question to ask is: 'Why a particular form should be fruitful of echoes or, in Bagehot's words, "more congenial to the minds around it". Why did the *Spectator* suit one generation and the *Rambler* its successors? Are we incapable of giving an answer?' (p.18)

Why, we might add today, did the Extension movement produce such a liberating alternative to Classics, and Oxford such a fettered imitation?

PART II
Cambridge 1919–29

CHAPTER 7

A space – and demand – for reconstruction

A deluge that would sweep away many landmarks

From January 1919 through 1920, an unprecedented group of students 'came back' to Oxbridge. They were the survivors, the remnants of the 1914–18 cohorts who had left school (or mid-course at university) to enlist, most of them as officers in front-line regiments.

Still largely members of a privileged class, schooled for higher public office (or membership of a leisured elite), almost all these men had been bred with deeply engrained assumptions, values and attitudes about Western European society and their future roles in it.

It was several years before any of these young officers could try to set down precisely what had happened to their class, after they left their cadet battalions – some ironically billeted in Cambridge colleges – and arrived at the Front. In 1919, apart from a few poems, those memories were more likely to be the stuff of nightmares.

Indeed, no public effort had yet been made to present what actually happened. On the contrary. First the popular press, then an official Propaganda Bureau, transformed the significance of rising casualty lists with images, stories and interpretations that would make the War Effort bearable, sustainable. For Russia, one of the Allies, even this had failed: realities broke through the mental defences by 1917. But for the victors, that didn't happen. Whatever might be going on east of the Rhine by the end of 1918, in Britain the official representations survived – with only minor challenges – and the War leaders had their reward in the electoral landslide of December 1918.

The images we see today, seventy years later, threaded together from film footage, for example, were repressed. But even now, the irony, scepticism and disillusion of the inner worlds of these men are difficult to imagine – simply because we are two or three generations away from the attitudes that crumpled into sham and the bitter withering of beliefs.

'Young men and not so young': they had been stripped of phoney slogans, sentimental appeals, patriotic myths, and the illusions of hope... But what they came back to had not – the Home Front had swallowed, with some exceptions, exactly what they had spewed up. So how would they respond, or accommodate, to an alien mentality?

Resistance and ideological conflict in Cambridge

In Cambridge, as it happened, there actually had been forms of resistance throughout the War. From October 1915 the rebel *Cambridge Magazine* – edited by C. K. Ogden, chair of the Heretics Club – decided to 'devote a considerable amount of space to a review of the Foreign Press'. It opened not only with French, Italian and Russian extracts, but also with brief translations by Mrs Buxton from Austrian and German sources. The *Neue Freie Presse*, in an article on war poetry, had protested against the stirring of international hatred; *Vorwärts* had an article, by a Jesuit priest, on the subject of truth in wartime. And there were more.

Substantial extracts on these lines were included weekly from then on. By 1918 they had won the magazine 15,000 subscribers – some of them men at the Front. Thus, in 1916 Sassoon's poem 'The Hero' was included, and early in 1917 Graves's 'The Dead Boche':

> Today I found in Mametz Wood
> A certain cure for lust of blood.

Patriotic letters of protest followed (and were published). Then, in 1917, at a time when the German free presses were becoming 'literary casualties', if not already 'bound and gagged', the London *Morning Chronicle* began a public attack on the *Magazine*, using an open letter from a group of fellow academics. But there were other academics who came to its support, and it pressed on, ironically claiming 'the largest circulation of any university weekly' (April 1917).

Throughout this period, like its official alternative the *Cambridge Review*, the *Magazine* continued to report and review university affairs, including public lectures and occasional books, and at regular intervals both of them published the long lists of former Cambridge men killed and wounded, and the awards for gallantry. To readers of the *Magazine*, some of them in the trenches, it must have felt a strange mixture: Roger Fry's exhibition at the Alpine Galleries; James Wood's talk to the Heretics Club on Cubism; Jane Harrison on the effect of the verb in the Russian novel; Professor Quiller Couch ('Q') on the Origin of the Ballad. Then the lists. Then, in April 1917, say, Sassoon's 'Base Details':

> If I were old and fat and scant of breath
> I'd sit with scarlet Majors at the Base
> And speed young heroes up the Line to death...

(The same issue contained a protest letter of a different kind: from A.J. Wyatt on 'The Animus against Anglo-Saxon': we'll be returning to that shortly.)

While the *Magazine* and its editor survived unscathed – till Armistice Night – some of its supporters did not. In January 1915 Cambridge had formed a branch of the Union of Democratic Control, a loose alliance of radicals and democrats, 'for the expression of individual opinion concerning foreign policy and the settlement after the war' (*Magazine*, November 1915). The local president was then Bertrand Russell, and information was available from G.H. Hardy of Trinity and Miss J. Baker of Newnham. Soon, there were public attacks on the 'curious pro-Germanism which prevails in certain circles' in Cambridge, and in the 30 October issue, the *Magazine* published Russell's letter to W. R. Sorley, declaring that 'so far from hating England, I care for England more than for anything else except the truth'. During November the Council of Trinity prohibited a UDC meeting from being held in the college and G.E. Moore (a junior fellow) wrote an open letter to the Council, suggesting the suspension of College Chapel in order to avoid maxims dangerous to patriotism, such as 'Love your enemies' (*Magazine* 27 November). Suspicion was not confined to the old, however. In June 1916 a UDC meeting addressed by Arthur Pigou on labour relations after the War was broken up by medical students (the main group still in residence, ironically), despite an appeal from the secretary – recently returned from the Front, wounded.

In the same issue (10 June) the *Magazine* reported that Russell had been fined for certain comments on the government in a leaflet on conscientious objection. When Russell – who was himself beyond the age for compulsory call-up – deliberately refused to pay the fine and was sent to prison, the Council of Trinity College sacked him from his lectureship. The *Magazine* took up the case, printing international comment as well as statements of support from other Trinity fellows. (It is ironic that in Berlin, Einstein too was opposing compulsory conscription at the time – a fact that was not forgotten by the student revolutionaries of 1919.)

In January 1919, then, Cambridge dons had experienced three years of bitter ideological division. The effects in such a parochial, introverted community can be imagined. ('Perhaps Cambridge is too much of a cave', wrote Virginia Woolf, thinking of the way Moore had aged in this period (Levy 1980: 297). And the divisions did not end with the Peace negotiations. 'Conditions for a Lasting Peace' was a major goal of the

UDC, and the theme of four earlier articles in the *Magazine* by Goldsworthy Lowes Dickinson. But by June the Cambridge economist Maynard Keynes had 'dragged myself out of [sick-]bed... to make a final protest before the Reparations Commission against the murdering of Vienna' and reported to Lloyd George, 'The battle is lost. I leave [the British representatives on the Reparation Committee] to gloat over the devastation of Europe' (5 June 1919, Lekachman 1967). He returned to Cambridge to write a book that won an international readership: *Economic Consequences of the Peace*. The blood-dimmed tide flowed on.

Improvising a new 'English' course

One local news item reported in the *Magazine* in 1917 had gone relatively smoothly, despite all this. Under the headline 'The Recognition of English' the editor welcomed the new proposals from a Special Board. They met the 'crying want' diagnosed in the *Magazine* as long ago as 1913 by the Master of Magdalene – Ogden's college. (In fact, from its foundation the *Magazine* had 'treated Q's lectures as news and helped the cause of English', said E. M. W. Tillyard.) The Board was congratulated, therefore, on the 'ingenious manner' in which it had 'provided that the conservative-minded can... go on almost as if nothing had happened' (a reference to Wyatt and all three tutors in the women's colleges) while others could opt for Section A, 'a very thorough knowledge of English *literature* from 1350 onwards, with its bearings to world-literature and world-criticism' (3 March). The irony was that, at the time, Wyatt was probably right to suspect that a hostility to things German – including Anglo-Saxon studies – had cleared the path for an English course without a philological demand.

So subscribers to the *Magazine* had advance notice of new options in the 'Modern Languages' tripos. The first exams for Section A were held in the summer term of 1919: inevitably there was only a short class list. But by the autumn, things had changed. In fact, Quiller Couch, the professor, was 'pretty well beaten to a rag' by the end of the spring term of 1920: 'We have some 160 men and women reading for the English Tripos... and the colleges *must* find people to take their essays' (Brittain 1944: 101).

It is not at all easy to account for the sudden shift. Lieutenant Basil Willey (later) thought that the ex-servicemen like him who filled Cambridge 'would stand no nonsense; they would be impatient of the pedantries and the textual minutiae of classical scholarship; they would insist on something more modern and actual' (1968: 13). A sense of rebellion certainly seems to have been essential. Thus, when he himself thought of taking Part II in English, 'my own College sighed, shook its head, and sent me for advice to A. J. Wyatt... [who] prophesied disaster for the new Tripos, and unemployment for me and anyone else deluded enough to take it' (p.14). 'Many, indeed most, of the Colleges... discouraged their undergraduates from taking it', he claimed later (p.14).

'In the early days... it was heartily despised', reflected Captain Eustace Tillyard (First in Classics, MC, three times Mentioned in Despatches) – but, while on leave, he was 'hypnotised' by his friend Mansfield Forbes and by Henry Chadwick to lecture for the Criticism paper as soon as the War was over. So eventually (in 1920) it was he who took Willey as a pupil, supervising 'two or three of us at a time', 'a happy band of pioneers' (Willey 1968: 14).

'Pioneers' was a polite word, so far as the staff were concerned; in fact, 'the only thing to do was to improvise something virtually new and to gather teachers as chance seemed best to offer' (Tillyard 1958: 12). Thus in 1917 Chadwick and Q had recruited Forbes, a Fellow in Modern History, who 'read the more advanced and exotic literary journals and was always on the look-out for true novelty and promise' (Tillyard 1958: 88). Forbes helped to recruit his friend Tillyard, who had rebelled against the course in 'classical literature, so-called' and chosen Archaeology for Part II, going on to the British School in Athens. And in the early summer of 1919 Forbes personally recruited a young friend of Ogden's, one of the Heretics, Ivor Richards. After getting a First in Part I in 1915, Richards had not returned to Cambridge till the summer of 1918, following a long struggle to shake off his third attack of tuberculosis. His more obvious qualifications were in philosophy, psychology and aesthetics, though he had been attending lectures in physiology with the dream, perhaps, of moving into psychiatry. He needed money badly and agreed to give a course on Contemporary Fiction as well as his main offer, 'a general theory of criticism'.

Perhaps the fact that the lecturers – apart from Q – were obviously 'young men in a hurry', 'progressives', (Tillyard 1958: 77); that they were all learning the subject, indeed, inventing it to some degree; that they had little sense of external controls (the established English Association leaders having queered their pitch by writing a letter in opposition to the 1917 proposals); and that they inspired and guided each other – such things, perhaps, showed through enough to affect bolshie students who had the temerity to think of opting for this new sort of subject.

Contributions of the teacher recruits

Significantly, it was not designed as a full degree course, but as a Part II to be taken after Part I in some other subject (Classics? Modern History?... Mathematics, in one notable case!). A one-year course, which included literature in a second language, it could hardly offer an ideal formation in 'Englishness', we should note. Students as well as lecturers had studied a good deal more than 'English literature, life and thought' or 'the general history of literary criticism'.

Admittedly, before long, even these titles did not stand for what actually went on. Richards had no interest in History – as a young anarchist student he had seen it as the records of corrupt power and successfully asked to drop the subject. His first set of lectures on Criticism, in the autumn of 1919, attracted an excited audience – sufficient, at 15 shillings a head for a one-term course, to cover his modest board and lodgings as a 'freelance' (not an established don). But the students were not offered the expected discussion of Classicism and Romanticism, 'or any historical questions'. Instead there was a pragmatic appeal to clarify fundamental concepts: first, Practical difficulties of criticism; then, *Experience* and what it means, *Truth* – and Intrinsically convincing presentation, *Emotion* and feeling; and finally *Pleasure* (Letter to Forbes, Carey 1984: 148, my emphasis). In a spirit typical of 1919, things are to start afresh. Aesthetics is to be 'a science' (Russo 1989: 59). Goodbye – and good riddance, presumably – to eminent Victorian thinkers, alive or dead.

'Forbes was the enthusiastic advocate of Richards's ends. I too found that Richards's doctrines were just the antidote I needed to the doctrines with which I had hitherto been familiar' (Tillyard 1958: 91). 'What Richards contributed most was leadership and a policy' (p.88). But something more than conceptual clarification was needed. In fact, 'Richards owed an incalculable amount to Forbes's inspiring faith and vitality and in matters of taste he relied on the sureness of Forbes's intuitions and the breadth of his reading' (p.89). 'Men having (the force and integrity of Forbes's enthusiasm for literature) do not often become dons', Tillyard acknowledged in a revealing aside (p.49).

It was Forbes, then, who had already lectured with 'a devoted interest in verbal effects in their subtlest and minutest manifestations... The kind of criticism he preferred was on a smaller scale: a detailed and subtle analysis of the verbal effects of the poems for which he had a special affection' (p.48). 'Two thirds of the way through [his 1919 course on the Romantics], Forbes was still exploring Blake's *Songs of Innocence* and *Songs of Experience* and giving us odd but evocative readings of them. He was developing a theory that words in poems had not only an exact stress and time (indicated by the metre, the rhythm and the sense) but that one must also discover a right pitch of voice for certain key words' (Bennett 1973). An analysis of language had begun.

Tillyard himself – a product of the Perse School, one of the most adventurous in the country – was caught up by the same tendencies: 'in my supervisions [about 1920]... I began to vary essay questions with detailed discussion of the texts themselves. I do not remember being put up to this by Forbes' (1958: 87). And that was precisely what Willey recalled about those supervisions: 'From the start his method was to direct our attention to particular texts and passages, to make us taste their diverse qualities, comparing and distinguishing... to avoid mere gossip, metaphorical vapourings and woolly mysticism' (Willey 1968: 15). The final words sound like a half-remembered quotation: certainly, they indicate what was out of favour, what in (serious thinking? plain, precise language? rationality?)

Nevertheless, rapid 'improvisations' of this kind in teaching, syllabus interpretation and assessment techniques had finally to be authorised. Here Tillyard's skill as negotiator came in, and his role as secretary to the Board: during the three or four years when ex-servicemen swelled the numbers, the senior member, Q, 'ended by agreeing to anything that Forbes, Richards and I had decided was desirable', given sufficient consultation (1958: 81). Thus, for example, from 1920 it became 'the habit to print a poem in one of the period papers and ask for comment on it' (p.103) – a vital precedent, as it turned out.

So the survivors came back to college – 'those who got back to Cambridge after all that slaughter... There was an atmosphere, such a dream, such a hope', Richards remembered (Russo 1989: 257).

Forces structuring innovation

Looking back at the experience now, what structuring forces can we posit? Why should Cambridge – where women were still denied a degree – become a place for cultural innovation?

(a) A group of students with unprecedented experiences were inevitably making new demands. Alienated from the language publicly used to represent – and evaluate – what they had been through, many seemed to want a fresh start, a new analysis of English life and thought, perhaps, 'a new day in which knowledge of our minds would give us enhanced control over ourselves and our destinies' (Willey 1968: 233).

The long gap between school and university, and what had filled it, gave them every reason to challenge the entrenched dogmas of their largely classical education. Furthermore, in rebelling against college prejudice and selecting the English (literature) Section for Part II, they came to this new study with more than usual commitment and a broad range in academic background – which their key lecturers could parallel.

(b) The sudden surge of demand for the Literature and Literary Criticism option resulted in makeshift arrangements. As it fell out, three enthusiasts from significantly different fields found enough common ground to give the official course a sense of unity and force. This was their own response to a demand and an 'atmosphere'.

On the one hand they projected a reciprocal demand for theory, for a new analytical clarity in thinking about reading and criticism. On the other, they made the act of reading texts and passages an object of discussion, detailed analysis and (joint) study.

In their choice of texts, too, that dwelling on Blake's *Innocence* and *Experience* – in 1919 – surely is significant? Forbes believed in selecting works that were relevant.

(c) The institutional freedom for such work arose from a situation peculiar to Cambridge. No mainstream degree in English Language and Literature had been developed prior to the War, though a literary 'amateur' – a classicist turned popular novelist – had been appointed the first professor of English Literature. But in 1917 he had joined in an agreement over the redefinition of the boundaries between Literature, Life and Thought; Literary Criticism; the Culture, Literatures and Archaeology of the Early Germanic and Celtic Peoples; and Historical Philology.

When a sudden rush of students opted for Section A, as the final Part of their degrees, Q's *laissez-faire* Liberalism and willingness to trust the young men gave the latter their head – for two formative years. Post-War confusion and overwork saw to the rest, so far as lecturing provision was concerned. (And in the spring of 1919, Q's son, who had survived the trenches, died in the Army of Occupation.)

As for weekly supervision (of 'essays'), very few of the men's colleges had dons competent or willing to cover the subject (thus Q's complaint above). From an Oxbridge point of view, this left unusual power with the lecturing team. Everything lay in their hands – and from 1923, it was their own students who joined in as additional 'freelances' (Joan Bennett, Tom Henn, Frank Leavis, L. J. Potts, George Rylands and Basil Willey). For a time, this helped to sustain the momentum, and to continue the sense of improvisation.

(d) Finally, we should add, during the early 1920s Cambridge was a world centre for 'the heroic age of Physics' (Rutherford) and the revolutionary implications of General Relativity (Eddington). Two former Trinity dons (Russell and Whitehead) and Moore, still lecturing there, were becoming world figures in the philosophy of Mathematics, Science, and Ethics (while, from the same school,

A space – and demand – for reconstruction 87

Wittgenstein's *Tractatus* – on the limits of language – was translated by Ogden and Frank Ramsay in 1922). Keynes's book on the Peace earned him an immediate world readership. Despite the War, then, and despite Britain's loss of world economic hegemony, great intellectual challenges were in the air – Cambridge expectations were probably higher than ever before, in certain respects.

This too was an 'atmosphere', which Richards especially was tuned to respond to. It was a good time to have a crack at fundamentals: The Meaning of Meaning, The Sense of Beauty (a typical pun!), Science and Poetry, Principles of Literary Criticism... especially when his friend Ogden was beginning to edit, and help to translate, the International Library of Psychology, Philosophy and Scientific Method. Surely they could produce between them something lasting in that field?

CHAPTER 8

New directions of theoretical interest

Opening up options for research

By May of the year 1919, that turning point in European life, Ivor Richards had found two friends who wanted to enlist him in their projects. The first was Ogden, the second, Forbes. Richards was penniless for the moment, and possibly near to breakdown. He went to London – presumably staying with family or friends – with two tasks in mind. First he had to prepare the lecture courses on Criticism and (for 'lucre') on The Contemporary Novel. The success of his lectures that autumn did end a 'hand to mouth' existence, temporarily, particularly as his lodgings, rented from Ogden, must have been reasonably cheap. But, second, Ogden had a bigger enterprise in mind, for which he very much wanted Richards's collaboration. And two attacks on his *Magazine* bookshops – one on Armistice Night, the other in March 1919 – had apparently driven him to take refuge in a friend's flat in Bloomsbury. So sometime that spring or early summer they wrote the first of their joint articles for a new model *Cambridge Magazine*. The interplay between these two friendly collaborations – with Forbes and Ogden – had significant effects on the development of Richards's thought and work during the next few years. The three of them are nodes for a key network. However, because Richards links the two, I shall deliberately simplify matters here by taking him as focal. Fortunately, too, in his case we have some graphic detail from later recollections – in Brower *et al.* (1973) and in Russo (1989).

From early 1918, it had become possible to believe that, one way or another, the War would soon end. Ogden's *Magazine* had built up a wide national and overseas readership by then; the question must have arisen, what new purposes could be given to a journal committed to international understanding? The issue of 25 April 1918 advertises a proposal to set up an Inter-University Section, with correspondents covering university developments throughout the world!

It was a long shot, but not untypical of Charles Ogden. Dora Black/Russell, current secretary of the Heretics and a close friend, saw a lot of him in 1919. She recalled that 'C. K. had a flair for knowing what was the latest thing, and its latest exponent, in a vast number of subjects, which made him invaluable to colleagues in work and to the Heretics Society. What is more, he could, by some subtle stimulus, prevail on people to speak or produce articles or books, a great gift for an editor' (Russell 1977: 43). Richards was an ideal partner, three bouts of tuberculosis having turned him into an omnivorous reader and autodidact, from schooldays on.

The remodelled *Magazine*, now nominally a quarterly, finally arrived in a double number for the spring and summer of 1920. Locally, its initial aims included: the emancipation of colleges from clerical influence; abolition of the pass degree and a greater extension of qualification by thesis rather than examination; the adequate endowment of scientific research; and doubling the numbers of Oxbridge students, by setting up a non-collegiate system side by side with the colleges. But it was thinking much more broadly, too.

An 'Inter-University Correspondence' section opened with H. G. Baynes on 'Psycho-Analysis in Zurich' and Eileen Power on 'Women's Degrees'. Following a successful exhibition of drawings at the *Magazine's* Art Gallery in December 1919 (including work by Matisse, John, Breszka, Hamnett, Picasso and Modigliani), this issue carried full-page reproduction of drawings by Stanley Spencer, Cezanne and Mailliol, together with children's work collected by Marion Richardson. Among the other contributions – from E. M. Forster, James Wood, P. Tudor-Hart, A. E. Heath, Bonamy Dobrée and others – were three by Ogden and Richards (under various names).

These articles introduced a theory of signs and proposed a new science of Symbolism – the work presumably of their spare hours. In fact, Richards was later to claim that all the leading ideas had been jointly developed in a characteristic moment on Armistice Night:

> Pandemonium broke out in Cambridge. I spent some time climbing up the pinnacle in the middle of the market place... I was sitting on top of that and enjoying the scene when I heard a name. I came down to King's Parade to see a crash of glass breaking. Ogden, by that time, was the owner of three shops in Cambridge; one was a picture gallery, the others were book stores. There he was standing by the door of one of them... nobody recognized him.
>
> I took my stand beside Ogden. Twenty or thirty drunken medical students were sacking the shop. Pictures were coming out through the plate glass in very dangerous fashion... Duncan Grant, Vanessa Bell, Roger

Fry... right out into the street; it was very lucky no-one spotted Ogden. He'd have been in the river. That night he came to call on me, to see if I could help him in recognizing any of the rioters. And later in the small hours, we stood together on the little winding stair... and for the first time we talked together – for three hours, outlining the whole Meaning of Meaning.

(Brower *et al.* 1973: 22)

Not surprisingly, the title of one of their articles in the second double number of the new *Magazine* was 'The Art of Conversation'! The same number (Spring 1920) carried their joint work into the field of aesthetic theory, with the help of James Wood.

During 1919–21, then, Richards was in some difficulty. He had several fascinating options worth following up, and seems not to have been clear – then as later – about which to choose, as between:

(a) developing a better psychological model of what goes on when people are 'contemplating a work of art' (1919), or more generally, are interpreting a wide range of symbols and signs (1920);
(b) developing general models of speaking and listening, first for the sake of 'scientific discussion' (1920), and second, for much wider purposes;
(c) analysing various types of confusion present in current philosophical discussion, including Aesthetics (1919), and especially our prevailing dependence on unconscious ambiguities in the use of various key words;
(d) carrying the above analysis into less theoretical areas of aesthetic and literary criticism, demonstrating the problems of verbal ambiguity and challenging the assumption that a single aesthetic model could cover 'all the valuable kinds of what is called Literature' (1920), let alone all art (1921);
(e) on a rather grander scale, radically improving 'the art of conversation' and raising the general level of communication 'through a direct study of its conditions, its dangers and its difficulties' – with all the further theoretical work and analysis this implied.

The outcome was that in November 1921 he signed contracts to produce *The Meaning of Meaning* with Ogden, and *Principles of Criticism* (sic) by himself. (And before those came out, Ogden, Wood and he turned their joint article into a short book with fascinating illustrations, *The Foundations of Aesthetics* (1922).) Yet, critically, throughout this period he was still a freelance, dependent on lecturing fees per capita, plus anything he could earn from examining. Only in April 1922 did Magdalene, his own college, appoint him to a lectureship – in English *and* Moral Sciences – at £100 per annum plus tuition fees. So now he had weekly supervisions to give (in two diverse subjects), as well as lectures. And a great international campaign to run, with Ogden – who by this time had taken on another journal, *Psyche*, for which Richards of course had to write.

The challenge of a new approach to language – in use

Arthur Quiller Couch and Henry Chadwick had jointly made it possible for students in an ancient university to drop philology and concentrate instead on 'literature, life and thought'. They could now ignore the 'Language' in 'English Language and Literature'. Instead they could focus on Literary Criticism – with a theoretical base – and follow literature (in English and another language) through to contemporary writing.

It seemed a new kind of freedom. As it happens, however, the Lit/Crit options had hardly got under way before Richards, working independently with Ogden, had proposed the foundations for a new study, first of language and thought, later of language and 'poetry'. Language reappeared, as a focal element within a general theory of 'signs and their interpretation'. A radical shift of interest was proposed – for a 'new or borderline subject', perhaps even for 'English' (*Meaning of Meaning*, 1923: vii)? The fact that this is ignored by Baldick and Doyle indicates, to my mind, how much Cultural Studies still has to learn about language.

What had Ogden and Richards in mind? It might have seemed natural enough for the latter – a student of McTaggart, W. E. Johnson and G. E. Moore – to keep to Language and Philosophy. Besides, at the time Ogden too was working in that very area, translating Wittgenstein. But neither was satisfied with so restricted a field. For Ogden especially 'The return of the exploiters of the verbal machine [the wartime propagandists] to their civil posts is a return in triumph, and its effects will be felt for many years in all countries where the power of the word amongst the masses remains paramount' (p.18).

Women had finally won the vote, in 1917. 'New millions of participants in the control of general affairs must now attempt to form personal opinions on matters which were once left to a few... The practical side of this undertaking [this new 'science of Symbolism'] is... to raise the level of communication through a direct study of its conditions, its dangers and its difficulties' (p.x).

Education beyond an elite seemed essential (and remained a lifelong commitment for both of them, too). However, for their central purpose, it was no use relying on existing subjects. 'Preoccupied as they are – ethnologists with recording the details of fast vanishing languages; philologists with an elaborate technique of phonetic laws and principles of derivation; philosophers with 'philosophy' – all have overlooked the pressing need for a better understanding of what actually occurs in discussion' (p.8).

Improving discussion for social ends is the baseline, then; that is where the (necessarily) abstract argument of *The Meaning of Meaning* (1923) begins and ends. But, using the models that are developed there, the authors began to sketch the possibilities for more effective discussion among philosophers (about meaning and interpretation) or critics in the arts (about 'aesthetics').

It was an immense project, undertaken part-time of course. What made it possible was their access to the two quarterlies that Ogden edited: the *Cambridge Magazine* and *Psyche*. He and Richards began placing short articles there in the summer of 1920, and continued throughout the decade. *The Meaning of Meaning* and *The Foundations of Aesthetics* (with James Wood, *et al.* 1922) simply plundered early articles, offering little further elaboration. As they said in the preface to *The Meaning of Meaning*, 'The authors have preferred to publish this essay in its present form rather than wait, perhaps indefinitely, until [they have leisure to rewrite it] in a more complete and systematized form' (p.x). It seems a reasonable excuse: even the second edition, in 1926, was apparently reshaped during a joint meeting in New York!

Signs and their interpreters

Nevertheless, during the period 1919–26, Ogden and Richards produced a set of models for communication and interpretation that are of lasting value, I would claim. To start with, what were their key choices in modelling?

They began (in the *Cambridge Magazine*, 1920) simply enough, it seemed:

> If we stand in the neighbourhood of a cross road and observe a pedestrian confronted by a notice *To Grantchester* displayed on a post, we commonly distinguish three important factors in the situation. There is, we are sure, (1) a Sign which (2) refers to a Place and (3) is being interpreted by a person. All situations in which Signs are considered are similar to this.
>
> (see *Meaning of Meaning*: 21)

Thus, what is needed is a theory of signs, of what they stand for or refer to, and of people interpreting.

The last element, we should add, is crucial – and the most often ignored, especially in literary studies. 'It is important to remember that interpretation, or what happens to (or in the mind of) an Interpreter, is quite distinct', Ogden and Richards went on to say (p.21). Perhaps they should have spent more time on it, there and then. After all, for one reader the signpost might mean 'Good – just five minutes and I'm home'; for another 'Drat! – I've missed the turning', and so on. The significance of the sign comes out in its various 'interpretations'. This was a major finding of Charles Peirce, whose work had already excited Ogden before the War and who was given a special Appendix. It was a major direction for investigation.

However, they continue, there is a further problem: the way we talk does not always make it clear that signs are involved. 'A doctor noting that his patient has a temperature and so forth is said to diagnose his disease as influenza... But if we say that the doctor interprets the temperature, etc., as a Sign of influenza' we begin to see similarities with the pedestrian's behaviour. And the same applies, they added later, to attending to marks on a printed page, or to the paints on a canvas surface. So there are situations when we are clear that we are dealing with signs and others when we are not – and may therefore fall into fallacies.

For example, said Richards later, 'We are accustomed to say that a picture is beautiful, instead of saying that it causes an experience in us which is valuable in certain ways.' It is not the signs, but the experience that is 'beautiful' – a valuable reformulation of the position he had recently been reading in Bradley! What is new is Richards's focus on language. This helps him explain the origin of the fallacy. 'Even today, *such is the insidious power of grammatical forms*, the belief that there is such *a quality or attribute, namely Beauty, which attaches to things* which we rightly call beautiful, is probably inevitable for all reflective persons at a certain stage of development' (Richards 1924: 21, my emphases). And we who have escaped this fallacy, he continues, recur to it. Hence a secondary, and important, direction for analytic work (deconstructing the grammar, you could say).

Inevitably, work on such fallacies affects work on (improved) interpretation, too. For in any modelling, 'the use of words as though their meaning were fixed, the constant resort to loose metaphor, the hypostatization of leading terms... conceal the very facts which the science of language is concerned to elucidate' (*Meaning of Meaning*: 3–4). The theorist's own uses of language had to be analysed.

When they applied this rule to leaders of the French school, the results were pretty devastating. Thus, after considering key examples, they rejected both Bréal and de Saussure, adding in the latter case that the device 'of inventing verbal entities outside the range of possible investigation [la langue and le signifié] proved fatal to the theory of signs which followed' (p.5). For to be of scientific use, they thought, a model must open the way to active experiment and investigation.

Thus, having noted that the new subject is one 'particularly suitable for collaboration' (p.viii) they continue:

> The person actually using a sign is not well placed for observing what is happening. We should develop our theory of signs from observations of other people... Those who allow beyond question that there are people like themselves also interpeting signs and open to study... [may then find] a framework within which their own introspection, that special and deceptive case, may be fitted. That this is the practice of all the sciences need hardly be pointed out.
>
> (pp.19–20)

So an investigative procedure is outlined: study people actually using signs and interpreting them. This implies studying signs in their context of use: 'By leaving out essential elements in the language situation [for example] we easily raise problems and difficulties which vanish when the whole transaction is considered in greater detail' (p.9). (That way, they might have added, there is a chance that defects in the model may show up – as some did.)

The scope was enormous: 'All experience, using the word in its widest possible sense, is either enjoyed or interpreted [i.e. treated as a sign] or both, and very little of it escapes some degree of interpretation' (p.50). Where was a start to be made?

In the circumstances, a primary goal was how to organise and communicate scientific analyses of language in use. But, as they point out, 'Besides [a] referential use which for all reflective, intellectual use of language should be paramount, words have other functions which may be grouped together as emotive.' Thus, when we speak, the signs we employ are caused 'partly by the reference we are making and partly by social and psychological factors' (p.10). Unfortunately, when people are trying to communicate a scientific analysis these other factors can complicate matters 'by emotional, diplomatic, or other disturbances' (p.10). In the worst case, they shift the listeners' attention away from the reference, to signs of the speaker's 'emotions, attitudes, moods, [and] the temper, interest or set of mind' (p.223).

(In passing, I cannot help noting the ironic fact that the authors themselves were soon attacked for their choice of the word 'emotive' to refer to these 'social and psychological factors'; presumably it was interpreted not merely as a reference to such things but – additionally – as a sign of a pejorative attitude. A perfect illustration of their point!)

The difficulty, as we have just seen, was that one and the same word (or sentence, or utterance) may convey an *explicit* reference while also *tacitly* evoking attitudes in the listener. Again following Peirce, the authors mark that difference by calling explicit reference a 'symbolic' function of language. Other functions, interwoven with it in 'almost every utterance', include 'the expression of attitude to referent; the expression of attitude to listener; the promotion of effects intended' (p.227). In silent reading, interpreting such functions depends on a complex process: treating the passage both as verbal symbols and as emotive signs. In conversation, of course, such signs are reinforced and assisted by other signs, in the voice, in gestures, in stance and so on.

So even children learn habitually to interpret (a) 'from symbols to reference and so to referent' and (b) 'from verbal [and other] signs to the attitude, mood, interest, purpose, desire, and so forth of the speaker, and thence to the situation, circumstances and conditions in which the utterance is made' (p.223).

Limits and potentials in their modelling

This analysis of Ogden and Richards's modelling is drawn largely from their first and last chapters – 'Thoughts, Words and Things' and 'Symbol Situations'. I have tried both to present their characteristic ways of thinking and to construct, from disparate material, a relatively unified position. It is fair to point out, though, that their language and modelling is less systematic than it might seem here. Is it 'language' – or 'words' – they aim to talk about, or more generally 'signs' and 'symbols' (which in actual utterances form a complex unity)? Is it sufficient to clarify 'language and thought', or must the model inevitably include 'interpretation'? Are they satisfied to place 'purposes', or must they take account of 'interests' and 'desires' too? Is the underlying situation a traveller looking at a signpost, or is it two or more people in discussion? And, whichever is the case, is the observer role of the theorist-investigator a vital part or not? I believe that, piecemeal, they answered all these questions, but they never returned in the light of those answers to revise what they had said previously.

Young men in a hurry? – and also Heretics, getting at the Old Men. In fact, 1919 was a year when many eminent Victorians were toppled from their pedestals. There is no doubt that Ogden and Richards enjoyed lending a hand. Thus, that curious mixture in *The Meaning of Meaning*: a serious appeal for a stricter focus on the symbolic function of language, couched again and again in emotive asides, allusions and examples. Play and iconoclasm kept splashing through the scientific intentions, disrupting and diverting them. The rebels were let loose.

I have to recall, too, that this was their first big chance to address an international readership (through the *Magazine*) about issues that orthodox Cambridge was not going to listen to. 'Prospectors' in a field of enquiry that lay beyond normal 'subjects', and the routine practices of 'instruction and examinations', they intended to mark out a vast post-War terrain for further work. Perception (and the role of signs) – accounts of imagery – verbal superstitions embedded in grammar and figurative uses – the linguistic practices and fallacies of philosophers and aestheticians – theories of definition and their practical uses... such fields, and the therapeutic Canons that might help to bring better discussion to them, were all to be targeted, critically exposed, and reshaped in a preliminary way.

Ironically, though, while blithely challenging institutional power themselves, they presupposed that 'scientific' discourse ought not to be 'disturbed' by such challenges. So, officially, they ought to have avoided 'emotive' attitudes, however necessary it might be in the real world to choose how to use them to advance their cause!

Caught in this tacit contradiction, *The Meaning of Meaning* was bound to fail in certain respects, you could predict that. All the same, it included lasting achievements. The attempt to develop a model for signs, and their interpretation in discussion, was especially opportune: this was to be a decade of great progress in that field, as we shall see later. And, at the international level at least, Ogden and Richards won immediate recognition for their new area of enquiry. In this 'radical study', wrote Edward Sapir, the originality lies chiefly in this: 'that it looks upon thinking as the interpretation of "signs"' (*The Freeman*, New York, 22 August 1923).

Looking back at this model of signs and symbols in action, then, crude as it may be, it seems of fundamental importance not only for effective social discussion, but for all university disciplines, including – perhaps especially – English 'literature, life and thought'?

For example: the words in a dramatic script manifestly refer to people and situations, which the reader must actively imagine. This, Bradley had made clear. But what more are they doing – and how? Following Ogden and Richards, we could say that, in considering how to perform a dramatic dialogue, we should expect to take into account:

(a) signs of the 'situation, circumstances and conditions' and the varied ways in which speakers are affected by them;
(b) signs of the speakers' 'interests, purposes, desires and so forth' in relation to what's going on;
(c) signs of their mood and temper;
(d) signs of their emotions and of their attitudes to whatever they are referring to as they speak;
(e) signs of their (shifting) feelings and attitudes to each other.

This is probably the most complex set of analytic prompts available at the time, or for many years after. Besides, it could equally well be applied to the analysis of social discussion. What's more, there are clear indications that Ogden and Richards do not treat it as complete or systematic – it is open to revision.

Despite this lead as long ago as 1923, however, to the best of my knowledge the general problem has still not been systematically tackled in English departments. There is nothing surprising about its absence in Eagleton, Baldick, or Doyle, for example – quite the contrary. Every English course includes texts, and it has been clear for over sixty years that 'in written English many of the most obvious signs of attitude etc. are necessarily lost; manner and tone of voice have to be replaced by various devices' some of them familiar in the technique of letter-writing, for instance (*Meaning of Meaning*: 224). But how do readers or actors actually use the printed signs to construct an oral or dramatic version? And what further signs do their spoken versions add in? The answer is still a mystery in English teaching.

Adapting the model for Criticism

A model of language as oral or written signs, used in specific contexts, must surely be one of the foundations of literary studies. Yet the problematic was not taken up, and some of the initial blame for failing to penetrate English teaching must lie with Richards. His promised book on Criticism (Richards 1924), which came out the year after *The Meaning of Meaning*, was after all the obvious place to spell out what the joint work on signs – and much more – implied for teachers of English literature, thought and life. But that was not to be. Despite the insertion of 'Literary' into the final title – and the fact that the original lectures were part of an English course – Richards did not hesitate to introduce central chapters on 'Looking at a Picture', 'Sculpture and the Construction of Form' and 'The Impasse of Musical Theory'; to sound off at length about viewing films; or to talk pretty generally throughout about 'the artist'. Obviously the extended scope cut down the degree of detail with which he could treat a major preoccupation, reading and criticising literature.

What's more, from internal evidence, it is not difficult to show that *Principles of Literary Criticism* (1924) represents three or four archaeological layers of thinking. All between 1919 and 1923 – what fertility! It must have been very tantalising to readers at the time. And, ironically, the excellent analysis of 'contemplating a sculpture' is more advanced, in some ways, than that of 'reading a poem'. However, it is these 'advances', as they seem to me, that I ought to focus on. I shall not try to trace here the lessons that Richards failed to learn, or half-learned. That has been done often enough, on both sides of the Atlantic.

He had set himself three clear goals in the new book:

> Criticism, as I understand it, is the endeavour to discriminate between experiences and to evaluate them. We cannot do this without some understanding of the nature of *experience*, or without theories of *evaluation* and *communication*.
>
> (1924: 2, my emphasis)

Starting with the experience of a work of art, he made 'a very clear demarcation between the object, with its features' and the 'experience, which is the effect of contemplating it' (p.23). This had been his position since the summer of 1919; however, the implication he drew was new. To a critic, he went on, 'remarks as to the ways and means by which experiences arise or are brought about are *technical* [let us say]'; by contrast, '*critical* remarks are about the values of experiences and the reasons for regarding them as valuable, or not valuable' (p.23 my emphases). The distinction is important, though it was often overlooked by Richards himself.

With regard to evaluating the experience, he had more difficulty, understandably. How could a philosophical tradition without a theory of society or of historical change approach the subject at all? In general terms, Richards did his best by starting from psychological categories like appetencies and aversions. These 'impulses', as he called them, were systematised, however incompletely, in social life. People seek satisfaction for the greatest number of impulses – without the frustration of 'equal or *more important*' appetencies. Thus, via Hobbes and Bentham, ethical codes became 'general schemes of expediency' for the satisfaction of impulses, or the avoidance of frustrations (p.48, original emphasis).

The missing link, I should add, was the way society systematised such matters. Richards trots us up to the brink, admittedly. Thus, 'acts which will debar (someone) from his normal relations with his fellows are often avoided, even at the cost of death... The case of the soldier, *or of the conscientious objector*, is thus no exception to the principle' (p.49, my emphasis). But – at this point – he didn't jump.

Many questions remain. Where, we might ask, is the place of signs – not to speak of 'works of art'! Signs must surely be used in the social organisation, control and operation of these systems of 'impulses', you would think, but their role is not considered – a fatal flaw even for his immediate purposes. The resultant role for Criticism is also left to the reader's imagination.

However, in discussing a 'bad poem' much later in the book, Richards characteristically hits on an answer:

> At present bad literature, bad art, the [sic] cinema, etc., are an influence of the first importance in fixing immature and actually inapplicable attitudes to most things. Even the decision as to what constitutes a pretty girl or a

handsome young man, an affair apparently natural and personal enough, is largely determined by magazine covers and movie stars (p.203)... [Thus] the nature and source of stock conventional attitudes is of great interest.
(p.202)

So the apparently 'natural' or 'personal' is actually socially inculcated – by signs and symbols. The critic and the sales manager, the poet and the advertising agent, have this in common. They 'suggest' or 'deliberately organise' key attitudes – 'a boy's "Idea" of Friendship or of Summer or of his Country' (p.202), for example. (Yes, the idea of 'Country'; a focus for attitudes that had just proved serious enough for the young men of Europe. Here was the context for an altogether new approach to 'Englishness'.)

So evaluating some works of art implies evaluating the attitudes their signs tend to incite, as Richards might have put it: attitudes with application 'to most things' in social life. How 'stock', 'conventional', 'stereotyped' were the attitudes that were promoted, he asked; or, more fundamentally perhaps, in what respects did they either 'withdraw us from actual experience' (p.202) or prompt us to re-engage with it? And we could add further questions now.

In keeping with this position, Richards made a sweeping new proposal:

Against these stock responses the artist's internal and external conflicts are fought, and with them the popular writer's triumphs are made. Any combination of these general Ideas, hit at the right level... of development, is, if suitably advertised, certain of success. Best-sellers in all the arts, exemplifying as they do the most general levels of attitude development, are worthy of very close study. No theory of criticism is satisfactory which is not able to explain their wide appeal and to give clear reasons why those who disdain them are not necessarily snobs.
(p.203)

So a new terrain for Criticism suddenly opens up. And, though in the event a sonnet from Ella Wheeler Wilcox's *Poems of Passion* was used as the introductory sample, 'the most able American advertisers are such that no critic can safely ignore them' (p.204). Advertising, the press, the cinema, best-sellers... become necessary objects of study, precisely in so far as they organise, suggest, or reinforce attitudes around central Ideas within a 'society'. Moreover, as Richards had indicated earlier, 'vast accumulations of anthropological evidence... establish the fact that as the organisation of life and affairs alters, very different experiences are perceived to be good or bad, are favoured or condemned' (p.44). So we could add that the study ought to be historical, and might expose conflicting tendencies at any given historical moment.

It is characteristic of the author that this brilliant new enterprise is launched in the middle of a chapter on 'Badness in Poetry' – not even in the chapters on Value or Judgement. The words 'immaturity' and 'disdain' also point to an unresolved problem on his own part, in attitude as well as in theoretical modelling, I would say. How can 'the best-seller' be disdained? Shouldn't one maintain a clear demarcation between the object and the experiences of people who contemplate it. Since you can hardly disdain signs, who are you left to disdain but the readers or viewers? But they are elsewhere seen as 'immature', caught in 'various halfway houses' of 'development' (p.202). Richards obviously needed to spend a good deal more time on this fascinating innovation in Criticism. Fortunately, five years later, he did.

A dynamic model of reading

For anyone but the anarchist Ivor Richards, his remaining theme in *Principles* – theorising communication in the arts – might have meant nothing more than following through the implications of his recent joint book. But not him. Instead, he made two significant discoveries in the course of writing *Principles*, I would guess – but the obvious paths were not taken nearly often enough! It is the discoveries I want to take now: first, a new, dynamic model for interpreting signs and, second, a growing awareness of the constructive role of the interpreter. These are not at all well signposted. The first occurs in the middle of a chapter on rhythm and metre; the second, piecemeal, but especially in the chapter on contemplating a sculpture.

What helped to produce a dynamic model? Enthusiastic students who attended his lectures of this period later recalled with gratitude how Richards transformed rhythm from an object into a mental process. This was the first, crucial step:

> The mind after reading a line or two of verse, or half a sentence of prose, prepares itself ahead for any one of a number of possible sequences, at the same time negatively incapacitating itself for others. The effect produced by what actually follows depends very closely upon this unconscious preparation and consists largely in the further twist which it gives to expectancy. It is in terms of these twists that rhythm is to be described.
>
> (p.134)

So

> *This texture of expectations, satisfactions, disappointments, surprisals,* which the sequence of syllables brings about, *is rhythm.* And the sound of words comes to its full power only through rhythm.
>
> (p.137, my emphasis)

A set of signs, we could say, was no longer being treated as a single unit (like 'To Grantchester'), but as a sequence stretching forward in time.

New directions of theoretical interest 101

Thus, the interpreter must be working piecemeal, giving one stretch focal attention while also anticipating what might be ahead – and we might add, integrating the current stretch with what had already been scanned and interpreted.

This novel view of rhythm proved to be the auspicious beginning to a model of reading itself as active 'expectancy'. For

> the anticipation of sound due to habit, to the routine of sensation, was merely part of a general expectancy. Grammatical regularities, the necessity for completing the thought, the reader's state of conjecture as to what is being said, his apprehension in dramatic literature of the action, of the intention, situation, state of mind generally, of the speaker, all these things and many others also give rise to satisfactions, disappointments and so on.
>
> (p.137)

Here Richards stopped. And there it was left. A promise over a hundred pages earlier – to show that rhythm, stress, plot and character are actually events in the mind – has, I suppose, been tacitly fulfilled. Well, in miniature, at least. It left a rather strenuous task of construction for the interpreting reader, I must say.

Nevertheless, arguing on these lines, plot, it could be said, was no longer a summary of past events. It was a set of expectations, feelings of dread, suspicions, premonitions and so on – sometimes prompted by the narrator or chorus, sometimes independently constructed by interpreters themselves. Character (as Bradley had half indicated) was another kind of construction, actively continuing at successive points in the story as the personae disappointed, fulfilled, or modified active expectations about their likely behaviour. So plot and character, on this view, entered into what Richards thought of as a macro form of rhythm, a counterpointed rhythm of anticipations and events.

Thus, interpretation is presented as a dynamic process, working at a very varied set of levels simultaneously – and the umbrella word Richards offered, 'expectancy', is a valuable guide to further investigation. What's more, he noted that

> the same definition of rhythm may be extended to the plastic arts and to architecture... The attention usually passes successively from one complex (of visual signs) to another, the expectations... aroused by the one being satisfied or surprised by the other.
>
> (p.138)

This dynamic model for reading, or for 'contemplating' a visual work, acknowledged new active, constructive elements in interpretation. By 1924, Richards was beginning to realise, I believe, how pervasive these might be. Indeed, in the chapter on contemplating a sculpture – which I take to be late in composition – a new conceptual frame peeps out.

'With sculpture perhaps more than any other of the plastic arts we are in danger of overlooking the work of the contemplator's imagination in filling out and interpreting the sign' (p.163). In such a context – alongside 'imagination' and 'filling out' – the sense of 'interpreting the sign' seems to me to be shifting. And a little later Richards moved a step further, talking about 'the imaginatively *constructed* statue-space' (p.166, my emphasis): it must be a very early use of that term.

I suspect that he was prompted, in part at least, by the fact that the sculpture he had in mind – modernist? African? Asian? – treated 'four aspects' fully 'without any attempt to fill in the intermediate connecting aspects' (p.161). Here, then, 'imaginative construction' filled out and combined. But a moment later, in retrospect, he acknowledged that it also selects. Through our selection among the *possible signs* present, form was 'within certain limits what we *like to make it*'. And, as it varies

> so do our further or deeper responses of feeling and attitude vary. But... out of the multitude of different forms which we might *construct by stressing certain of the signs* rather than others, the fixing *even temporarily of a part of the form* tends to bias us towards so interpreting the rest as to yield responses accordant with those already active'.
>
> (pp.166–7, my emphasis)

This is a fascinating advance in his modelling. As readers, we have some choice, it seems, among the signs to be 'stressed'. But in making such choices we begin to 'construct' a specific 'form'. And this in turn biases our further choices of what to stress, and thus how we actively interpret a text in a given reading. Whatever the case in sculpture, in poetry or prose I certainly believe he was right, and can easily be shown to be. For instance, the possible intonation, or speech tune, of a written sentence is rarely if ever fully determined by the textual signs: it is the reader who makes a constructive choice.

His naive notion of 1919, that there existed a 'standard interpretation' – that of the artist – from which a 'permissible range of variation' could be drawn up by some 'literary logician' (p.226) was crumbling, it seems to me. And about time! He was now having to take account of imaginative work by the interpreter, filling out signs, selecting for stress, and imaginatively combining what they stood for. And all this partly depended on developing expectations. There were certainly limits – but you did 'make what you like'.

Something exactly similar is true of my interpreting him now, of course: that has to be acknowledged, too. Only, in my case, the reasons explaining why I select, stress, and fill out here seem to me part of a necessary cultural and ideological analysis for any acts of interpretation. More of that in Part III.

CHAPTER 9
Experimental investigations in an English course

Teaching, investigating and learning

In 1925 came a shift in Richards's interests that I still find startling. For a pupil of G. E. Moore, with friends like Ogden and Wood, the articles and books up to 1925 could be seen as projects within a tradition. If so, what happened that year was a sudden lurch in strategy, from an elaboration of 'Principles' to the analysis of 'Practice' in criticism.

But is this true? As early as 1920 he and Ogden had specifically included an 'interpreter' in their model, claiming that – unlike Saussure – they were opening the way for active experiment and investigation. After that, the first group of interpreters that came to hand were the students at Richards's lectures – readers of literary texts. Given the model, reading experiments were an obvious first step, you might say. 'Obvious', that is, to anyone who could actually step aside from formative traditions in reading and in teaching.

For in choosing to experiment as he did, Richards put new demands on himself, not simply as a lecturer now, but as a teacher. Tact, understanding and concern for the volunteers would be called for. He was asking them – anonymously, it is true – to take part in an investigation, to hand in their personal 'comments' on a series of poems (grouped in fours), for critical analysis in public lectures. And each group of poems, he hinted, 'were perhaps a mixed lot' (*Practical Criticism*: 4). What he promised them in return was not only a detailed survey of the obstacles that caused many of them to misinterpret a given text, and consequently to under-or over-value it, but also a glimpse of the psychological activities at work during reading in general.

In some respects, this new project was unprecedented. It was one thing for Tillyard – and no doubt Forbes, Richards and others – to discuss a poem with two or three students during a supervision. It was quite another to submit relative failures or successes of interpretation to detailed analysis, and attempt to account for them, in terms of reading practices and psychological processes. In fact, so novel was the idea that – unfortunately – when Richards left Cambridge, no one attempted to take this type of investigation further, then or later.

Instead, there has been a litany of protests, on both sides of the Atlantic, at the crudeness of his methodology. Baldick and Graff are just two of the most recent voices. Like the rest, they are ready to criticise details of Richards's experimental method – which certainly is fairly crude – without showing the slightest interest in investigating for themselves what readers are doing, and why. It seems as if an experimental approach in the humanities – on this scale especially – depends for its very existence on a favourable social and intellectual context.

What gave Richards his chance, initially? I believe it was the era of 'improvisation'. Then the notion of experimenting emerged piecemeal, it seems to me. Willey recalls Tillyard trying out poems and passages. Tillyard remembers putting a poem for comment in an early tripos paper – and no doubt that gave the examiners (for the first time) clear evidence of the uneven quality of reading that was going on. Jean Stewart/Pace reported to me something a step further on: a series of analytic sessions in Richards's attic room in 1 Free School Lane, when she and a group of other students were given, for example, a passage to comment on (a chorus from *Samson Agonistes*, it turned out – 1924?).

Yet that was not enough. Students had to find the process rewarding, unthreatening, and – ideally – fascinating. But this called for supervisors who saw them as developing, who made the best of positive signs, who anticipated a slow maturation – and didn't show disdain! A genuine interest in psychology and human development: that was essential.

How did such things emerge from the spirit of the time? Well, Ogden for one was just publishing the work of one of the greatest developmental psychologists of the century: Jean Piaget. His brilliant observations of children at play (culminating in *The Language and Thought of the Child* translated in 1926) hypothesised an 'egocentric' phase in early speech that might well suggest egocentric readings later on.

As for tutorial styles, Raymond O'Malley's recollections of Frank Leavis's methods, a few years on, seem doubly significant – given the latter's reputation for dogmatism in later years:

> He listened. In particular, he always searched for the sense behind a student's seeming nonsense. There was one such occasion when I had been asked to study in advance a piece from G. M. Hopkins. Hopkins was not yet widely known, and to me was quite unknown. I was absorbed, but puzzled. When invited to name a possible source, I could think of no one

but Donne, and I knew that to be an impossibility. The mistake could have been a mere embarrassment, but became the occasion for an especially helpful study of 'the intolerable wrestle/With words and meanings' conducted by two men so far apart and close together. *There was nearly always this sense of discovery, for teacher as for taught, in the supervisions.*
(O'Malley, in Thompson 1984: 54, my emphasis)

Leavis's teaching methods – important for their effects in both the women's colleges, where he regularly taught during the mid-1920s – seem to fit the kind of people Gwen Freeman reported in a letter home: 'Last year [1925, Richards] started a wonderful experiment. He believed that the way in which different people read poetry would give it quite a different interpretation. So he and Forbes, his friend, worked together.' After Richards had given a reading, Forbes came in and gave his. Then, as Queenie Roth and a friend told her with amusement: 'Richards got up and said, "Oh, Mr Forbes I never thought of that interpretation before. How wonderful it is", and the experiment ended in perfectly tumultuous stamping' (in Thompson 1984: 14).

The notion that teachers *as a group* are learning – *expect* to learn from each other, in experiments – *show* they learn from the discussion sparked by a student's exploratory response – creates a special kind of intellectual climate. It makes space for students to think and speak more freely, without the sense that a final, authoritative judgement is always waiting round the corner. (And, I would add, the fact that their interpretations and evaluations were inevitably provisional – though never *experimentally* exploited by Richards – was an essential factor in making his report-back sessions so rich an opportunity for further learning.)

The new course in 'practical criticism', then, became a kind of contract. Volunteers would hand in pieces which said – which explored – what they thought and felt after a week's readings. The lecturer would report back, fitting exemplar pieces into a sort of map that they could comprehend and study. This mapping would inevitably throw new light on the textual signs, and on the challenges, dangers and potentials for interpreters like his audience. On each occasion the undergraduates and seniors who attended would hear their interpretations – or others like them – analysed. They would begin to see relationships between contemplated experience and text (as interpreted vocally, or sub-vocally: a significant rider). Then, by implication – and usually not as a result of direct comments – they would try to understand *for themselves* how full, partial, incomplete, or wrong-headed their satisfactions or aversions had been. (And I know from personal accounts that, on occasion, some were quite prepared to resist a particular leaning that the lecturer indicated – with the Hardy poem, for instance.)

Incidentally, students of those days whom I have talked to reminded me how young they were then. For many of them, I now realise, it was the effects on their own powers of literary criticism that mattered. That was quite enough to hold on to as they listened to the rich material of the lectures. This is important for its effect on the later impact of the book.

The first course, in 1925, was recognised as a historic event. Forbes, Eliot, and many other seniors were present, as well as undergraduates drawn from many a tripos besides English. By the second series (1927) Lionel Knights recalls sitting up on a window sill because of the crowd, and thinking it was like going to Abelard's lectures:

> I went as a hero-worshipper... It was as if new powers of the mind were being activated. Richards showed us the obstacles to criticism, and the interinanimation of words. He set our minds working – my adolescent mind really came alive, while he was providing the stimulus. We knew this was intellectual activity: other people were still summarising plots!

Raymond O'Malley found the third course (1928) very challenging – 'but then, we were young enough to like being challenged'. He remembers poring over the poems – making difficult decisions and feeling that'll sound very silly if it gets read out, but one's got to make up one's mind. There was the excitement of a new venture, real innovation: something was happening which ought to have happened before... It felt as if criticism began in 1920! Lots of things being written were so chaotic and disordered: Richards was establishing a map, as far as we knew for the first time... After the lecture, O'Malley (no doubt like many others) used to talk it over with a student friend who was reading science or maths. On one occasion, a group in his college argued on into the night, he remembers, seeing in the dawn (interviews with Raymond O'Malley and Lionel Knights 1990).

'Practical criticism', then, was a new way of teaching, investigating and learning – for all concerned. After the three series, Richards – a college fellow with an assured salary at last – took the time to write up a book dedicated 'to my collaborators, whether their work appears in these pages or not'. It was to be the last major product of his Cambridge years (completed April 1929). On reflection, it seems, he slowly began to realise the immense implications of this joint enterprise. After he left for China, though, the most original of them were ignored – as they are to this day.

The signs and their potential

Any study of interpreters and the products of their activities can move in at least four major directions. By 1929 Richards was fully aware of this. We could sum up the first as follows.

(a) Investigators can sift through a range of critical responses, relating them (perhaps systematically?) to signs in the text. Thus, they can progressively elucidate, for themselves as well as others, a set of potentials for those signs, and thus (a range of) interpretations that may arise when the signs are attended to with sufficient care.

Forbes, Richards and others had already made half this process familiar by 1925: they were prepared to spend a whole hour's lecture looking at two lines, if necessary. What Richards added was the practice of attending – with a rather similar scrupulousness! – to a group of interpretations, to see what they alerted one to. As he put it: 'The effect of all this is remarkable. When the first dizzy bewilderment has worn off, as it very soon does, it is as though we were strolling through a building that hitherto we were only able to see from one or two distant standpoints. We gain a much more intimate understanding *both of the poem and of the opinions it provokes'* (Richards 1929: 9, my emphasis).

Parenthetically, I still wonder why he reverted to talking about 'the poem' in this ambiguous way. Why not use his 1919 model? – we learn about the potential of the 'signs', the 'experiences' derived from them, and the evaluations people make as they 'contemplate' those experiences. This kind of ambiguity is characteristic of the language of *Practical Criticism*, for whatever reason.

Nevertheless, as he rightly claimed, he was inventing 'a new technique for those who wish to discover for themselves what they think and feel about poetry (and cognate matters) and why they should like or dislike it' (p.3). Compare what others have said with your current reading, he was telling them, in effect. Do you now notice signs – perhaps whole sets of them – that you have ignored, or underplayed, or misconstrued? And in general, can you now see the partiality – if not wrong-headedness – of many interpreters, yourself included, on one occasion or another? For it turned out that readers did not divide neatly into 'good' and 'bad'; by the end of the course, many of them proved to be 'mixed'. 'They would pass, with contiguous poems, from a very high level of discernment to a relatively startling obtuseness, and often force one to consider very closely whether what appeared to be so stupid did not mask unexpected profundity', as Richards wrote after the event (p.316).

If we ask ourselves which dimension was most important to the students who attended the course, my guess is that this is the one. Most of the students were young (18–20); many, ardent readers of poetry no doubt – otherwise, why attend? No one was compelled to go. The revelation that pretty well all of them were prone to misinterpret, and demonstrably so, must have been shocking, challenging and stimulating. But, as a good teacher, Richards then met the need he had created.

What he showed them was that language 'has not one but several tasks to perform simultaneously' (p.180). Thus, as a provisional model, he offered 'four types of function, four kinds of meaning': 'sense', 'feeling', 'tone' (attitude and relation to listener), and 'intention'. It may seem only a start, but it was immensely superior to the tacit models of the grammar books they had all been steeped in at school. They had indeed the sense of a new 'map' for elucidating which aspects of the text they were neglecting, or treating without sufficient care. Richards also helped them to elucidate how misconstructions in one function fed back into all the others.

The comparison of their comments – 'protocols' as he called them – thus led them to examine and work on the 'disciplining' of their own acts of 'interpreting'. This was a positive gain all of them could aim for during the course.

However, in doing all this, Richards actually gave the word 'interpret' a specific and restricted sense. For he believed (part of the time) that the main thing to be solved was 'the communication problem'. 'When we have got, perfectly [sic], the experience, the *mental condition* relevant to the poem, we have still... to decide as to its worth. But the latter question nearly always settles itself' (p.11). It was simply a matter, we must recall, of the calculus of 'impulses' tacitly working itself out. With 'lyric' poems, on the borderline of song, that may seem plausible; but how about novels or drama? If students faced problems of value, it seemed he had no further help to offer – except, as we shall see, inadvertently.

The character of various misinterpretations

Once this approach has been opened up, a second line of enquiry follows immediately, using the same material. I could put it this way:

(b) Investigators can group interpretations, studying let us say all those who make a characteristic misreading, or prefer a characteristic reading. What, they may ask, tends to produce such effects? Is it reading practices – like (inadequate) attention to the sound and rhythm, or (failures to) work on construing the sense? Or are there any signs of common psychological factors – a tendency to sentimentality, or to inhibition, say?

One obvious result of such enquiries is 'to prepare the way for educational methods more efficient than those we use now in developing discrimination and the power to understand what we hear and read' (Richards 1929: 3). But the interest in the interpreters may become more personal and psychological: we may study 'the mental operations' of characteristic groups of interpreters, whether naive or subtle, and possibly over time discover 'stages in development' (pp.6, 9).

This fascination with the 'mental goings-on' of *readers*, and not simply of poets, opens a new world for the teacher. And it calls for a new discipline, as Richards realised. 'When views that seem to conflict with our own pre-possessions are set before us, the impulse to refute, to combat or reconstruct them, rather than to investigate them, is all but overwhelming. So the history of criticism... is a history of dogmatism and argumentation rather than a history of research... We cannot profitably attack any opinion until we understand *what it expresses as well as what it states.*' Yet, 'even the firmest resolution will constantly be broken down, so strong are our native language habits' (p.8, my emphasis). And our social assumptions, he might have added.

We see, then, why Leavis listened. Within this circle, a positive interest in O'Malley's 'mistake' is more than understandable; ideally, it is to be expected.

Of course, as Richards noted, anything so revolutionary called for a reconstruction of the teacher's habits, a fundamental change in his 'attitude, his direction of attention, his order and plan of interpretation'. But precisely this kind of disciplined change had already been achieved by 'the alienist'. This gave grounds for confidence: 'Normal minds are easier to "follow" than diseased minds, and even more can be learned by adopting the psychologist's attitude to ordinary speech-situations than by studying aberrations' (p.7).

Behind this reference, we too have to make further constructions. In Cambridge immediately after the War, W. H. Rivers and Head had been welcomed back with great respect, almost reverence, because of their therapeutic work with shell-shocked men from the Front. (We now have the story of Sassoon and Owen meeting at their clinic in Craiglochart.) These would be the typical 'alienists' that many older members of Richards's audience would have had in mind, I imagine.

Actually, of course, Richards's own disciplinary practices as a teacher–reader ebbed and flowed – as my liberated students helped me to realise in the early 1970s, when we studied the protocols on Lawrence's 'Piano', together with the analysis (see p.115). All credit to him, nevertheless, for achieving that theoretical position in the universities of the 1920s.

In addition, Richards certainly began to make very interesting observations on current reading practices. To take a central example: from the evidence, it seemed that, in first reading a poem, many students suffered 'distractions' from the rhythmic and sound effects they created. Some said as much; others betrayed the fact – by their simple misconstructions of the grammatical sense, for instance. Perhaps an incantatory way of reading – with marked pauses at the end of each line – led them to relegate the sense to marginal attention? Whatever the case, the teacher should 'regard them with the commiseration we extend to those trying to do sums in the neighbourhood of a barrel-organ or a brass band' (p.190).

The answer lay in further teaching. Forbes, for instance, tried to introduce a markedly different practice: 'Great emphasis was placed on reading slowly, aloud, giving full attention to pitch as well as stress, and to variations of tempo, so that the fascinating interplay of sound qualities upon sense and sense upon the quality of the sound might be explored' (Carey 1984: 83). Richards reinforced the call for 'several readings' – if necessary including one where 'we disentangle and master the sense' – so that 'varied factors may fit themselves together' (1929: 190).

The very use of the terms 'pitch', 'stress' and 'tempo' – characteristic of this pioneering group – indicated a fresh attempt to analyse, discuss and steer practices in this complex domain of signs (much as 'intonation' and 'speech acts' might do today). The 'movement of verse' was recognised to be highly dependent on the reader, and to be signified by several interacting systems within a text – many of the (sets of) signs being easy to overlook or override. (And this was elsewhere recognised to apply to prose, too – only more so!)

More difficult to steer, perhaps, were psychological tendencies or sets – inhibitions, stock responses, prejudices, and naive expectations of various kinds. Yet evidence of their effects was pervasive. Consider this series of comments on Christina Rossetti's lyric, 'Gone were but the Winter':

- To begin a poem with such a line as 'Gone were but the Winter' gives the show away...
  Rhymes such as 'boughs' and 'house' grate on one's ear
- What does the air mean when it sayeth softly we spread no snare
- Idea of living with a mossy stone singularly unattractive
- The sun cannot shine shadily; it can only cause shadows to be cast
- it is simple, almost childish, without being charming
- this is a wish for a lazy and 'secure' life rather than a longing for peace
- consolatory... [which] makes indulgence seem rather childish and cowardly. Make-believe has its after-effect of increasing rather than decreasing present discontent. To make this experience an end in itself is to ignore our responsibility to society etc. etc. ...
  while temporarily to indulge is mental 'dope'
- A more serious subject fits better my serious working mood

These seem to Richards to fall into two groups. In the one case 'Instead of trying the poem on, we content ourselves with a glance at its lapels or its buttons' (p.35). These readers resisted constructing an experience (or contemplating its product). In the other case, an experience has emerged in varying degrees, but within a frame of mind that expected something more – less childish, less lazy in its longing for security, less self-indulgent and irresponsible, more serious...

Obviously, demands like these are not to be altogether dismissed, but are they appropriate? In this context, to expect something 'charming' or 'more serious' seems a shade beside the point, and 'lazy' is surely imprecise? A resistance has been evoked somehow, probably through 'moral qualms' (p.37).

What Richards does in such cases, is to give a place to alternatives (including some within the same protocols!)

- Assonance, rather than strict metre, is used to heighten effect of simplicity
- full of delicate changes of metre...
  the whispering air is wonderfully suggested in the last verse...
  'the sun shineth, most shadily'... at once suggestive and concise
- delicate movement of the rhythm as it changes from the fine clear tone of the 3rd and 4th verses to the gravity and steadiness of the last two... 'mossy stone'... at once produces the intended atmosphere of quietness and undisturbed peace
- in its own tiny way... quite exquisite...
  a light little thing... but expressing certainly the pleasant feeling of joy and peace one feels in the spring
- the lines inevitably associate themselves with an experience which I value

As a teaching methodology this is fascinating. Moral qualms are not upbraided; instead, alternative evaluations are introduced. Partly this affects the treatment of detail, so that various moments in the experience are constructed in new ways. Partly, there is a different interpretation of the intent. Finally, in a later lecture, the character of various resistances or obstructions is discussed separately, in general terms.

However, by the time he came to write the 'Introductory Part I' of *Practical Criticism* – after completing much of the book, I suspect – even this breakthrough did not satisfy Richards. Characteristically, neither direction (a) nor (b) is given pride of place. Instead, a whole new subject of study is broached, as his primary 'aim'. This calls for a section in its own right.

Criticism and ideological field-work

'In part', says Richards, 'this book is the record of a piece of field-work in comparative ideology' (1929: 6). What did he mean by that?

(c) 'First, [he aimed] to introduce a new kind of documentation to those who are interested in the contemporary state of culture whether as critics, as philosophers, as teachers, as psychologists, or merely as curious persons' (p.3).

Thus, the investigator, by organising and analysing characteristic responses to lyric poems, could throw new light on 'the vast *corpus* of problems, assumptions, adumbrations, fictions, prejudices, tenets... the whole world, in brief, of abstract opinion and disputation about matters of feeling' (p.6).

'I need only instance', he goes on,

ethics, metaphysics, morals, religion, aesthetics, and the discussions surrounding liberty, nationality, justice, love, truth, faith and knowledge... As a subject-matter for discussion, poetry is a central and typical denizen of this world... It serves, therefore, as an eminently suitable *bait* for anyone who wishes to trap the current opinions and responses in this middle field for the purposes of examining and comparing them, and with a view to advancing our knowledge of what may be called the natural history of human opinions and feelings.

(p.6)

So far, so good. Already, it has to be said, there are pretty clear marks of the investigator's own ideological assumptions: he is thinking in terms of 'natural', not social history, thus evading the question, Where does the person doing the 'examining and comparing' stand? But a bigger practical problem looms ahead. How is a book organised for enquiries (a) and (b) going to cope additionally with (c)? And the simplest answer is that it did not try to.

Indeed, once again the reader has to wait well over a hundred pages before Richards gives this highly subversive aim a second chance.

However, the outcomes prove worth waiting for, I believe. They take us into a new speculative model of 'interests or desires', 'stock responses', 'sentiments', and organising 'ideas'. As an early lead in cultural studies, this model had – perhaps still has? – fascinating implications.

Richards begins with 'stock responses': he treats these as 'active systems of feelings and tendencies', organised in the form of 'ideas' (p.242). Thus, we might say, during the Great War the idea of 'Your King and Country' was used pragmatically to evoke certain feelings and the tendency to act in certain ways. And, though Richards omitted to do so, we should note that the subtly related ideas and feelings evoked by such a stock phrase were being organised by signs. Signs of this type, that is to say, serve to promote 'feelings' and 'tendencies' to behave in certain ways – including, it must be conceded, resistant tendencies, too.

For this reason alone, Richards like Ogden was interested in 'stock responses' – of which the Cambridge protocols gave repeated evidence. And he was not thinking only of their effects on interpreting poetry.

> [The intervention of stock responses] in all forms of human activity – in business, in personal relationships, in public affairs, in Courts of Justice – will be recognised, and any light which the study of poetry may throw upon their causes, their services, their disadvantages, and the ways in which they may be overcome, should be generally welcome.
>
> (p.240)

First, their services: some stereotyping of action and response was not to be avoided, Richards thought. 'A stock reponse, like a stock line in shoes or boots, may be a convenience... Indeed, an extensive repertory of stock responses is a necessity. Few minds could prosper if they had to work out an original, "made to measure" response to meet every situation that arose... Clearly there is an enormous field of conventional activity over which *acquired*, stereotyped, habitual responses properly rule' (p.241, my emphasis). So much for 'practical exigencies'. (I have to note, at this point, that he does not elaborate how such organised tendencies are 'acquired'.)

In everyday action, however, our stock reponses may be put to the test. If they are not appropriate or complex enough, we sometimes stand to find out. The difficulty comes when ideas are 'handed to us by others', or sometimes, 'produced from within': they can become 'a beguiling substitute for actual experience in evoking and developing our responses' (p.246).

> An idea – of soldiers for example – can stay the same through innumerable repetitions; our actual experience of soldiers may distressingly vary... [Yet] even in the presence of the Army it is by no means certain that what we perceive will not be as much our idea as the soldiers themselves.
>
> (p.246)

People who live in a world dominated by signs, with only limited fields of action – teachers and academics especially, we could say – have to be particularly cautious about the possibility that stereotypical ideas will promote a withdrawal from experience. Was he thinking perhaps of the public-school sermons that had dinned the glory of war into hapless pupils: *Dulce et Decorum est Pro Patria Mori*? Certainly, 'a child, being too easily persuaded what to think and feel, [may develop] parasitically'. Equally, 'when insufficient experience is theoretically elaborated into a system [it] hides the real world from us' (p.246). So theoretical ideas too could be used to promote stock responses.

Understandably, then, poetry that prompted Richards to reconstruct the forms of experience (or any such use of language, he might have added) had a particular value. Yet manifestly, even the 'good' poems he offered his audience quite often failed to have that effect! How could this be?

There seemed to be only one answer. 'Nine-tenths, at least, of the ideas and the annexed emotional responses that are passed on – by the cinema, the press, friends and relatives, the clergy... – to an average child of this century are [...] crude and vague rather than subtle and appropriate' (p.248). We are back, here, to a dominant theme of *The Meaning of Meaning* (give or take a tenth).

Characteristically, though, Richards wanted to take the model a stage deeper now. How about ideas in competition with each other, for instance? 'We shall not understand the phenomena of stock responses unless we regard them as energy systems which have the right of entry, unless some other system of greater energy can bar them out' (p.242). So a dynamic form of the model emerges:

> Every interpretation is motivated by some interest, and *the idea that appears is a sign of those interests which are its unseen masters*... The interpretation (a reader) puts upon the words is the most agile and the most active among several interpretations that are among the possibilities of his mind.
>
> (p.242, my emphasis)

Marx could hardly have put it better, you may be thinking! But Richards, significantly, did not pause to elaborate this fleeting discovery – in fact, he momentarily trivialised it. (Punning on the word, unconsciously, he proposes as a major 'interest' the 'desire to read faithfully'.) However, some pages later, he recovers:

> All our ordinary ideas about objects that matter to us, that are, as we say, *interesting,* are coloured by our emotional and practical relations to them. We can hardly help thinking that our nation, for example, is, on the whole, the best. Naturally enough, we are usually blind to this subjective colouring.
>
> (p.247)

His example pretty obviously belongs to the later Empire: it sounds less convincing today, I suppose. Nevertheless, the notion is clear. We use signs to refer to things that matter to us. Inevitably, these signs also evoke certain feelings and tendencies to act in certain ways. Thus they form an inextricable part of our practices, guiding and affecting them – so that, in general, the feelings and tendencies to act in those ways, and no other, are reinforced. Thus, in such cases, signs organise the whole system in the form of stock responses. Yet the question of 'what matters' remains primary. We may be unconscious of the shaping power of our 'interests', except – Richards adds – when they become explicit 'desires'.

It is worth trying out this model, briefly, even though Richards did not. Suppose we take some typical stock responses to Lawrence's poem, 'Piano'. In general terms this was characterised by some students as:

- silly, maudlin, sentimental twaddle... revelling in emotion for its own sake... nothing short of nauseating
- perfectly nauseating... utter puerility... the attitude to music is disgusting– wallowing in a warm bath of soapy sentiment
- it makes me angry... I feel myself responding and I don't like responding... I feel hypnotised... A lot of emotion is being stirred up about nothing much. The writer seems to love feeling sobby about his pure spotless childhood and to enjoy thinking of himself as a world-worn wretch
- simply sloshy sentiment
- some 'Vain [sic] inglorious Milton' has unhappily been moved by that mawkish sentiment with which we so often think of childhood...

These are fascinating responses to a 'speaker' who, in outline, has said: 'Softly, in the dusk, a woman is singing to me... In spite of myself the insidious mastery of song betrays me back... So now it is vain for the singer to burst into clamour... I weep like a child for the past.' Even allowing for the fact that the nostalgia for his old home is powerfully evoked ('the heart of me weeps to belong/To the old Sunday evenings at home' etc.), he hardly seems to deserve such an unmitigated outcry.

So how might we account for it? What resistances to weeping, to nostalgic (*Pears Annual*) memories of home, to the glamour of childish days, and so on were likely to have been inculcated into some, at least, of Richards's Cambridge students? Where could these students have picked up the key phrases: 'feeling sobby' about 'pure spotless childhood'; 'perfectly nauseating'; 'wallowing' in 'soapy sentiment'; 'silly, maudlin, sentimental twaddle' and so on? I can imagine at least one plausible context, for a start: the rites of induction to preparatory or public boarding school. And, of course, in such a context, the stiff upper lip was a cruelly necessary shield at the time: the repression of feeling by stock phrases was indeed 'what mattered'.

From such influential centres, stock reponses could spread quite widely – in this case, among the upper middle class, especially. Even 'sentiment' itself, I note, had gathered its group of associated feelings, attitudes and resistant tendencies, expressed here by 'mawkish' – a word for the parent, master and prefect? – or 'sloshy' – for your sisters, or the fellows in your dorm, perhaps?

Whatever the case, such signs in the 'protocols' manifestly did organise a passionate resistance to any signs in the text that evoked nostalgia, weeping, or abandonment to feeling. They were part of a culturally organised system for regulating practices, I would say, to sum up. But, in fact, they excluded the possibility in this case of attending to other, countervailing signs within the text and, thus, to other feelings and tendencies within the potential experience to be derived from it. As stock responses they are therefore 'disadvantageous and even dangerous, because they... prevent a response more appropriate to the situation' (p.241), in poetry as in everyday life.

So much for a brief attempt, then, to weave the strands of Richards's model together and apply it directly to the documentation he offered of 'the contemporary state of culture'. It is already richly suggestive for cultural studies, I believe. But there were still two afterthoughts added by Richards in later chapters. One concerned 'sentiments', the other 'beliefs' – something he had first tried to define more closely in the Moral Sciences Club in 1915.

You may already have felt some disadvantages in Richards's use of the word 'idea' to cover not merely 'the sense' we make of liberty, nationality, justice, love, truth and so on, but also the varied feelings, attitudes and tendencies to action we actually use the words to promote or inculcate. Richards himself may have been aware of this. In some respects he may have preferred what he takes to be 'the psychologist's use' of the word 'sentiment':

> Love, for example, is a sentiment, if by love we mean, not a particular experience lasting certain minutes or hours, but a set of tendencies to behave in certain ways, to think certain thoughts, to feel certain emotions, in connection with a person... A sentiment, in brief, is a persisting, organised system of dispositions.
>
> (p.260)

This was a very useful proposal, it seems to me, providing we add that such sentiments are organised by signs. Thus, the sentiments appealed to by the use of 'Your Country' in 1914 were more than ideas, we could agree, though ideas were involved, in close relationship with feelings and tendencies. The notion of such signs organising our 'dispositions' underlines the pragmatic force of language, too.

As for belief, Richards proposed two ways 'in which we can entertain an assumption: [first], intellectually, that is in the context of other thoughts ready to support, contradict, or establish logical relations with it; and [second], emotionally, in a context of sentiments, feelings, desires and attitudes ready to group themselves round it' (p.274). From this point of view, intellectual 'belief' implied the testing of an assumption within a system of ideas, of alternatives perhaps. But 'emotional belief is a different matter.'

> Given a need (whether conscious *as a desire* or not), any idea which can be taken as a step on the way to its fulfilment is accepted, unless some other need equally active at the moment bars it out. This acceptance, this use of

the idea – by our interests, desires, feelings, attitudes, tendencies to action and what not – is emotional belief.

(p.275)

The proposal is exploratory still, I take it – thus the force of 'and what not'. The grammatical assumptions of the second sentence, in this form, certainly seem rather shaky. But for cultural analysis, the sophistication of this dual – and interacting? – treatment of beliefs seems suggestive.

Thus, there has often been a temptation on the Left not to place ideological 'belief' within an actively formed system of desires and needs – to treat the agents rather naively as power operators, self-deceiving opportunists, or alternatively as scientific materialists. So they may have been, on occasion. But in the last decade the roots of ideological belief have begun to be taken more seriously.

Discriminating among poems

Finally, one further aim of the experiment must at least be mentioned. By offering a 'mixed lot' of poems each week, Richards initially hoped, I suppose, to be able to find out how discriminating students were, when left to make their own judgements – whether, indeed, they 'preferred some poets to others' (as Robert Graves had recently been accused of doing, in his college Collections – 1922: 86).

Unfortunately, this notion fell at the first hurdle. With so many readers betraying signs of partial, incomplete, or wrong-headed 'interpretations' of the text, any evaluations of the experience were rather beside the point. For, analytically at least, without an experience based on scrupulous reading of the verbal signs, evaluations were simply further evidence of culturally inculcated dispositions.

Within the book (and possibly the lectures), it is true, Richards was able to organise his protocols in ways that prompt or steer a careful reader, so that s/he progressively realises how much – or little – a given text had to offer to an imaginative interpreter. And thus, he might be said to offer an indirect way of teaching greater discrimination, perhaps.

However, as Richards rightly saw, the whole investigation suggested that reading must be improved, and that it might be better if interpreters held back their ongoing evaluations, suspending judgement till they had made a much better job of exploring the potential of the signs.

Perhaps for this reason, he ruefully acknowledged that four poems were probably too many for one week – given the demands of other courses, I suppose. He might also have told himself earlier, after his first course, say, that the 'mixed bag' idea was premature. It encouraged some students to 'have a go' at a poem, not without encouragement from the lecturer, who spoke disparagingly of 'havering, non-committal, vague, sit-on-the-fence, middle-body opinion' (p.18). No doubt sitting on the fence does have its penalties. But surely the first lesson of the protocols was that tentativeness was to be commended, and that both readings and appraisals had better be treated as provisional?

Whether in promoting or probing 'discrimination', then, (or other, more positive, forms of appraising, we might add), the experiment was not a success. This is not altogether surprising.

Richards, after all, had no tradition to work in – he was inventing one. From their later behaviour, few if any of his colleagues or most brilliant students were concerned to develop the experimental method he was pioneering. He was very much on his own, without friendly criticism or advice, it seems. And the nearest discipline, which in Britain would be current psychology, offered little encouragement or help for his kind of investigation.

Looking back, many possibilities come into focus. Richards himself had probably not fully clarified his experimental aims. But then, with his agile sense of plural aims for his projects – from *The Meaning of Meaning* on – perhaps he can be excused for wanting to grasp more than he could hold? Why, we might ask instead, was so little done, first in Cambridge and later at Harvard, to build on these foundations? What factors, in the institutions, their ideologies and their practices, resisted any such tendencies? And in many cases, continue to do so today? This seems to me a much more serious question than the limitations of a unique experiment.

CHAPTER 10
New discursive options and theories

Discourse, knowledge and institutional forms

Practical Criticism, I would claim, heralds a revolutionary change in the discourse of literary and cultural studies. Consider the mainstream tradition in 1919. In the classical curriculum, where canonical texts formed the basis of instruction, the teacher's role was to produce, or more often reproduce, an authorised commentary. The authority lay in the teacher's long acquaintance first with an alien language and second with a disciplinary tradition established by earlier commentators. That was 'knowledge'. The standard edition by Jebb, say, was emblematic of such a tradition: on any page you could see a dozen lines of the original text (above) and two dozen lines of commentary (below). 'Learning' was an ability to reproduce commentary in the spirit of this tradition. Students could be tested on it, and their comments or translations minutely corrected. 'Discovery', if it ever emerged, came after years of work in the field.

Admittedly, at Cambridge there was a Classics course called 'Pure Scholarship', introducing the select few – like Eddie Marsh, editor of *Georgian Poetry* – to the actual disciplines of critical editing. But normally the teacher had authority, the student none.

Compare this with 'English', in the hands of Forbes, Richards and their allies. There was no agreed canon for the modern novels – and later the contemporary poems – they brought into lectures in the 1920s. In fact, nationally, there was heated debate around 1925 about the poems of Richards's friend, Tom Eliot, and when Leavis wrote to the Home Office formally, asking permission to import a copy of Joyce's banned book, *Ulysses*, he was put under surveillance by the local police. What is more, as they well knew, this radical break was widespread in all the arts during the period 1910–30; the painters kept in Ogden's shop had actually been forerunners. It was not just in the Heretics Club that an appeal to canonical authority was being ruled out.

Besides, the tradition of reading set up by a classical education from the ages of 8 to 18 was demonstrated by these 'English' radicals to be inadequate. Cambridge students from elite schools could not even interpret quite elementary poems in their own language. Not that the fault lay with them: the supposed 'discipline' they had been taught was based on fundamental misconceptions about language in use – and naive models of 'the poem'. 'Meaning', they were now being shown, was far more complex than they had been led to believe. The authority of the 'Old Men' was being undermined.

From this perspective, the vanguard of 'English' teachers were seen as a revolutionary group. By introducing new theory and practices, they wanted to change the meaning of 'knowledge', 'discovery' and 'learning'. That implied radical changes in discourse. But unlike the Extension lecturers, they were working within an established centre of power, with its own institutional forms. 'Supervisions' left some room for innovation; could lectures and examinations be radically transformed? And if not, could any alternative forms be introduced? What constraints – and internal conflicts – were they laying themselves open to? Within the political setting of Cambridge, could these be resolved?

A context for discovery

So far as I can see, Forbes's lectures on the Romantics, early in 1919, initiated the new direction. Joan Frankau/Bennett has three clear recollections. 'Two-thirds of the way through the term, Forbes was still *exploring* Blake.' In other words, there was something more important than regular coverage of authors – and Forbes saw his job as 'exploring' that. This involved 'odd but evocative... readings' of the *Songs of Innocence* and *Experience*: so it was not the text, but a vocal rendering of it that was under consideration. And, she adds, he was 'developing a theory' that one must 'discover' an exact stress and tempo, with 'a right pitch of voice for certain key words' (Bennett in Brower 1973: 47).

Now, pitch, stress and tempo are three types of sign we use in speech to evoke mood, feeling, attitude, relations with listeners, intent (and more). If you become more precise in choosing these signs, therefore, that implies becoming more aware of precise nuances in the moods, feelings, attitudes and so on that go to make up your 'experience' of a poem, on a given occasion. It is a familiar matter for musicians attending master classes. With poems, we have an additional advantage: we may be stimulated to search for linguistic expressions that communicate (and steer) the shifts in thought, feeling, attitude and so on that begin to emerge.

> How the Chimney-sweeper's cry
> Every black'ning Church appalls;
> And the hapless Soldier's sigh
> Runs in blood down Palace walls.

The way such lines are said expresses, in part, 'what they mean' to the person reciting them. The voice may express sympathy or antipathy; it may pity, accuse, or protest; it may register a grim irony, a restrained anger... and so on. Reading the lines in an 'exploratory' way, and talking over potentials in the signs, sets up an opportunity to steer further readings – and what they now communicate to the audience. This is a step beyond Bradley, because spoken signs of various kinds can be referred to (more) exactly and a (more) precise significance evoked *or* described (a contrast we will come back to).

How did that fit the expectations of 'lectures'? Not very well, it appears. By the mid-1920s, according to Leo Salingar, Forbes:

> seemed to be thinking aloud, talking for us but not to us, inviting us into a kind of labyrinth of ideas, in a style of amiable digression, with a range of comparisons, anticipations and afterthoughts that I couldn't get into focus...
>
> I got the sense of a new way of thinking about literature, and more than literature... Forbes seemed to want to explore.
>
> (Carey 1984: 79)

The mention of 'anticipations and afterthoughts' is a valuable clue. For efficient communication, it may be best to keep a rein on thoughts, stick to the known, and focus on the people listening to the lecture (keeping their interests and needs in mind). But, when 'thinking aloud', speakers must ask the indulgence of their audience to some degree, for second thoughts will intervene, or avenues for later exploration suggest themselves. 'Digression' from the immediate theme may seem worth the risk – though it may not pay off on a given occasion.

The contrast in discursive choices with the classical tradition could hardly be more sharp. As it happens, Hughlings Jackson had only recently observed and described it: in the traditional lecture, the speech was 'old organised', he would have said; with Forbes it was 'new now organising' (1932) – quite possibly marked by long hesitations or fillers, with frequent retracings and false starts, we could add.

As an induction to disciplinary practices, 'new now organising' discourse makes special calls on the listener to think alongside the speaker – to anticipate and actively foresee possible routes ahead, and to make a running synthesis of the mental work in progress. It demands great mental agility, naturally, as well as some familiarity with the speaker's characteristic positions.

Most important of all, if the lecturer is struggling to articulate new thinking, there is a certain invitation to the student to do likewise. For their essays, Forbes actually advised his students to jot down any ideas that occurred to them, on one large sheet. Then they could underline important ideas. Then join associated ideas, using 'circles and lines'. This allowed for an organised form to arise from considerable diversity – side-tracks and all (Carey: 77).

His student, Hugh Carey, who recalls these things, notes also Forbes's 'emphasis on creativity'. He wrote poetry, and assumed his students did. From time to time, too, he would submit his poems to the class, for criticism.

This final switch of role – from teacher to 'learner', from 'student' to 'teacher' – may not surprise us today. At the time, though, it must have amazed many in Cambridge.

What did this say about the lecturer's authority? – and the students'? Besides, how could such improvising, such thinking on the wing, count as knowledge? Was it conceivable – or appropriate – that a lecturer should be learning, in public? What kind of example was that setting the students? It was pretty lucky for Forbes that his reputation placed him somewhere between a mooncalf and an archangel (in Queenie Roth's words). But if we take those same questions seriously, it is obvious how subversive – and mentally liberating – his practices could be.

Didactic or collaborative investigation?

If Forbes seemed to want to explore, Richards – by contrast – 'wanted to expound', thought Salingar. To judge by other evidence this seems a fair comment on what became his regular lecture series, on Criticism.

Joan Bennett recalls technical defects in the first series, it is true: too much scribbling on the board, or drawing diagrams, with his back to the audience. Undoubtedly on this subject he felt he had a good deal to say, and, while he broke many pieces of chalk as well as new ground, the overall effect was 'spell-binding'. Three or four years later, however, M.A. Scott noted, 'Richards was fine again, analysing the experience of reading a line of poetry with the aid of little diagrams. *He is always very clear, in spite of being so subtle*' (in Phillips 1979: 161, my emphasis). Richards was shifting the focus of his attention to his audience, by the sound of it, shaping 'old organised ideas' for effect. It is no surprise that by the later 1920s, 'Richards shews some very Welsh qualities as an orator', according to Muriel Bradbrook!

The three series on 'practical criticism' were discursively more complex, that is clear. Richards is certainly maintaining an authoritative position: it is he who chooses the poems, he who selects, organises and comments in various ways on the 'protocols'. Nevertheless, to judge by the book, it is not his comments but selected protocols that have the last word – and rarely a single protocol, at that. In the book at least, his own comments are rarely direct: he genially teases, evokes suspicions, suggests a note of query... pretends to be puzzled. This already marks a major shift in his social relationship with his audience (his voluntary assistants in the experiment).

Muriel Bradbrook, one of the students present, would go further: 'with Richards a new art of reading evolved. The study of literature became a collaborative social exercise' (1973: 63). This was certainly a potential that Richards himself was aware of, as we have noted. Whether he ever fully developed it, I rather doubt. Nevertheless, a degree of 'collaboration' is essential, even in reading the book: the readers too are invited to take part in the experiment, and – to some degree – are left to reach conclusions on the basis of conflicting evidence. You can see why, after the lectures, students went on arguing into the night: there was still work left for them to do.

Indeed, given the prevailing teaching traditions, there are conspicuous absences: no explicit, magisterial summing up, in most cases; no final, *ex cathedra* analysis of the poem by the lecturer himself. The teacher may hint, suggest and occasionally allow his own judgement to emerge. But I have never had the feeling that the 'case' was being rigged, for example, by the suppression of contrary evidence in the protocols. And, from personal experience, I know the value of submitting those same protocols to a new generation of student-readers, for *them* to analyse independently. That is something Richards did not do; but his discursive practices mark a new direction – towards collaboration, rather than direct instruction.

Scope for 'original composition'?

Teachers lectured; what opportunities did students get to hold forth? And when they did, were they simply expected to reproduce what the authorities had said?

In the case of one student we have detailed recollections of what happened in his early supervisions. Although he had read Maths for Part I, 'He seemed to have read more English Literature and to have read it more recently and better', said Richards, 'so that our roles were in danger of being reversed'.

At about his third visit he brought up the games of interpretation that Laura Riding and Robert Graves had been playing with the unpunctuated form of 'The expense of spirit in a waste of shame'. Taking the sonnet as a conjurer takes a hat, he produced an endless stream of lively rabbits from it and ended by 'You could do this with any poetry, couldn't you?'... so I said, 'You'd better go and do it, hadn't you?'

(Richards in Gill 1974: 4)

Two or three weeks later, the student, William Empson, returned with the central 30,000 words of a book.

Naturally, we cannot take this prodigy as a representative case. More important is the question: what scope was given to prodigies – and others – anyway? Were the 'essays' students were regularly asked for simply a means of covering an existing syllabus of topics, or was there room and encouragement for them to propose their own?

As a topic, this is a particularly fascinating example, too. The idea of 'an endless stream' of multiple meanings ran contrary to Richards's earlier notions – if it did not contradict them. It does not come easy to any teacher to encourage blatant opposition, you might say. But he did, apparently, and the resultant work – submitted as an optional 'original composition' – did not prevent Empson from getting a starred First in 1929.

How often this kind of thing occurred, I do not know. The evidence may no longer exist. In a sense this in itself is significant, of course. The examination system introduced in 1926 did not insist on 'original composition', as a sign of competence. Despite the *Cambridge Magazine*'s call for 'a greater extension of qualification by Thesis rather than Examination', the notion that students might have anything original to say (whether individually or as a group), was institutionally treated as an exception, an optional extra. (Even with newly emerging Ph.D. theses, there seems to have been no organised route to publication, in part or in full. In the 1900s Oxford had certainly done better for their earliest B.Litts. – dull as they often were.)

When it came to the writing, the composition of *Seven Types of Ambiguity* is very much what might be expected of a student of Forbes and Richards. Just as in Richards's published work of 1919–25, some of the best ideas emerge in asides or unexpected elaborations. As with Forbes, the tone suggests at times someone genially thinking aloud, relying on a certain indulgence from the reader. Deeper discursive choices had been internalised by this student, it seems to me.

'Original' thinking was at a premium, perhaps, rather than 'composition'? Unfortunately, as with the brilliant theses started during the period – *Fiction and the Reading Public* (Leavis 1932), and *Drama and Society in the Age of Jonson* (Knights 1937), especially – I get the feeling of someone thinking independently, but individually. They do not seem to be part of a circle where friendly criticism, close collaboration, or the give and take of argument, has an inevitable place.

Leavis's thesis, we must recall, was supervised by Q; Knights's by Tom Henn – though his best help came informally from Tawney. Only Queenie had Richards as supervisor, and neither left any comments that I know of, to reveal their respective roles. Did Forbes ever supervise postgraduate work, I wonder? – there is no mention of it in Carey's biography.

Thus, though there were rebels, an alternative 'school' was not being contemplated or developed. And to some degree, this meant that the politics of discursive alternatives was not being theorised, either.

Theorising functions of critical discourse

Forbes and Richards, as we have seen, were jointly stimulating students (and some of their colleagues) to think more explicitly about signs in lyric texts, and – equally important – in vocal interpretations of them. Although, if anything, Richards seems to have simplified the kind of frame available in *The Meaning of Meaning*, rather than continued to elaborate it, in practice their students were used to very delicate, subtle analyses as lines were recited and explored.

Where is our evidence? Well, there are recurrent moments in the *Practical Criticism* protocols, for a start. And fortunately there is the testimony of various students of the time. But why, you might ask, can we not turn to their own published critical practice? The simple answer is that during the 1920s, Forbes published nothing on poetry, and Richards only two general, introductory essays, one on Eliot (a *New Statesman* review, reprinted at the back of *Principles*), the other on Hopkins (in *The Dial*).

So far as they were concerned, then, critical discourse was oral, not written. And it is not difficult to see why. How can you get onto a page the sound of the voice reciting – and enjoying – a lyric poem? How can you show the exploration going on? And, given the kind of theoretical frame they have elaborated, how can you draw on it without distracting or actively repelling the very kind of reader you want to be enjoying the poem? (There was one possible answer, through the new BBC Radio Service, but either they neglected it or they had inadequate access.) So throughout the 1920s, Forbes, Richards, Leavis, and perhaps others, developed their approach to criticism in lectures or 'practical criticism' sessions.

This may account for a curious omission: so far as I know, during this period Richards never applied his analytical frame to critical discourse, in order to offer an account of what was going on – or what ought to be.

Fortunately, the omission did not escape his student, William Empson. So, buried deep in *Seven Types of Ambiguity* – like many another original idea – there is a lucid account of what his teachers were trying to do. (It is the best kind of tribute from an enterprising student, you might say.)

> On the face of it, there are two sorts of literary critic, the appreciative and the analytical; the difficulty is that they have all got to be both. An appreciator produces literary effects similar to the one he is appreciating, and sees to it, perhaps by using longer and plainer language, or by concentrating on one element of a combination, that his version is more intelligible than the original to the readers he has in mind. Having been shown what to look for, they are intended to go back to the original and find it there.
>
> Parodies are appreciative criticisms in this sense, and much of Proust reads like the work of a superb appreciative critic upon a novel which has unfortunately not survived.
>
> (Empson 1961: 249)

I cannot resist including the aside, but nevertheless let's address the main point so far. Empson is interested in the critic as a person using language to communicate with a group of readers. What typical kinds of effect is the language intended to produce, he asks. It is an original question. And in the case of 'appreciative criticism' – the achievement of Bradley's generation, say – the answer is already revealing: they were trying to produce 'literary effects' similar to those of the original. (This is a point we have already discussed.)

Then comes a typical Empsonian aside: parody is a way of producing something comparable to the original, thus some appreciative criticism should be parodic! Before we proceed, let me demonstrate that Empson is being, as usual, both witty and serious.

Some chapters earlier, he had been discussing the kinds of contradiction used in jokes, and took the paragraph which describes the appearance of Zulieka Dobson as 'a pretty example'. He starts like this:

> Zuleika was not strictly beautiful.

'Do not suppose that she was anything so commonplace; do not suppose that you could easily imagine what she was like, or that she was not, probably, the rather out-of-the-way type that you particularly admire'; in this way (or rather, in the gambit of which this is a parody) jealousy is placated, imagination is set free, and nothing has been said (what *is* this strict kind of beauty, anyway?) which can be used against the author afterwards.

(p.176)

All the passage in single quotes, as he points out, is a quasi-parody here: it is an attempt by the critic to elaborate on what a person like the narrator might be expected to think as he says, 'Zuleika was not...' It is longer, and it focuses on the narrator's paradoxical play with ambiguity, slightly sending him up as it does so. A parodic element, then, might be especially appropriate in appreciative criticism of the comic – entering into its spirit of play.

To return to his major distinction now, how about the analytical?

> The analyst is not a teacher in this way; he assumes that something has been conveyed to the reader by the work under consideration, and sets out to explain, in terms of the rest of the reader's experience, why the work has the effect on him that is assumed. As an analyst he is not repeating the effect; he may even be preventing it from happening again.
>
> Now, evidently the appreciator has got to be an analyst, because the only way to say a complicated thing more simply is to separate it into its parts and say each of them in turn. The analyst has also got to be an appreciator; because he must convince the reader that he knows what he is talking about (that he has the experience which is in question); because he must be able to show the reader which of the separate parts of the experience he is talking about, after he has separated them; and because he must *coax the reader into seeing that the cause he names does, in fact, produce the effect which is experienced.*
>
> (p.248, my emphasis)

Language explaining an effect does not repeat it, then. On this model, some part of the poetic experience must be separated out, and the causes of it 'named'. This is a strictly intellectual process. There is, admittedly, just a hint that in naming the parts – in pointing to the signs – the analyst must also do something more: relate them to 'the rest of the reader's experience' *beyond the work*. If that had been pursued, it would have been a new and highly significant corollary. However, it was not, at this point. To see something of the analyst typically in action, let us take another comment on the description of Zuleika:

> No apple-tree, no wall of peaches, had not been robbed, nor any Tyrian rose-garden, for the glory of Miss Dobson's cheeks. Her neck was of imitation-marble. Her hands and feet were of very mean proportions. She had no waist to speak of.

The negatives in the first sentence throw a prim pattern over its lush fulness, force one to think 'no, the tree had not', and give it, as a doubt in the background, exactly the opposite meaning, as by an Italian or vulgar-English double negative. In the second, of course, her neck could only *imitate* marble, but was it imitating *imitation-marble*?... And then, since *mean* may be medium, small or without quality; since a waist is at once flesh and the absence of flesh; we are left in doubt whether the last two sentences mean that her beauty was unique and did not depend on the conventional details, or that these parts of her body were, in fact, not good enough to be worth mentioning, or they were intensely and fashionably small.

(p.177)

References to each sentence (each part), to 'negatives' (to vulgar-English 'double negatives' indeed), to opposed meanings, to three senses of the word 'mean', and thus to three explanations of the last two sentences – these indicate the focus is on analysis. Nevertheless, on re-analysis, signs of Empson trying to 'convince' and 'coax' are pretty clear. (How about: 'prim... lush', 'of course... only', 'flesh... absence', 'intensely... fashionably', for instance, and their 'effects'?)

What should we be looking for in critics, then? Empson himself puts it this way:

The process, then, should be one of alternating between, or playing off against one another, these two forms of criticism. When you have made a quotation, you must first show the reader how you feel about it, by metaphor, implication, devices of sound, or anything else that will work; on the other hand, when you wish to make a critical remark, to explain *why* your quotation takes effect as it does, you must state your result as plainly (in as transferable, intellectually handy terms) as you can.

(p.250)

'Show how you feel' and 'state your result plainly': these are expressed as polar but complementary processes. Still, you might reply, any quick student of Richards would surely have recognised by that time that critical language was mixing referential and emotive functions. The answer is surprising, even rather shocking. Among the younger teachers – from George Rylands to Frank Leavis – there is little or no evidence of this kind of theoretical frame. By the 1930s, like Richards, it was vanishing from Cambridge.

Already, in Empson I seem to hear premonitions that this may happen. 'You may say that this distinction (between appreciative and analytic) is false, because in practice one must do both at once, but I think it is useful' (p.250). The point was to recognise the 'antinomy'. True, in reply to 'the cult of irrationalism', 'it might be said that the business of analysis was to progress from poetical to prosaic, from intuitive to intellectual, knowledge'. But weren't these 'just the same sort of opposites [as appreciative and analytical], in that each assumes the other is also there' (p.251)?

Empson, in the poetic tradition of wit and irony, would continue to keep the analytic aspect firmly in view. True, under the influence of basic English maybe, he tended to keep to words and neglect other vocal signs. Nevertheless, his brilliant articles in Ogden's *Psyche* during the next decade indicate a continuing interest in Richards's projects, and especially the analytical interest in language – with which Cambridge progressively lost touch.

CHAPTER 11
A brake on innovation, despite new demands

Changing structures of degrees and power

It was the year 1926 that marked the end of the 'informal oligarchy' of Forbes, Richards and Tillyard (1958: 122). Pressures from several directions saw to that. In part, their very success had created problems: a one-year course intended for students who had already studied some other tripos began to feel inadequate. Besides, this made English (Section A) dependent on other departments, and – Tillyard hints darkly – they were increasingly 'disappointed at the small flow of men from classics'. Competing with other subjects for students entering their third year was inevitably risky. There was irritation in some quarters that English was not 'a piece of post-war folly that would soon die down' (p.117). It was actually here to stay.

Perhaps for that very reason, on the one side, Modern Languages 'were in the act of making the popular combination of English and a single modern language next to impossible' (p.107). On the other, Chadwick's Section B, on Early History and Literature, specifically intended 'for the few', was not an adequate partner: it could not produce the numbers they hoped for. The obvious answer seemed to be a new English Tripos, Parts I *and* II. So, in 1925, discussions began. Chadwick, Q, Coulton, Attwater and Richards were involved, with Tillyard as secretary of the Special Board.

In October 1926, however, following the report of a national University Commission, there were structural changes of many kinds at Cambridge – one of the foremost being that women dons were given recognition at last. From that term the number of University Lecturers with tenure in the subject expanded to include: Attwater, Bennett, Coulton, Downs, Forbes, Lucas, de Navarro, Richards, Tillyard, and from the women's colleges, Murray, Paues and Philpotts (all philologists by training). The result, as it turned out, was a much more conservative tendency. The oligarchy and their experiments had to give way. Even their ally, Chadwick, had to move his Section into the Faculty of Archaeology and Anthropology, to avoid pressure from traditional philology.

To external eyes, things went very well. Six Firsts in 1925; fourteen in 1928, the year of transition; and in 1929, ten in Part I and eleven in Part II. 'The new Section C, which now became Part II, was an immediate success', Tillyard recalled: the Italian set books were congenial; English Pastoral, a compact special subject, led to thorough study; the English Moralists appealed, and Willey responded (1958: 120).

What became of the new investigatory approach, however? What happened to the theoretical foundations for Criticism? In the new Board, they were no longer central.

As an index of the change, someone might trace the changing notion of 'practical criticism'. In 1925, 1926 and 1928 the basic reference would be to the investigatory courses Richards was running, with a minor reference to the kind of work with college groups that Leavis was encouraged to do at Girton and Newnham. It was primarily a teaching approach, based on experiments in which students collaborated.

By 1929 at the latest, however, Richards had also begun to show its underlying possibilities, as an instrument of research. Practical investigations raised new theoretical problems about 'interpretation', 'culture' and 'ideology'. These were not taken up, then or later, by colleagues in the department – though two rebellious research students, Queenie Roth and Lionel Knights, were obviously deeply affected.

Instead, somehow, a semantic narrowing occurred, until finally the key reference becomes the exam questions in the paper on 'Passages of English Prose and Verse for Critical Comment' – introduced with the new tripos. To sum up: what set off as an experiment was reduced to a test. Significantly, as that happened, the student was placed in a simplified relationship with institutional power: the chance of this being a liberating experience had ended.

What steered and enforced this shift of direction? In part, it has to be answered, the 'oligarchy's' compromises with the original Section A syllabus. By 1920 Richards had demonstrated the need for a new theorising of Criticism. In addition, throughout the early 1920s, Forbes, Tillyard and he had proposed a new focus for teaching: on the detailed study of texts in order to give an interpretative reading (aloud), as a preliminary to any evaluation. In 1925 he had shown – devastatingly, one would have thought – that it was absurd to 'think that the whole of English Literature can be perused with profit in about a year' (Richards 1929: 317).

A quite different discipline of reading was a prerequisite for the new tripos, that was clear. What is more, as he and Forbes already knew, this called for a frame of analytic categories, in order to clarify the multiple potentials of texts at any given moment of reading aloud. (And in 1928, in the course of early supervisions, his brilliant student, William Empson, had opened up a further vein in this area.)

In the heady days of the young Section A, a little group of colleagues had kept up with such things. (Indeed, Leavis continued to attend all three series on practical criticism, rather to Richards's embarrassment!) Not that the majority of 1926 lecturers were actively antagonistic. Rather, in published work at least, the leading ideas sketched above had not been taken up, critically assimilated, revised, or developed.

Nor were they adequately discussed elsewhere. The sole professional journal, *The Review of English Studies* (1925–), was looking in the opposite direction: 'the academic *apparatchiks* were in full command' (Gross 1969: 209). The small periodicals of the time were often sympathetic, but none offered a broad enough base, and most lapsed intermittently, after a run of two or three years. The reforming group at Cambridge depended, therefore, largely on personal influence.

However, if there was a possibility before 1925 of applying their power and influence to change syllabus requirements, the 'oligarchy' were slow to use it. Forbes and Richards could afford wry references, they thought, to 'the godlike lords of the syllabus world'. This turned out to be politically naive. But even in 1926, there must have been many forces restraining any impulse on their part to give things a radical shake-up.

For a start, this was the year that Richards, having been made a Fellow, left Cambridge in March on a world trip that ended only in September 1927. More important, while he was away, there was a sudden, harsh intensification of social conflict, gripping the whole country during the Miners' Strike. Dons and students were involved, on both sides – 'undergraduates in plus fours and fellows of colleges (actually) marched off in organised gangs to break the workers' strike', Queenie Leavis remembered (1943). And afterwards, the moral was clearly drawn in the conservative camp: 'We've had the Great Strike, and in some ways it's going to be as valuable as the Great War [sic]... We shall feel the benefit of the public object lesson to Labour for the rest of our lifetime at least', wrote G. S. Gordon, Oxford's Professor of English. Even if his time-scale was overly optimistic, the 'lesson' was pretty generally applied to anything with a whiff of revolution to it. Cambridge, already politically split, was all the more unlikely to give considered treatment to any radical proposals for reshaping its traditions: so much must have been obvious.

Retrospect and new questions

This group of friends, then, with Richards as an inspiring link, had introduced and theorised a significant shift in literary and cultural studies. Its implications were revolutionary, too much so to find an effective or permanent home in Cambridge University. Because the set of new possibilities emerged piecemeal and were never synthesised, it was easy – even for the proponents – to develop one or other of them partially, while neglecting the overall frame of practices and their shaping theoretical 'ideas'. But theoretical synthesising itself depends on a social context: an active, developing argument among schools with enough differences to keep the frontier open. In 'English' departments of the 1920s, this was conspicuously missing, especially in England. If Cambridge failed to respond, Oxford and London were worse. (Later, Harvard proved to be just as bad, too.)

Still, this is no excuse for failing to make such a synthesis today. From our vantage point, and in our terms, what had this group to offer? The following is my selection and organisation, but the 'ideas' and language are theirs:

(a) They began with a theoretical frame for analysing language in use. It was probably the first in Europe to escape so systematically from the presuppositions of Classics – the study of dead languages, through texts, not speech. What was required, as they saw it, was a theoretical analysis of signs and interpreters, in a 'context of situation'. The 'situation' was easily overlooked, but their binary interest, in the interpreters as well as the signs, remained fundamental.

(b) Thus, studies of language in use, they saw, would necessarily be investigatory. The investigators would observe people in discussion, or readers interpreting (not that metaphysical entity, a 'text'). Their analyses should seek to diagnose why given people interpreted (or responded) as they did, on a specific occasion.

(c) During such investigations, it turned out that students and teachers could collaborate – to greater or lesser degrees.

(d) The act of interpreting called for a dynamic model, acknowledging the texture of expectations that arose, as the incoming signs were actively organised. Words in current usage that suggested static entities ('plot', 'character' etc.) embodied fundamental fallacies, and had to be transformed to take account of reading events.

(e) In reading, as in social life, signs were seen to be organising 'sentiments' – systems of thoughts, feelings, and dispositions to act. How fixed or open to change were such systems? The answer could be crucial, and reading poetry (among other things) offered a suitable bait for eliciting evidence about this. Thus, a new analytical study of cultures and ideologies was conceivable.

(f) The field of study was not simply responses to canonical texts, then – nor even to imaginative literature. It might range out to the

A brake on innovation, despite new demands 133

discursive practices of any institution with dominating effects on 'responses': the cinema, the press, advertising (or the clergy, business, Courts of Justice...). It should be a critical study of their influences and effects on signs in action – in reading, in personal relationships, in public affairs.

(g) As for reading literary texts, a complete renewal of practices was necessary, steered from this theoretical base. For a start, the focus should be on vocal interpretations, sifting the plural potentials in textual signs and making constructions beyond them. (In part this was in line with Bradley and similar rebels of the previous generation.)

h) However, in communicating with an audience, in the course of repeated readings, a critical interpreter must adopt two interlocking roles, one appreciative, the other analytical. These made two contrasting sets of demands on the potentials of language, imagination and intelligence.

To go no further, this is still a staggering achievement, it seems to me. And yet in retrospect, its limitations were already becoming painfully obvious too. I am thinking of three strikingly original essays of the Cambridge students of the later 1920s: Queenie Roth/Leavis's thesis on *Fiction and the Reading Public*, Lionel Knights's on *Drama and Society in the Age of Jonson*, and finally, Frank Leavis and Denys Thompson's primer on *Culture and Environment*.

What they learnt from the new tradition is pretty obvious from the titles. There were novels and there were readers; plays and a social audience; cultural products and an environment. You could not study one without, in some way, investigating the other.

But how, and precisely what, to investigate? By roughly 1930, the answers were not simple. They might involve learning how to study:

(i) The social impact of new economic 'activities', in the form of influential 'industries', 'finance', 'markets', and 'trade' (L.C.K.).
(ii) The ways in which these somehow structure 'reading habits' and theatre 'audiences':
– directly, through a 'book market', with 'middle men' organising the 'supply of reading matter', and thus the relations of 'author and public' (Q.R., D.T. and F.L.);
– indirectly, through 'advertising', 'education' and 'forms of mass production' (D.T. and F.L., Q.R.).
(iii) Resultant social 'attitudes' and the 'appeals' made to them in various forms of 'popular culture' (all four).

For questions like these, no one in Cambridge had a theoretical frame or a methodology. The ambitions were heroic, but the answers very uneven. That was to be expected.

It had been obvious from the start that Ogden, Richards, and possibly Forbes were interested in certain contemporary issues, but not in history. Without that interest, what hope was there for any efforts to place 'culture' – or to define it? – within a social and historical 'context of situation'? Here, Richards was as 'immature' as most of his students.

Knights gets furthest, by arguing with Marx and enlisting friendly help from Tawney. Nevertheless, in my view, the final titles of the two parts of his book, 'Background' and 'The Dramatists', spell out the problem he was unable to resolve; within this metaphor, there was little hope of establishing adequate relationships. Besides, until Empson (1952) had shown how key 'ideas' like 'honour' and 'honest' had developed historically, among conflicting social groups, I wonder if an adequate methodology at the semantic end was available within their tradition? It needed a new infusion, new international contact. And, ironically, this was available – though the link was never made.

INTERCHAPTER 12
A revolutionary theoretical alternative

Language, psychology and culture

Language, psychology and culture: there had to be complex connections in this field, Richards and his allies were sure. A theory of signs... a model to define their interlocking functions in speech or writing... scientific investigations of interpreters in action... a dynamic model for reading processes... analysis of the effects of stock responses (inculcated by verbal formulae)... Sixty years later, it is not difficult for an observer to imagine how fruitful this advancing project might have been. But it was never given institutional recognition or power – and the key handful of people separated, and moved on.

Ironically, during the same decade, and working within the same field, another group produced a remarkable alternative – only to find exile or death in the 1930s. Their published work of the 1920s went unnoticed in Western Europe and was later suppressed by their own government; when it was finally republished and translated – in the 1960s and 1970s – amazingly, it had lost none of its original force and relevance. (Does that suggest something about 'Western' thought in the meantime?)

The Bakhtin circle and their theories were the product of a revolutionary society. Despite the grim terror of civil war and foreign intervention, despite the inexorable shift to despotic power within the Bolshevik party, this circle, and others around them, produced ideas that would stand being buried for thirty years – and still prove vital. These were people – let's remember – who had put their heart into a radical change in social life. One or other of them had taken part in 'alternative' People's Universities; campaigned for mass literacy in the revolutionary armies; taught in the burgeoning teachers' colleges (introducing new psychological labs); set up reading circles and local journals; experimented with theatre in mass education; been in on the founding of new universities in Central Asia; lived and worked together, in communes...

All of them believed in group work: in discussion and argument; in collaborative projects; in laying new theoretical foundations, jointly. Fortunately for them, in the field of language, psychology and culture, Marxism was relatively undeveloped; a party orthodoxy had yet to be enforced. In fact, the leading intellectuals of the period, associated with radical experiment in the arts, were Formalists. For a few years, then, the group around Mikhail Bakhtin (and also Lev Vygotsky, as we shall see) had an opportunity to place language, psychology and culture within their own versions of a Marxian frame. In doing so, they produced a startling new perspective on the problems tackled by the Cambridge group.

Marxism and the Philosophy of Language (Volosinov 1929) seems to me the central, mature product of those years of discussion in the Bakhtin circle. Unlike *The Meaning of Meaning* – which has so many interests in common – it is powerfully analytic and historical. Thus, it scrupulously places the two prevailing theorists in contemporary linguistics, Saussure and Vossler, after a detailed, critical study of their assumptions. What the circle were obviously seeking was a historic break – into something more comprehensive, theoretically, and yet, more practical. Where they used Marx, they did so soberly enough. By comparison, it is the Cambridge tradition that is cursory and polemical in its criticism; and, because it did not take opponents seriously, it didn't stand to learn much from analysing them. The Leningrad group recognised themselves as more than 'Heretics' – as part of a historical process that includes the traditions they rejected. For brevity's sake, in this chapter I am going to ask one simplifying question: what alternative frames could the Bakhtin circle have offered the Cambridge group?

They began with something elementary, and quite fundamental. Ogden and Richards had observed a person interpreting a signpost; Volosinov, Bakhtin, Medvedev and their circle analysed a group in dialogue. The difference it made was immense. They looked at themselves listening, and realised they were already productive. They looked at themselves writing and saw they were in dialogue – still! They looked at their thinking, and realised the way dialogue entered into consciousness itself. Using these insights, we can transform the work of the Cambridge group *and* the Extension lecturers, while still recognising how often they prepared the way.

From modelling monologue to modelling dialogue

Twentieth century linguistics, like nineteenth century philology, was still unconsciously based on texts from the past, thought Volosinov. These fragments from past cultures – often surviving in relative isolation, he added – became written 'monuments' and were treated as such. Suppose that, instead, you thought about contemporary production, with books alongside speech: how did that change the model?

> Any utterance – the finished, written utterance not excepted – makes response to something and is calculated to be responded to in turn. It is but one link in a continuous chain of speech performances. Each monument carries on the work of its predecessors, polemicizing with them, expecting active, responsive understanding, and anticipating such understanding in return. Each monument in actuality is an integral part of science, literature, or political life [and so on]. The monument is set towards being perceived in the context of current scientific life or current literary affairs... [or] that particular ideological domain of which it is an integral part.
>
> (Volosinov 1929: 72)

Like everyday dialogues, then, contemporary written monologues are historically enmeshed in a discussion with others. *The Meaning of Meaning*, we could say, is part of a chain (or better, a network) of post-War argument. It arises, in response to other writing in the field; it seeks and prefigures responses in its turn. In fact, several responses to the original articles are published within the book. It is itself already a 'dialogue'.

And precisely the same is true, we could add, for any reading of the poems of Richards's friend, Tom Eliot. You don't have to go further than the first couple of lines:

> April is the cruellest month, breeding
> Lilacs out of the dead land...

April cruel? But where is 'Aprille with his shoures soote', and the 'swete breeth' of the season? Yes: Spring, the sweet spring. What kind of speaker is this? – blighted by old age, shell shock, mental depression or something, has s/he lost all faith in life and renewal?

So, the 'monologic' utterance was 'already an abstraction'. The poem, like the polemical book, enters into dialogue with other texts, as it is produced and as it is read. Just as in spoken dialogue, it calls up and is greeted with further signs from the reader.

Ogden and Richards, it has to be said, had come very close to admitting as much. They made an explicit distinction, let us recall, between the words on the signpost and what went on in the mind of the interpreter. But Forbes and Richards's delight in reading the text aloud, in savouring all the vocal potentials of the written signs, had distracted them, you might say. They became fascinated with the signpost, rather than the mental goings-on of the interpreter.

What was going on, then? Take an everyday utterance, says Volosinov, like: 'What is the time?' This has a different significance whenever it is used, according to the situation. I take the point today. At first, we might object that an utterance like that is just a signal to us to look at our watch and read off the time. If we were feeling very dull – a bit like a computer – that might sound plausible. But what time? – the hour? – the minutes? – the seconds? – all three? We have to fill in a situation, it seems. Suppose we are all waiting for the last bus, when someone raises the question: then it might imply, 'Is it after midnight? – Has it gone already, perhaps?' Now we aren't just 'listening', passively, we are actively thinking about the situation too.

That passive role for the listener/reader was a fiction: a product of philological scholarship, Volosinov claimed. In social life, listeners had to be active. But he goes one stage further than that; he places the listener/reader's understanding within a theory of signs.

> To understand another person's utterance means to orient oneself with respect to it, to find a proper place for it within the corresponding context. For each word of the utterance we are in process of understanding, we, as it were, lay down a set of answering words...
>
> *understanding is to utterance as one line of dialogue is to the next.*
>
> (p.102, my emphasis)

At first sight, this notion may appear paradoxical to say the least, especially to anyone brought up on a 'receptive' model of reading. How can you combine reception and production? But first, consider the bus-stop request for the time. Our reply, likely as not, would be governed, not by the verbal string alone, but by our responsive construction of its 'significance' *within* the situation: 'He's thinking the bus may have gone already', and so on. That 'construction', the Bakhtin circle realised, is itself signified (how, we shall see in a moment).

But to return to Richards – and Bradley. They too had been referring to responsive constructions. Bradley explicitly defined the 'reflective product' that we need to form, temporarily breaking out of the experience of the drama. This 'product' – this production by the reader – implies the use of signs. These in turn will affect our reading when we continue.

Equally, consider those 'expectations' and so on that, as Richards reminded us, are aroused even by a simple narrative. Or, in the case of discussion and argument, think of the 'resistances' that may be aroused – to go no further. An expectation and a resistance both imply signs, in however fragmentary a form. Such terms must point to various types of signs that are being produced in the very process of listening/reading.

In active reading we must be producing responsive signs, however fragmentary, then. This insight has revolutionary implications for

A revolutionary theoretical alternative 139

practices in reading, learning and teaching. It took most of us till the 1980s before we began to see them.

Dialogue, inner speech and active response

The notion of a productive 'answer' arising in the course of reading could still have been puzzling, at this stage – if only from a strictly practical point of view. How could the brain cope? Here, a revolutionary group of psychologists, inspired by Lev Vygotsky at the Moscow Institute, came to the rescue. From experiments with young children (aged 4–7 especially) they had developed the idea of 'inner speech'.

What happens is this. From around the age of 2, children can take part in dialogue, especially when their parents offer supporting structures:

Father: What does grandad do?
Robert: Fwow water!
Father: And what does Robert do?
Robert: Wun awaaaay!

Early utterances are brief, context-dependent, and often steered by the parent's initiative. Somewhere around 3–4, though, as children play with 'toy' objects or undertake social tasks on their own, they normally begin to talk to themselves about it. They start producing a type of monologue, which scans and organises their solo play:

> That's going on...on... on the carriages. That's going to go next to the carriages – you see? And we shall put the brake on, you see? ... Then fall down like this... Oh that's going to go – on this do you see?
> (Dixon 1967 – see Part III)

Among younger children, these forms of self-organising speech are at first fully audible – even though other people around them are not being directly addressed. And dialogic forms are often retained (like 'you see', 'isn't it?' and so on). The children behave as if an active listener was present.

Vygotsky's group investigated what happened next. Their work showed that the forms gradually became more fragmentary, though obstacles experimentally introduced would elicit more articulate forms again. Finally – they hypothesised – the fragmentary forms were fully internalised, around the age of 7. Children continued to use language to steer and organise their actitivies, but in the form of 'inner speech'.

This was a fascinating lead. Starting from social dialogue, in which they played a dependent role, children were learning to 'address themselves', in order to organise their own thoughts and actions, independently. In doing so they were internalising their social world. From dialogue with others they were moving to dialogue with themselves. And the verbal signs they used, which began by being external and elaborated, ended – it seemed – in fragmentary forms. So it would no longer be surprising to find fragments of 'inner speech' accompanying many kinds of personal and social activities, as a normal part of conscious life.

How could such fragments be understood, though? From a formal grammatical perspective, this seemed a profound difficulty. Fortunately for Volosinov, in working on everyday spoken dialogues, Jakubinskii (1923) had recently shown that even 'explicit' verbal signs worked normally as 'hints'. Given shared social experience and a common situation, listeners could readily transform verbal fragments into more articulate forms – as their responses indicated, Volosinov pointed out.

Here, the Bakhtin group developed one of their most daring and profound ideas. What is linguistically articulated anyway? Normally, only a fragment, they would say. Any string of linguistic signs inevitably depended on the situation for its 'significance' (its 'theme', as they called it). The semantic force of a string like 'What is the time?' could be thought of as a 'lower limit' of meaning: 'it only possesses potentiality – the possibility of having a meaning within a concrete theme' (1929: 101), in an actual situation. There *has to be* a dialogic construction, it seems, by a listener who scans the situation and spells out part of that potentiality in more explicit terms.

In describing understanding as 'a response to a sign with signs', then, Volosinov was being quite precise. Where was Robert? At the seaside, of course. Where was grandad standing? In the shallow water. What did Robert do first? Walk, with glee towards grandad... *You* may need these signs now to put you in the picture. None of this was said at the time, though; the father and son had other signs to draw on, in shared memories (stored images and enactive schemata, at Robert's stage, I would add).

At a later stage in human development, Vygotsky was saying, the child (like the father) would have inner speech – even if no external speech occurred at the time. Then, responsive, verbal signs *would be* operating, throughout such an episode. Indeed, through all of conscious life! So there were major implications, as Volosinov and his group recognised, for consciousness itself. This is how they saw them:

> Consciousness takes shape and being in the material of signs [images, words, meaningful gestures...] created by an organized group in the process of social intercourse.
>
> (p.13)

A revolutionary theoretical alternative   141

Latent in this view, there was the call for a new focus in contemporary psychology, whether Pavlovian or Behaviourist.

Experience, consciousness and social evaluations

Within society, as Volosinov saw, signs are implicated 'in literally each and every act or contact between people – in collaboration on the job, in ideological exchanges [in science or art, say], in the chance contacts of ordinary life, in political relationships, and so on'. Signs are organising and implementing, on the one hand, relations between people, and, on the other, their joint practices.

The concept of inner speech added a new dimension. It placed each individual consciousness in dialogue with others. For, in order to exist at all, inner speech (together with the non-verbal signs that accompany it) must internalise these socially active signs and their functions, using the product to shape personal awareness, to organise personal activity, to interpret what's happened or what's going on, and to project into the future. Suddenly, it must have struck the group that this notion revolutionised their definition of 'experience' itself:

> *experience exists even for the person undergoing it only in the material of signs...*
> If we disregard the sign function of inner speech and all the other expressive activities that together make up our psyche, we would turn out to be confronting a sheer physiological process.
> (p.29, original emphasis)

It is fascinating to note that Ogden and Richards had come very close to this statement, but had not followed it up. Obviously, it would have immense ramifications, especially for anyone brought up on Locke. Volosinov paused only to sketch those in social psychology.

The ramifications for literary studies are especially fascinating. For example: it is now possible for us to return to Bradley and Richards's concept of the 'poem' as an 'experience' and transform its potential. The reader would indeed be constructing beyond the 'lower limit' of the verbal signs themselves. There would be moods, feelings and attitudes in this new inner event, as well as an imaginary situation in the mind's eye, a 'world' of people and their setting constructed from the references, let's say, to pianos, parlours, Sunday evenings and so on. There would be images, sketchy or full, of a child sitting under a piano, and pressing his mother's poised feet. And there would be a relationship with the participant/narrator too – concerned, resistant, or whatever. But where does the reader get all this from?

> The understanding of a sign is, after all, an act of reference between the sign apprehended and other, already known signs; in other words, understanding is a response to a sign with signs.
>
> (p.11)
>
> Thus each of the distinguishable significative elements of the utterance and the entire utterance as an entity are translated in our minds into another, active and responsive, context.
>
> (p.102)

So this stream of inner events readers are constructing, in the form of inner signs, is indeed an 'experience' on a par with any other they construct in everyday life from *verbal reports*.

What's more, if we take due account of inner speech, this type of 'experience' also shares many of the features of events we actually observe. For it would be a gross mistake to treat such events as physiological or given; they too are scanned and ordered by verbal signs, in however fragmentary a form.

Thus, if we consider 'the whole aggregate of life experiences', an atmosphere of 'unsystematized and unfixed inner and outer speech... endows every instance of behavior and action and our very "conscious" state with meaning' (p.91). But here a new point was made – a vital counter to Cambridge assumptions.

Ogden and Richards had sketched many functions for language in their provisional models, but one seems to have been steadily omitted – or lost in the vast range of the word 'attitude'? Throughout consciousness, social dialogue, and the written monologues that arise from it, the Bakhtin group recognised that:

> There is no such thing as words without evaluative [colour].
>
> (p.103)
>
> New aspects of existence, once they are drawn into the sphere of social interest, once they make contact with the human word and human emotion, do not coexist peacefully with other elements of existence previously drawn in, but engage them in a struggle, reevaluate them, and bring about a change in their position within the unity of the evaluative purview.
>
> (p.106)

So, whether within a society or a small group, signs signify what is worth referring to – and what is becoming worthless. They dismiss some things as mawkish, and find others pleasant or exquisite. The struggle over evaluation penetrates every name: you are a 'bolshie', she is a 'comrade', he is a 'lackey of Imperialism'... And it infects every reported speech, most obviously 'with the help of *expressive intonation*' (p.103).

How people who called themselves 'Heretics' failed to foreground evaluation takes some explaining! The very name of the club testified to their desire to resist or transform existing social evaluations. Suppressing such desires must in its turn arise from deeper, ingrained assumptions about what to bring to the surface in social experience.

Again, Volosinov can assist. His circle contrasted the level of everyday behaviour, or acted-out ideology – where inner and outer speech leave values unsystematised – with the level of ideological systems 'crystallised' out of it. Obviously, there was an interplay between the two. But 'newly emerging social forces find ideological expression and take shape first in [the level of everyday behaviour] before they can succeed in dominating the arena of some organized, official ideology' (p.92) – in poetry, ethics, science, or religion, say.

In the case of Richards, and possibly Ogden, the dominating influence of organised assumptions (perhaps from Moore?) seems to relegate evaluation to the ineffable – to 'our own inmost nature' (Richards 1929: 11). The social 'inculcation' of values was actually admitted, but on the whole deprecated: it stood for war-time propaganda and the orthodoxies of the Old Men. Leave the natural individual free, Richards seems to say, for a personal organisation of impulses, 'by ways which we know nothing about' (1924: 57). This Robinson Crusoe-like image of humanity was deeply entrenched, as Marx had noted; it steadily resisted the evidence of language in social dialogue – and among many linguists, does so to this day.

Reading, culture and evaluation

At this point, then, we are well placed to take a critical look back at *Practical Criticism*. First, the very form of the investigation. A focus on readers in action opened the way for a dialogic theory of reading. In terms of method, this was a step beyond anything the Bakhtin circle attempted. And, whatever the distractions, Richards was beginning to head in similar directions. He could see that, in reading, relations were being set up between the text (the crystallised ideological product) and sentiments or stereotypes laid down in everyday experience (acted-out ideologies). He recognised that poems were just one kind of 'bait' for catching such everyday ideologies in action: law reports, the press, the cinema might have done equally well, he knew. He was indeed pioneering an analyis of 'culture'.

However, he simplified what was going on, principally through not isolating and analysing the signs that are used to organise thoughts, feelings and dispositions into unified 'sentiments'. In particular, he made no analysis of the evaluative force of words. The way evaluations were being contested within his society – sometimes by his own friends! – was also missing from his frame.

Rather, orthodox 'society' out there was seen as betraying the individual by 'emotively' 'inculcating' these things willy-nilly. The notion that evaluations inevitably arose in social dialogue – and might be willingly internalised – ran counter to ingrained ideological stereotypes of his own.

Of course, Richards like everyone else, had to rely on social dialogue to reshape and develop his model. At the time, no one did so at all systematically. So, to end this 'interchapter', suppose we imagine a group of intelligent readers in 1929 who had just read and enjoyed Richards's and Volosinov's new books. What questions might they have proposed for cultural studies?

Using the model of 'dialogic reading'

- How to elicit and explore readers' dialogic constructions?
- How to analyse relations between text and dialogic responses?
- What kinds of social dialogue to set up, as between selected writers and selected readers?

Using the model of 'inner speech' and 'products'

- How to capture early moments of inner response and organising? (For example, in jottings, question marks, underlinings and other abbreviated signs alongside the text?)
- How to trace developments in successive readings? (For example, in greater articulation and explicitness?)
- How to get evidence of the effects of successive 'products' like these on the reading that followed? (For example, in taped prefigurings and retrospective responses alongside each oral reading?)

Using the model of 'social conflict' over emerging social meanings

- How to draw on conflicting (and ambiguous) ideological potentials in contemporary texts?
- How to relate the texts selected to ideological conflicts between various groups of readers?
- What features within the texts to take account of in selecting and analysing?
- What other crystallised forms besides lyric poems?

Finally, try to imagine the forces – historical, social and institutional – that made such questions unthinkable at the time.

PART III
Restructuring an elite system 1960–79

CHAPTER 13

Pressures for radical change in education

The Space Race, telecommunications and curricular reform

In 1867, the British state was making world history; by 1957 – when the first sputnik went up into space – it was a minor agent, a smallish part of an immense power block dominated by the United States. The 1960s, therefore, saw British institutions reacting, culturally, socially and politically, to world-wide historical movements.

As the two great powers emerged from Cold War into an uneasy Co-existence, the sputnik came to symbolise a change of strategy. It was a Soviet challenge to the spirit of capitalist enterprise – to its inventiveness, technological daring, and capacity to organise innovating production. There was going to be a Space Race, with resources pouring into research and development, into new technologies and, briefly, into the educational base itself – which was suddenly seen to be alarmingly inadequate.

When the US government gave the lead (from 1958), Britain and other European states followed. In project centres across the United States, there were suddenly funds to develop for the schools a New Science, a New Math, and (five years later, after much lobbying) a New English – all in an atmosphere that encouraged inventiveness and original thinking. In Britain, over the decade, teacher education colleges went through a revolution, while universities doubled their intake, and new types of institution – technology colleges and, finally, polytechnics – were hastily set up in major cities.

This, we could say, was the innocent face. But, inexorably, within both the Soviet Union and the United States the technological race reinforced specific centres of power, and characteristic ways of enforcing it. The 'military-industrial complex', which Eisenhower had warned against in 1961, inevitably had the dominant voice not only in rocket production but also in the communications systems that controlled it.

With television spreading across the globe, a new form of imperial power became possible: 'Telecommunications had progressed... to being also an instrument of foreign policy' (Schiller 1969: 12). In the struggle for world hegemony, as it was now seen, 'a powerful communications system exists to secure, not grudging admission, but an open-armed allegiance in the penetrated areas' (p.3):

> Through the use of modern instruments and techniques of communications systems it is possible to reach large or influential segments of the national population [in a target state] – to inform them, to influence their attitudes, and at times perhaps even to motivate them to a particular course of action.
>
> ('Winning the Cold War', Report to Congress No.2, 1964; in Schiller 1969: 12)

The radio and television systems of the USA, already the most commercialised in the world, were unable to resist the pressure to become the 'voice of America'. So, when the 'penetration' became increasingly bloody, costly and inhuman – as it did notably in Vietnam throughout the 1960s – new forms of spectacle and a specific kind of Newspeak were developed and broadcast world-wide, to keep the 'free world' away from difficult questions. The face of experience, of power in action, was officially veiled. Ironically, though, in their competition for viewers, networks also vied with each other to secure the most powerful pictures of violence, from Vietnam to Chicago. Contradictory pressures found an outlet.

The conditions of the undeclared 'war' on Vietnam (like the later war in Afghanistan) were bound to provoke resistance, especially within the United States itself. The age-group due for call-up were mainly students, especially in the more liberal states, where over fifty per cent were entering college. Already a grass-roots Civil Rights movement earlier in the 1960s had shown them how civil disobedience could be used against injustice and human degredation. Moreover, as the outrage over Vietnam grew, US students spread and fuelled the protest, from Japan to Western Europe, including Britain. In all these countries, too, television coverage came to their aid, magnifying the images of war, resistance and protest. (And out of the blue, even in China, it seemed, a new wave of intense ideological conflict was beginning through the mass student movement, encouraged by Mao.) With an explosion of sects on the Left, there were millenarian dreams of world liberation from exploitation, oppression and manipulation.

A world-wide movement among students began, in Berlin in 1968. Radicalised by violence – including the shooting of student demonstrators – the demands broadened. In Italy, the whole curriculum was under attack. In Paris, the unions joined the students in mass demonstrations. 'Alternative' classes, workshops, counter-courses and universities were set up: subjects, lectures, exams, and the ideological assumptions underlying these structures were all under fierce analysis and attack.

The responsibilities of scientists, of communications researchers, of universities themselves as corporate institutions, were suddenly put under interrogation. Some people in them had manifestly power over life and death. What uses of that power – what political answers – could they offer? And where did the so-called Humanities stand? What testimony were they giving about the life experience of dominated people: Blacks, the industrial working class, Third World peasants and (voices at last began to add) women?

Rejecting a system biased towards exclusion

In the UK, the complex historical forces sketched here – and much more that's omitted, too – slowly but inevitably affected English, and many other subjects, from 1960 on. I will simplify matters, by concentrating to start with on the first phase, which ran roughly from 1960 to 1969.

In 1960 there was no 'higher education' system in Britain – just the universities and the rest. The taken-for-granted structure of education, you might say, was an echo of the class structure. First, the upper class: the proportion of the age-group destined for university was four per cent. They were drawn almost entirely from the so-called 'public schools' (selecting by cash and class), or from the 'grammar schools' (selecting by tests at the age of 11). Compared with other modern states, like the USA, Sweden, or the USSR, their numbers were ridiculously small.

Nevertheless, university demands dominated the curriculum of these prestige schools. By the age of 14 almost half the future Arts students were taking no course in the sciences. For their two pre-university years they were studying only three subjects – almost always in the Arts (the Robbins Report 1963, chapter VII). If those subjects included 'English' there was only one option: English Literature – a course covering nine or ten set books, starting with Chaucer and Shakespeare. The tiny minority who were accepted for degree courses in English Language and Literature then went on to study... Chaucer, Shakespeare, and the rest.

So much for the elite and their formation. A group of about the same size – roughly four per cent – formed the next social layer (the middle class, you could say). They were studying for vocational certificates. Part were in residence at 'teacher training' colleges for a two-year course; they were destined for non-grammar-school teaching. The others were attending colleges of 'further education' as day students on technical and business courses – all but the few fortunates who were at the new

Colleges of Advanced Technology. As far as full-time education went, that was the end of post-school provision. (The lower class, made up of part-timers, had too high a failure rate to count.)

In Britain, then – and especially in England – the state education system and the exams that governed it were biased towards exclusion. At the age of 11, over seventy per cent of children were excluded from 'academic education' – were labelled, in fact, as 'unsuited' for it. Most of the twenty per cent selected went on to grammar school, where they were taught largely by graduates; a small minority went on to 'technical schools', with lower prestige. At the age of 16 these selected students were again selected by examination. The survivors – under half – entered the sixth form. After two years they were again selected: the chosen few joined the public school elite at Oxbridge, or else went to London and the 'civic' universities. The others – many of them women with similar qualifications – had to choose a vocational course or start work.

Remembering the democratic hopes for education a century earlier, it was an ironic outcome. Worse, the system did not make sense, even in its own terms. Selection tests at 11+ were a sham. The English Literature papers at 16+ had been condemned twenty years earlier (in the Norwood Report, 1941); the English Language papers were officially condemned in 1964 (by the Lockwood Committee). And from a wider perspective – politically, economically and educationally – by 1960 the whole system was under repeated attack. In the decade that followed, alliances of socialists and liberals struggled to make three key changes:

- First, to abolish selection at the age of 11, and to form 'comprehensive' secondary schools;
- Second, to reform the 11–18 curriculum, so that the majority of comprehensive school students could follow a common core;
- Third, to reshape 'higher education', bringing in: regional 'polytechnics' with a commitment to day students of all ages, whether part- or full-time; degree courses in all teacher education; and an Open University, using modern media as well as correspondence for 'teaching at a distance'. Meanwhile, the number of university places were to be doubled and a range of new universities founded.

Schoolteachers undertaking the reform of English

In the event, it was not the universities that took the lead – in fact, many teachers in them resisted any kind of change. So, for the first time in their history, it was the schools that made the initial moves. The prestige 'grammar school' curriculum was officially recognised to be pretty irrelevant. New science and maths courses would have to be constructed (and Colleges of Technology instituted, to attract thousands more students into new engineering sciences).

So experiments started, funded by the Nuffield Foundation and others, and bringing some of the most dynamic professors from the universities into dialogue with a very select group of schools. (In fact, with millions of pounds donated by industry, the 'public schools' shouldered their way to the front.)

In English and the Arts in general, nothing was planned at first. But by 1960–1 things were moving: small groups in state schools were struggling for themselves to define new directions, and finding allies, not in the university English departments, but in the departments (and colleges) of Education.

What – beyond the international call for a New Curriculum – gave this rebellious minority a unique opening, and the confidence to take it? Politically, it was a renewed searching for 'democratic' traditions in the British Left, I believe. This was the spirit of the *Universities and Left Review* and the Left clubs and forums it set up in the late 1950s. After the Hungarian Rising of 1956 and the defeat of the Eden government over the invasion of Suez, there was an extraordinary willingness to exchange experiences in an undogmatic way, and one of the focal themes became the struggle to establish democratic schooling: to break the prevailing system of selecting children at the age of 11 and submitting them from then on to an 'academic' or a 'practical' curriculum, within segregated types of school.

What enriched those discussions were the different strands the clubs brought together: an older generation, many of them tutors from the Workers' Educational Association, including Raymond Williams, Richard Hoggart and Edward Thompson; the generation fresh out of university, with Stuart Hall and Raphael Samuel keenly involved; and many younger teachers like myself from innovating schools (the new comprehensives especially) or from 'vocational' colleges defining a new 'liberal studies' option. *The Uses of Literacy* (Hoggart 1957), *Culture and Society* (Williams 1958), *The Long Revolution* (Williams 1961), and *The Making of the English Working Class* (Thompson 1963) became four of our key books.

Within this kind of forum, and in networks that built out well beyond the Left itself, a growing number of secondary English teachers learnt:

- To value working-class experience, and slowly to find ways of encouraging kids from city or country to discuss, probe and write from experience (in poetry, prose and dramatic scripts). Here, an early stimulus was the documentary film tradition, from Karel Reisz

on, and later the Radio Ballads of Charles Parker, Peggy Seeger and Ewen MacColl.
- To see drama and reader's theatre presentations as a key form of access to imaginative literature (later, adding a background of improvised drama). Here, Joan Littlewood's theatre at Stratford, London, was an early inspiration, soon swept into a renaissance in drama studies and dramatic presentations (both 'in the round' and on television.)
- To take the broader view of 'literature', to bring issues of our time directly into discussion, and specifically to include work by Blacks and other culturally dominated people (though not yet consciously, women).

Thus, to discuss press items and television or radio programmes, the cultural products that the media were fashioning with a teenage market as their target; tentatively starting to make films with classes, too, and linking up with the British Film Institute's new education department. (See *Reflections: a Walworth English Course* by Clements *et al.* (1963) and *The Popular Arts* by Stuart Hall and Paddy Whannel (1964).

It took time: for most of us this meant turning upside down our own grammar school and university formation. We had to recover oral traditions of story-telling, in classes of 30-plus; to write poems and stories alongside our class on occasion; to turn poetry texts into choral recitals and novels into dramatised scenes, with Brechtian narrators; to draw ideas from the actors, when directing plays; to interview positively, eliciting detailed knowledge and experience (and encouraging our students to do so); to take the chair and guide discussions that exposed real differences, challenging our own positions; to study partial and conflicting reports in the press; to set up groups to probe press and television extracts for language in use; to analyse the visuals alongside the text in the new colour supplements; to start watching film and television as possible directors or editors...

The groups involved were lucky to share the excitement of pioneers. Fortunately for us, there were also strong allies in teacher education. And by 1963–4 institutional structures were set up nationally, to support the informal networks. First, a National Association for the Teaching of English (NATE); then – under a liberal Conservative minister, Edward Boyle – a Schools Council for England and Wales, to promote curriculum research and development. English was one of its three target areas, and the sixth form curriculum another.

For an active minority in schools, then, the period 1960–69 meant undreamed-of possibilities – and achievements – in young students' work in English, starting from their capacity to discuss, to think

Pressures for radical change in education 153

independently in a social group, and moving on from there. In this way, we believed, they could wrench a kind of independence for themselves from the intensifying threat of cultural domination and passive consumerism. But what was happening in the universities meanwhile?

At first, so far as the English departments were concerned, there was little change. In fact, Frank Leavis, in his 'retirement', finally became a cultural hero, defending imaginative literature against the dragons of technology and utility. Ironically, a man – a representative of a tradition – that Cambridge had held at arm's length for so long had at last won through, after a fashion. (No one proposed to implement his earlier dream, though, of a joint analysis of culture and capitalism in the 17th century.) Yet the acclaim was pretty general: 'As a critic, Leavis is a landmark that has yet to be surpassed', conceded a leading young Marxist, as late as 1968 (Anderson). For others, of course, his work became a useful excuse for intransigent English empiricism.

By the mid-1960s, however, the UK universities had reluctantly agreed to double the number of students within the decade. New universities were being set up in Sussex, East Anglia, Warwick, Lancaster, Stirling and elsewhere, giving promise of a curricular break. Something more was going on than a struggle simply to ensure that the Arts and Humanities expanded in line with the now dominant Sciences (physical, biological and social).

Severe doubts were being expressed, for instance, about the current curriculum on the Arts side. In fact, Penguin produced a best-seller on *Crisis in the Humanities* (1964), edited by the liberal historian, Jack Plumb. 'England is no longer the centre of literary creation in the English language', conceded one of the contributors, the Cambridge professor, Graham Hough: faced with that fact, a course in *English literature* – omitting American, African, Australian, West Indian and Anglo-Indian – seemed to him an anachronism. As George Steiner put it a year later: 'If these new literacies are to be excluded from our curriculum... will the student of English literature be taught in a kind of museum?' (in 1967: 82) (The use of *'will'* here is academic politeness, of course: the typical mainstream student *was* in a cultural museum, the Oxford course, for instance, still ending at 1870.)

But Hough tentatively went further than that:

> Other quite recent forces have made for a sort of literary modern internationalism – the rise of film as an art-form, and the ease with which it transcends linguistic barriers; the rapidity with which the most effective drama gets translated and produced outside its own national borders.
>
> (p.105)

Live drama, film... television (?); where might that line of thought have taken him? However, he had no pioneering experience to offer in this domain. Rather, Raymond Williams's new film courses in Cambridge were going to be rigidly excluded from recognition in the syllabus.

Thus, while it was possible for Hough to recognise 'a change *almost comparable* with the invention of printing' (my emphasis) and to see that 'youth is in rather a mess' – that 'the insulated teen-age sub-culture' had its manifest dangers – it was unthinkable at the time to go on from there to question the English department's responsibility for the cultural splitting.

This was not an individual matter, needless to say: Hough had at least the decency to step out of line, almost to transform the title – from a crisis in the humanities, to a cultural crisis in which youth stood to pay the cost, both ways. But a wrecking elitism was hard on his shoulder. The minority who knew best had no intention of making room for outsiders. 'More means worse': following that slogan of the time, let the majority succumb, undiscriminating, to the revolutionary media, and then let the few survivors submit, willy-nilly, to the old canonical texts. (While we middle-aged, middle-class lecturers looked on?)

Even in 1964, there was one place where that answer couldn't stand up: the colleges of education. The international movement of curriculum renovation inevitably brought radical change in teacher education. To build a graduate profession, courses were lengthened, and – later in the 1960s – extended to include an 'honours' B.Ed. option. The recruitment of English lecturers from the schools brought in the new curriculum: writing from experience, dramatic presentation, interviewing and 'documentary', critical discussion of the press, film and television, and longer personal 'essays' and cultural investigations... In higher education, it was some of the colleges that first faced the question: what was to be done about a split culture?

The initial challenges for teaching and learning

It is one thing to have a sense of crisis within a culture; it's much harder – at the time – to define it, and in such a way as to produce a programme of action. It would be easy, in retrospect, to underestimate the difficulties in the 1960s when groups set out to transform the disciplinary practices of their education – and to do so within an international power block that had quite different irons in the fire.

Think, for a start, of the range of questions troubling that network of teachers for whom Hoggart, Williams and Hall were three of the important nodes. Here are some that raised the most searching difficulties:

(a) Who is to be taught, and what, for what social ends? What institutional changes are vital in education, and what immediate changes in courses credible or feasible?
(b) What about our formative training in teaching literature: what fallacies did it entail, what questions did it hide from us? How can we equip ourselves to move into the new media, too?
(c) What place must we give the making of culture, within structures hitherto defined in exclusively critical terms?

Each of these would take a generation's work or more to answer, inevitably. But it was essential to have a sense of direction. How was that done: let me be more specific.

'We speak of a cultural revolution', wrote Williams in 1961, 'the aspiration to extend the active process of learning, with the skills of literacy and other advanced communication, to all people rather than to limited groups' (p.11). 'The active process of learning'? In secondary and higher education we had only just started to take 'learning' and 'learners' seriously, as possible partners. As for 'other communication': at that moment, the UK had not even a research and teaching centre for film education, let alone education in radio and television.

For TV, in any case, technical problems were decisive: teachers would have to wait two decades, till videotape recorders became readily available. Film was partly a surrogate, in the meantime. Thus, early in the 1960s, the Society for Education in Film and Television, a network from schools and colleges, began to pioneer courses and shortly after the British Film Institute's education officers were actually producing packs of material. But the problem remained: how to gain recognition for such work within universities that had still no thoughts of joining in – or saw these things as right outside their 'discipline'?

Of course, Williams had forecast it was going to be 'a long revolution'. 'If we take the criterion that people should govern themselves... it is evident that the democratic revolution (like the industrial) is still at a very early stage' (p.10). But what would more democratic practices in the classroom, and in education generally, imply? New kinds of discussion, manifestly, with a focus on the class's ability to contribute to developing ideas? – new forms of group work? – a committee structure, maybe, in which joint projects were discussed and negotiated?

All these things had to be invented, against the grain of the dominant exams. It was clear enough at the time that, for the teachers themselves, 'we [had] not nearly enough institutions which practically teach democracy' (p.339) and plenty that taught something very different. How hard it is to transform your role as teacher! In the London Association for the Teaching of English network we learnt this (to our dismay), when portable recorders became available in the mid-1960s and a group with Nancy Martin began to tape 'poetry lessons'. Throughout each taped 'discussion' we teachers had insisted on asking the questions and holding the initiative.

We recognised the crassness of our formation more fully, too, when BBC education officers joined in and taped small groups of students discussing on their own. We had never realised their potential (see *Language, the Learner, and the School* – Barnes et al. 1969). Yet the resistance to such findings went very deep in the society. The first university project to analyse 'class discussion' managed to pass over this evidence: what they produced instead was a classic analysis of the teacher-dominated dialogue we wanted to escape from. (And it has to be added, university classes were excluded – in Sinclair and Coulthard 1975.)

It was necessary, in fact, to question precisely those practices that had given most of us, as graduates, our sense of having 'mastered' a subject. Thus, 'We are not *primarily* concerned with whether "highbrow" books will be read in a society dominated by mass communications', wrote Hoggart, in his dogged way; 'we have to ask what will be *the quality of the life expressed through all the arts* and at all levels within such a society' (1961: 151, my emphases).

After the first shock, it made good sense. What practices in the arts could involve our young students? What, for instance, could they make of writing poetry, or prose, or scripts? The answers delighted us, just as their first efforts at film did. But we ourselves had no inevitable competencies here, as we felt we had in reading. And whereas in schools, active teachers could seize opportunities to experiment, in higher education the pressures on them up to 1969 were much more constraining. After all, compared with all the subtleties of 'close reading', what had 'creative writing' to offer? (The last work on writing theory, surely, had come from the Scottish Enlightenment, hadn't it?)

From this new perspective, 'English' was an odd-one-out in the Arts; it suffered from a long-established asymmetry. 'As far as institutions of [post-16] education are concerned, painting and music are things you do, but literature is something other people have done', as James Britton, a founding member of NATE, put it in 1963. Thus, full-time education in literature for the sixth form and beyond, 'will have nothing to do with writing it, nor even performing it... I cannot accept that view of my subject this evening', he continued. 'If I were to submit to the limitations imposed on themselves by the universities, I should be doing grave injustice to the schools' (p.34).

This view was widely accepted in the new National Association. At 16 or 17 a gap was opening between what many in the schools knew and wanted and what was thereafter authoritatively excluded – with predictable effects on the next generation of schoolteachers.

During the 1960s, there were growing numbers who agreed that for teaching, 'the deepest danger, now, is the external division (pushed by the media, ratified by education), between those arts which are thought of as serious, academic, and old and those which are experienced as lively, personal, and new. To underwrite this division harms the traditional work and misses the chance of creating real standards in the new' (Williams 1962: 105). For decades, every exam syllabus for English at 16, 18 and 21 had insisted on this division. They had to be changed. And the first break was actually made, in 1965 – in alternative English exams at 16-plus. Which way would the struggle go beyond that age, we wondered?

CHAPTER 14
Theoretical guidance for new approaches

Setting directions for research

In 1960–65, the situation was fairly crude, simple, and visible to any detached observer. The media of the 20th century – film, radio and television – were manifestly becoming the dominant cultural force in the world. The British (and European) universities had not begun to research or teach in these fields, though their students were increasingly affected. Through TV especially, the recent UK decision to allow advertising of mass products on a national channel was exerting profound new influences on cultural production. Internationally, the USA or USSR (according to your power block) was consciously gearing up to win a new kind of struggle, for world hegemony in ideological penetration and control.

From a democratic standpoint, there had to be widespread countervailing action – at many levels. In 1960, the UK Colleges and Departments of Education recommended that every teacher should have courses in film and television. (In 1960, too, the Ecole Pratique des Hautes Etudes in Paris set up a Centre for Studies in Mass Communications – joined by Roland Barthes.) In 1962, 'Two kinds of body are urgently required', wrote Raymond Williams: 'a Communications Centre with a staff able to supply catalogues of existing material... and an Institute of Communications Research, at university level, undertaking long-range research and analysis' (p.109). Still little happened.

In 1963, Richard Hoggart – who had just helped to produce the Pilkington Report on Broadcasting (1962) – seemed to have made the break: he was appointed to Birmingham University, to set up a Centre for Contemporary Cultural Studies (CCCS). For his inaugural lecture, he spoke on 'Schools of English in Contemporary Society'. In a deliberately inoffensive, muted way he proposed a study of 'the interrelations between the sophisticated and the popular arts, interrelations which are both functional and imaginative'. 'Some secondary schools attempt it; they do not get much help from university English departments' (1963: 253). Thus, 'the mass or popular arts... in which there is room for developed critical practice', he suggested, 'include: film criticism; television and radio criticism; television drama... popular fiction of all kinds... the press and journals of all kinds; strip cartoons; the language of advertising and public relations; popular songs and popular music in all their forms' (pp.257–8). It was a very wide remit to acknowledge.

Besides, such studies should also include the social context of production. But on UK sociology of literature at the time, he commented: 'how little we know... about interrelations between writers and organs of public opinion, between writers, politics, power, cash and class... and how few foreign comparisons we have made' (p.257).

This lecture was immediately published in *The Use of English* (edited by Denys Thompson) – one of the two journals read by almost all NATE members at the time. And in Spring 1965 Stuart Hall outlined to NATE the first proposed programme of studies. Nearer home, however, one of the first responses was 'a blistering attack' from colleagues in sociology, warning that if the Centre took on the study of contemporary society (not just its texts), without proper scientific controls, it would provoke reprisals (Hall 1980).

As for the production of cultural studies, by 1965 Penguin Books had funded Hall as Research Fellow and the university had allocated a prefabricated hut, as I remember. (Meanwhile, in Perugia, an Italian Centre for Mass Communication Studies was set up, with Umberto Eco submitting a joint paper in 1965 on the semiotics of the TV message.)

At this point, then, it looked as though the (still-expanding) universities would leave the critical problems in British culture to a minor centre, which might sink or swim. The initial hope of enlisting English departments in some kind of break was crumbling. UK sociology – still using positivist arguments in its bid for belated recognition – was shown to be touchy. In fact, 'inter-disciplinary studies', and the teamwork which was manifestly needed, had few supporting institutional structures yet (though within five years, the CNAA would begin to develop them seriously). And there were still key issues to be faced: Culture or Communications – where was the research focus to be?

An international seminar on English

Yet, ironically, just at this point, research funding for English in schools was about to mushroom – stirred, there's no doubt, by US Office of Education grants empowering twenty-five university centres to define a

New English (and answer the Soviet challenge). So in 1966, while the new Centre for Cultural Studies was struggling for grants and staff, the Carnegie Foundation funded a month-long international seminar on the Teaching of English. There were fifty participants, including twenty from schools, colleges and universities in the UK. It was their first effective chance to take stock together.

(Incidentally, by a further irony, Hoggart and Hall were too preoccupied to attend, Stuart Hall having to turn down a commission to write the report for the profession. This came out in 1967 as *Growth through English: a report based on the Dartmouth Seminar*, Dixon.)

The alliances struck up there, and the new syntheses proposed, were to have international effects for nearly two decades. Equally important, they strongly affected some of the key Schools Council research groups that started work in the UK immediately afterwards.

Thus, for a start, Denys Harding and James Britton combined to give a new perspective on 'literature':

> it is impossible to separate response to literature sharply from response to other stories, films, or television plays, or from (students') own personal writing or spoken narrative. *In all of these the student contemplates represented events in the role of a spectator*, not for the sake of active intervention. But since his response includes some degree of accepting or rejecting the values and emotional attitudes which the narration implicitly offers, it will influence, perhaps greatly influence, his future appraisals of behavior and feeling.
>
> (in Squire 1968: 11, my emphasis)

Learning to contemplate represented events, on this view, was a fundamental goal for English teaching. But placing, and responding to, tacit values within the narrative was an essential part of it. Maturing readers learned to establish a relation not only with the events, but with the author, as Harding emphasised at NATE conference the following year. Thus came 'the stage of criticizing a novel for its improbabilities, inconsistencies, exaggerations, sentimentalities and brutalities'. For students, that step was decisive, for it indicated an incipient awareness that:

> fiction is a social convention, an institutionalised technique of discussion, by means of which an author invites us to join him in discussing a possibility of experience that he regards as interesting and to share with him attitudes towards it, evaluations of it, that he claims to be appropriate.
>
> *(English in Education:* 1967: 13)

For its time, this was a remarkable statement. Fiction was suddenly recognised to be one side of a dialogue. The interests and evaluations it offered, tacitly or explicitly, 'invited' a response. What did readers make of this 'possible' world – from the standpoint of their own existing versions? What did our students want to say – or write back – in reply, and what varied forms might that 'discussion' take? We had to look for a range of new generic strategies.

Besides, this way of putting it gave rights to the student reader, and suggested a problematic: what kinds of 'experience', 'interesting' to whom, with whose notion of 'appropriate evaluations'? In this institution, Harding was implying, both sides had a necessary role.

But discursively, more than 'discussion' was involved. In tracing the continuities beween gossip and fiction, Barbara Hardy had argued in the seminar that 'narrative, like lyric or dance, is not to be regarded as an aesthetic invention used by artists to control, manipulate and order experience, but as *a primary act of mind transferred to art from life'* (1968: 5). As she later added:

> I take for granted the ways in which storytelling engages our interest, curiosity, fear, tensions, expectation, and sense of order. What concerns me here are the qualities which fictional narrative shares with the inner and outer storytelling that plays a major role in our sleeping and waking lives. For we dream in narrative, daydream in narrative, remember, anticipate, hope, despair, believe, doubt, plan, revise, criticise, construct, gossip, learn, hate, and love by narrative. *In order really to live, we make up stories about ourselves and others, about the personal as well as the social past and future.*
>
> (1968: 5, original emphasis)

For many teachers of English this was a crucial synthesis. Why encourage students to write, knowing they couldn't match some of the texts already on offer? Because, from this perspective, they – like us, the teachers – were inevitably engaged in story-telling, *for better or worse*, throughout their lives. It was a form in which everyone made sense of *personal and social* experiences. So why not make space for some of those everyday stories (and dreams) to be elaborated, reflectively, in class? In fact, how could it be questioned that learning to represent and contemplate life as you meet it (or want it) had a place in education? Couldn't a vital aim be to foster an interaction between such activities and the institutionalised representations of fiction? Here, John Berger and Jean Mohr's book, *A Fortunate Man* (1967), gave us a perfect exemplar in a doctor whose (partial and incomplete) project started from reading Conrad.

In effect, this joint formulation on narratives set up a major problematic for cultural studies. What opportunities were socially available for those stories to emerge and be elaborated in oral traditions? And what were their potential qualities? Here teachers in NATE began to follow up the pioneering work of Charles Parker (BBC Radio) and Paul

Thompson (Oral History Group). The publication of Studs Terkel's radio interviews (in *Division Street, America*, 1967) and of Ronald Blythe's *Akenfield* (1969) gave us further inspiration.

In what respects, we began to ask, were those everyday stories for self inevitably being penetrated by the terms and figures of stories from powerful institutional centres – and with what effects? How could democrats set up with their students, and perhaps a wider community, ways to develop, resist and transform these forces? This was a focus – often less conscious – of the contemporary movement for personal or 'creative' writing. But an adequate cultural analysis did not emerge at the time.

In any case, the seminar questions had not stopped short at narrative. Jim Moffett, then working at Harvard, proposed a new effort to organise the 'universe of discourse' in terms of 'abstraction levels' within our representations. First, and primary, drama: the physical presentation, the acting-it-out. Then, narrating, especially by retrospective narrators, with their capacity to construct related 'events' from what might well have been initially experienced as a flux. Then, generalising, thinking about types and in abstract categories, rather than particularising. And finally, speculating and theorising, turning back on the discourse to analyse and vary its categories and assumptions (1968).

A sketch of a discursive range: but what questions it already raised for teachers of English – whether in school, or in higher education. Thus, in our university formation, we recognised the inadequate treatment of generalisation; the virtual absence of any invitation to speculate or theorise; the recurrent neglect or marginalising of dramatic enactment. Equally, when the London Writing Research group went on to analyse some of the effects of secondary schooling on writing 11–18, using a developed version of Moffett's model, they found narrative itself was progressively excluded. This was not a product of rational choices within each subject domain (including English); rather, it was a crude by-product of that central institution in the grammar school and university curriculum, the essay-paper examination.

Constructing a theory of (student) writing

In the 1960s, the universities, like the schools, had no general theory of writing. (Even now, I wonder what account many lecturers could give of the discursive demands of some typical exam questions.) Yet it was by their writing that British students were judged and selected, in English especially. During the period 1966–70, then, this problem was taken up by the London Writing Research group. At the same time, as it happened, the Birmingham CCCS got funding from the Rowntree

Foundation for a historical study of the popular press. Both research groups developed models of written communication appropriate to their domain of interest: it is worth considering the two together.

The London research group (LWR) made short work of the well-worn textbook categories that still survive today in North America: Narrative, Description, Exposition and Argument. Hidden behind 'narrative', for instance, were critical differences of function, between a fictional story and a factual report, or a scientific account and an advertiser's anecdote. What's more, at one pole narratives could in effect generalise, by dealing with typical events (Britton, Burgess *et al.* 1975). To get beyond this kind of diffuse concept, a multi-dimensional model was essential.

But what dimensions? Here the group's contact with pioneering schools and colleges raised the central questions:

- We all wanted students to be more independent and active: how could a theory place the pedagogic relationships we hoped for between students, as they wrote, and their teachers?
- We wanted to make writing a flexible resource for thinking and learning: how could a theory expose the way schools – across the curriculum – were constraining or developing such resources?
- We wanted to escape from restricted traditions in writing: what light could a theory throw on the way those restrictions had unconsciously been set up – and could now be broken down?

To answer such questions, the LWR first drew explicitly on George Herbert Mead and Lev Vygotsky – finally translated in 1962, as part of the Thaw. From the start, the group made a clean break with communication theories that treated listener/readers simply as an objective addressee: instead, they proposed an analysis of 'sense of audience', the way (to judge by the text) listener/readers were progressively constructed in inner speech, and relationships with them set up.

Students internalised their sense of audience from the real context, of course. And in current school traditions (as in university essays), the context for writing was severely simplified: 'it is almost always the teacher who initiates the writing and who does so by defining a writing task... [and nominating] himself as audience' (p.64). Teachers' comments in response to the tasks, I should add, then signalled their selected role: when their side of the dialogue consisted in a mark and a perfunctory evaluation (Not thought out – Full stops and caps not clearly written – Errors of fact – You write a letter as briefly as possible – Needs more careful thought – Not developed – Padding... to quote from an actual set (DES 1979)) the role was roughly that of Authoritative Fault-finder. In response, most students were taking on the role of a right-answer machine, as American friends put it.

In the 1960s, however, some secondary teachers were learning to change their roles – in lessons as varied as Science, Maths and English. It seemed to the researchers and their readers' panel that one teacher was being construed as an examiner/judge, another as an instructor/guide, a third, as a trusted adult. These tacit roles were affecting the social construction of the writing task – and suggested a reciprocal role for the student, we might add. In students' writing of the time, they had some crucial effects on what it was possible to think and say.

The prevailing relation, the research group found, was still student to teacher-as-examiner. Put on the defensive, students hung on to discourse as 'teachers have structured it and textbooks reinforce it' (p.198). They avoided generalising for themselves, for instance; instead, they reproduced ready-made generalisations. A vital ingredient in their thinking was missing.

To restore active thinking, teacher and students had to set up the tasks and *'each write for the other'* in new roles. Work in progress – thinking on the wing – might be just as well worth responding to as a finished product. Student writers had to learn that teachers (of all people) might be deeply interested in their *provisional thinking* – their mental goings-on, as Richards would have said. They had to write as equals for their peers, as guides and advisers for less experienced readers, and as imaginative and intellectual explorers with teachers as mature (but not infallible) guides. They must 'abandon [their] inferior status' (1975: 65). And this would depend on social relations built up throughout classroom discourse – especially in talk. For it would be the social interaction of the classroom that students internalised when they came to write.

Thus, if we took Harding seriously, students must learn to feel themselves in dialogue with the writer, the narrator and the personae – but this would never happen, the LWR indicated, unless we teachers learned to feel ourselves in dialogue with our students. How we responded to their oral and written ideas became the key question.

There wasn't always an easy answer, either. In the inner city some students came to us already on the defensive. The LWR group put it this way:

> The pupil operates in *a context of culture* which will exercise an influence not only on the values he expresses but also on the ways he expresses them. It will also lead him to construe his audience (let us say, teachers) partly or wholly in the way his culture construes them. In some degree the pupil and teacher will share a common culture, but frequently there will be dramatic divergences – such as inner urban working-class pupil with parents from overseas, and university trained, suburban middle-class teacher.
>
> (p.63, my emphasis)

Theoretical guidance for new approaches 165

Without the assurance of a common culture, there would be further obstacles for students. When a culturally distant teacher-examiner dominated the writing (setting, specifying, marking), 'it may be shaped solely by the demands of [this perceived] audience and not by complementary pressure to formulate ideas in ways which satisfy the writer' (p.64) or which answer to the writer's own cultural experience. This effect was very general, I should add: it was crippling literary studies in the 18+ exams, and still may, well beyond the exam questions themselves (see Dixon and Brown 1984/5).

On this model, then, all writing internalised a social relationship with the imagined other. In effect, this confirmed and developed what Ogden and Richards had proposed in the 1920s. But the LWR went further in their model: most writers also made tacit choices of a focal function and 'abstraction level'. The latter was of particular interest to literary and cultural studies, I believe. Jim Moffett had already roughed out some key contrasts between enacting an experience, narrating it in retrospect, and generalising from a set of similar experiences. What the LWR did was to elaborate on this set of contrasts, using the results to analyse current writing across the curriculum between the ages of 11 and 18.

This threw into relief some severe tacit constraints on students' choices. First, narrative was progressively marginalised. Second, theoretical thinking – the discussion of alternative category systems – was rarely if ever reached, even in the most selective sixth forms. Third, I would add, and predictably, scripts for dramatic dialogue – once the mainstay of Greek and medieval thinking – were absent. By the sixth form, British students were annually producing in the order of 250,000 words in their writing, I would estimate; most of the time, this took the form of 'low level generalisation'. But why? No theoretical justification was available. Is it now, I wonder. And what tacit choices on this dimension are being made today, in English or Cultural Studies departments – whatever their theoretical tendency?

There were more dimensions to the LWR model, but these already indicate its direction and lasting importance. At the same time, there were characteristic limitations. The group acknowledged that, in placing a student's text on various dimensions, they and their panel must be tacitly drawing on evidence in the textual signs. But, in spite of their close relations with Michael Halliday (also directing a project for Schools Council), they did not take that further.

Equally, their underlying assumptions were explicitly 'developmental' – strongly influenced by Piaget and Bruner. Manifestly, much that was going on in schools and universities ran counter to those assumptions: it amounted to an ill-considered 'formation' of the writer, largely governed by long-term, tacit exam traditions. But the developmental assumptions,

I suspect, limited the group when it came to experimenting with alternative, more liberating, kinds of formation.

In one experiment, however, they did give a taste of future possibilities. Sixth-formers were invited to comment on the writing they were doing, with interesting results:

> ...I enjoy English more as a subject, but I find writing for history somewhat easier. English essays demand an organisation of ideas which is also necessary in history, but the difference is that ideas in English often have to do with verbalising feelings, while history essays deal with what you think. English demands a rigorous examination of your own reaction to a novel or poem, while in history the difficulty is not so much the formulation of ideas as the marshalling of facts, and the clarification of notions which you had all along. It is because English has more to do with the non-cerebral part of your mind that it is more difficult to write about and more satisfying at the same time...
>
> ...though an individual part of an English essay may be satisfying, the longer length of time spent on it means one is more aware of its failings and shortcomings, and yet powerless to correct them (due to tiredness, or boredom, or something else). A history essay can conform more closely to a perfect and almost attainable plan set by teacher.
>
> (Dixon 1979)

Here is a student, I can imagine, who might well make sense of the sorts of models for discourse discussed in this book – and learn to question habitual practices by doing so?

Social transactions between journalists and readers

In schools and universities, the problem was to release writers from traditional forms of subordination. With the popular press of the 1960s, the problem was normally inverted: it lay in the corporate writer's efforts to dominate the reader's ideas, feelings, attitudes and dispositions, penetrating and transforming their narrative culture – their own stories of personal and social events. Fortunately, in the historical study of the *Express* and the *Mirror* 1935–65, the CCCS group rediscovered an alternative tradition, built up during a period of national crisis. Thus:

> First, an astonishing proportion of the [*Mirror*] in 1945 was given to readers' letters, and stories derived from readers' own experiences. Sixty-five per cent of the election coverage on July 4 was contributed by readers, and from June 13 to July 5 readers contributed on average nearly thirty per cent of the paper's electoral material...
>
> The second striking element in the relationship was the directness of the paper's address to its readers, felt as much in its sympathy with

distressed readers as in its brusque admonitions to others... in a difficult time. The latent but powerful function of the mode of address was that it had about it the feeling of democracy, of people talking straight to each other in 'real' language about their lives and hopes, and by the same token an anti-authoritarian feeling: we, the people, can get things moving, and done – anyone who directs us can only do so with our consent.

(Smith 1975: 63)

To test that relationship, to establish that such letters were more than a manufactured pretence, and to examine the straight talking in detail, the research group had to set aside the demand – which they faced explicitly at the time – for standard 'content analysis', and develop alternative, 'literary-analytic' methods. The sense of a personal 'voice' among the named journalists, their roles as experts, their willingness to consult readers' experiences, their ironic parodies of upper-class speech and contrasting use of working-class idioms, the friendly but rather bossy tone of the women writers... these and similar readings had to be justified within specific extracts.

Then, standing back from the analyses of both papers, a clear direction for cultural research emerged:

> Such matters as style and appearance are not simply referable to the production and presentational choices of the editorial team and its managers. Though speaking to readers from a position outside their 'world', and about topics on which it is well informed and they are relatively ignorant, the newspaper is, nevertheless, the product of a *social transaction* between producers and readers...
>
> Newspapers must continually situate themselves within the assumed knowledge and interests of their readership, consciously and unconsciously adopt modes and strategies of address: they must 'take the attitude of their significant others', their 'imaginary interlocutors'... Language, style and format are therefore the products of *a process of reciprocal symbolic interaction between the newspaper and its audiences.*
>
> (Hall, in Smith 1975: 22, my emphasis at the end)

What knowledge and attitudes journalists assumed in the reader, what interests they projected, what strategies of address they adopted – these became evidence for an internalised interaction, a sense of self in relation to a potential audience. 'Our working hypothesis was that every significant stylistic, visual, linguistic, presentational, rhetorical feature was a sort of silent witness, a "meaningful disguised communication", embodying and expressing that relationship' (p.23) with a constructed reader. That – and not just content – was a primary focus for investigation. In particular, was the relation with the reader democratic, or dominating?

This new theoretical position had profound implications, well beyond the teaching of writing. Within English Studies, it meant thinking again not just about the contemporary press, but also about those other journalists, and more than journalists – Simone de Beauvoir and George Orwell, Marian Evans and Charles Dickens, Will Hazlitt and Mme de Staël, William Cobbett and Mary Wollstonecraft... Not simply as producers of texts now, but in social interaction with imaginary others. And which others? How deeply, or schematically, internalised? With whose interests in view? Implying what relations of power or co-operation?

Whatever the reaction in the academy, these new questions for Criticism were certainly not lost on the 'underground' and 'alternative' newspapers that sprouted up from the late 1960s on.

Reading for social and historical meaning

These imaginary (and occasionally real) transactions, these speech acts with their desired, projected responses, were framed within institutional structures. And here the Birmingham group made a distinctive contribution.

A paper like the *Mirror*, they began, used 'a structure of meanings in a linguistic and visual form' to reduce 'the formlessness of events to that socially-shaped, historically contingent product we call "news"' (Hall 1975: 18). Thus, for the press, a 'grid of existing "common-sense" categories' both pigeon-holed the data and generated distinctive idioms – for treating 'the front-page news story', 'gossip', 'sport', 'the leader column' and so on. (And I suppose, in retrospect, that something rather similar happened to thinking, in school and university?)

These categories of the press became 'so routine that they seem the natural way for making up newspapers'. In fact, new categories of the time, like the *Observer's* Business Section or the *Guardian's* Women's Page, suggested – or assumed – major shifts in the paper's appeal and readership and, thus, 'indirectly, in its cultural assumptions' about 'the pattern of readers' interests'. In this sense, the categories 'represented on-going schemes of interpretation... intended to awaken in the reader contexts of awareness, appropriate referential associations' (p.19).

Such categories, then, were partly organising readers' versions of life, partly responding to their existing, everyday ways of organising it. Their divisions placed and consolidated the appropriate kinds of story, language and attitudes for every area of social experience they marked out. Thus, your sport was your 'time out from politics *and* women, masculine and competitive' (p.20).

Turning in the same year, 1970, to BBC Radio's *World at One*, Stuart Hall gave this whole model a new cutting edge. The BBC had a less socially stratified audience than the press. How did radio journalists and

Theoretical guidance for new approaches 169

editors select – on their behalf – who to interview as witnesses, how to address them, and how to place their news? The professionals seemed to have 'some unstated and unstatable criteria of *the significant*' (1973: 86). These were part of unwritten codes developed in the institution.

News selection was framed by categories like those of the press. It made assumptions about the listeners' knowledge, attitudes and interests. And, equally important, it made *'inferred assumptions about society'* (p.86, my emphasis).

Thus, in the *World at One* bulletins, news items were consistently mapped into areas of consensus, toleration, or conflict. Consensus implied 'accredited witnesses' in mutual agreement about the terms of the discussion; toleration, more 'maverick' but still 'sympathetic' witnesses, negotiating between competing definitions; and conflict, an 'un-accredited cast of witnesses' – protesters, activists, militants, hippies and so on – with alternative definitions in play. But in deciding who should count as 'consensual' witnesses, the British media had a steady, unwitting bias for the status quo:

> The operation of unwitting bias is difficult either to locate or prove. Its manifestations are always indirect. It comes through in terms of who is or who is not accorded the status of accredited witness: in tones of voice: in the set-up of studio confrontations: in the assumptions that underlie questions asked or not asked: in terms of the analytical concepts which serve informally to link events and causes: in what passes for explanation.
> (p.88)

Within those questions, more specific categories like Violence had a key role. Suppose you labelled as 'violent' every incident 'from skinhead attacks on Pakistanis, to Ulster, to protests against the South African [rugby] tour'. This established a certain way of 'seeing and understanding' a complex set of public events. (As Richards would have agreed – J.D.) In fact, 'once the category of "law and order" had come into existence as a legitimate news category, whole orders of meaning and association can be made to cluster together' (p.87). Terms reserved for crime could be transferred to new events – like political demonstrations.

As for the 'explanation' of a reported story, by 1970 some new lessons were being learnt:

> As events like political confrontation and civil disturbance escalate, so the [media] coverage is doubled, quadrupled. As coverage expands, so we become more alive to the actual 'violent' events and overwhelmed by the vivid sound and image. But as this coverage takes the characteristic form of *actuality without context*, it directly feeds our general sense of a meaningless explosion of meaningless and violent acts – 'out there' somewhere...

> 'Out there', let us note, is a rapidly expanding area, covering most of the rest of the globe – Indo-China, Latin America, the Middle East, the Caribbean, Berkeley, Chicago, Tokyo – as well as some growing enclaves closer home. Events of this order play straight into an *ideological gap* in the media.
>
> (p.92, original emphasis)

The effective question in Britain – where radio and television could be challenged about their statutory duties – was 'Do/can the media help us to understand these real events in the real world?', 'Do the media clarify them or mystify us about them?' Without social and historical context, only mystification was possible. Hall took a recent example, the Black Power rioting in Trinidad:

> The background to the foreground-problem of riots in Trinidad is the persisting poverty of the mass of people, intensified by the basic conflict of interests between the coloured middle class inheritors of the 'end to colonial rule' (one of the most conspicuous-consumption classes anywhere in the Third World) and the mass of peasants, workers and urban unemployed, who also happen to be black. Without this knowledge, the large-scale migration from the Caribbean to Britain, which has occupied so much 'foreground' space in recent months is, literally, unintelligible. It is another of those meaningless events...
>
> The gap between the urban and rural masses and a native bourgeoisie, grown flush in the hectic, post-colonial years of neo-imperialism, is *the* political fact about vast tracts of the Caribbean and Latin America.
>
> (p.93)

What was foregrounded instead? – 'small groups of vandals', 'disaffection in the army', 'resignations from the government', 'detachments of marines'... 'The Prime Minister'... Breakdown and restoration of Law and Order. And what was the verdict? 'A tragedy', said Alva Clark; inexplicable, said Sir Leary Constantine.

This developing analysis, I can see, was putting new challenges to the Media, and to Education. Most people, after all, relied on such everyday stories for their sense of a 'world' beyond face-to-face contacts. They inevitably had to place *themselves* – immigrant and native Brits – within it, imaginatively and historically. Yet without historical categories like class, colonisation, slavery, imperialism, and the socio-economic systems that succeeded it, what sense would the News make? Wasn't that a serious subject for discussion and study?

Equally, we might have asked in the schools, what help were our students getting from the other stories – the imaginary worlds – they were meeting in English courses? Was a focus on 'character', or 'themes', as far as they went? Or were signs of wider social forces being brought into the foreground too? Were they facing the social world of *Robinson Crusoe* with the same kind of ideological gap as the *World at*

One? (And, if so, what would happen when protest erupted among the likes of them? As it did.)

What's more, the testimony of 'witnesses' in the Media, like the writing of students in Education, could no longer simply be analysed as 'texts' for 'reading'. A new set of factors had to be considered first: the social context of production. Both in Education and in the Media, institutional structures – often unseen by those who operated them – were forming what was said, and framing its reception too.

Thus, for all its explanatory power, the 'communicative' model of the 1920s would have to be transformed. The 'context of situation' had now to be unpacked analytically. And the results would set up new enquiries, among other things into the social production of literature and the institutional forces that had shaped *it*.

CHAPTER 15

A second phase: rebellions, challenges and liberation

Student rebellions

As this historical retrospect reaches 1968, and the decade that followed, a new phase begins.

I'll start, for reasons that must now be obvious, with the movement among students. Probably the triggering event for the UK was the sit-in at the LSE in 1967. It followed a pattern that shortly after became predictable. First, a demonstration by an active political minority, against the Vietnam War or against current racism, say; then, a sit-in by a much wider group, in protest against the college or university's disciplinary action; then, through teach-ins, workshops, or alternative 'courses', a wider questioning of rights, justice and the organisation of intellectual life, from utopian liberal, anarchist and socialist positions; then, attempts to change power structures within the institution or beyond it (Atkinson 1969).

Outbreaks were sporadic, but within three or four years, many students felt they had seen power laid bare – not just within higher education, but in the family, in school, in the media, and in traditional political machines (Labour and the Communist Party especially). The conflicts within 'liberal democracy', the compromises enforced by an elite formed in 'public school' and Oxbridge, though widely taken for granted – or passively suffered – became intolerable to these utopians and revolutionaries. Their sympathies were with under-classes everywhere, and their targets established power and its systems of hierarchical control (which excluded 'participation').

Many teachers in higher education were hit in the raw. The power relations of teaching and learning had been invisible parts of their role. They had no responsibility for inventing them, certainly, and, in the universities at least, no history of questioning them either. If anything, the lecturers' own sense of power within larger, more bureaucratic, institutions was becoming insecure: it was not a good time to face challenges from students – especially when those challenges explicitly analysed a 'hidden curriculum' in which teachers counted as undercover agents.

Thus, within the 'Humanities' of all places, why should teaching so often contradict its supposed values? As Joe Spriggs put it in the revolutionary manifesto, *Counter Course* (1972):

> Let us say loosely that one of the functions of literature is an invitation to share and widen experience by creating representations of man's [sic] social and material relationships...
>
> In Real Life across the centuries men have done all sorts of things in, around and in response to literature: re-enactment, retelling, re-expressing in different forms; 'using' it as illustration in arguments, discussions or thought concerning why people behave in such and such a way and so on. The Eng. Lit. essay does none of these...
>
> [Thus, by a final reduction,] a recent telly programme showed two York Eng. Lit. academics sitting down after a seminar solemnly discussing whether Jim Smith's 'intervention' in the previous discussion on Wilde was worth 64 or 65 per cent...
>
> How come ideas and original thought... have intrinsic gradeable value? Where is this 'value' situated? In a consensus of liberal intelligence? Is Leavis alpha beta or straight alpha? How would a liberal consensus grade a polemic against the liberal consensus? Who is doing the assessing for whom? And on what qualifications?
>
> (p.224)

Many quite unremarkable practices of this kind now came in for a beating. Was it Literary Criticism – was it History – they stood to produce? Hardly: instead they confined the subject within a specially designed institutional genre, the student essay. That was a form of knowledge in which students' thinking, no matter what its potential, was effectively trapped. But after the final exams, three years on, suddenly there came a change of role and status. Promoted to teacher in school or higher education, the graduate – with the shake of a fairy wand – escaped ugly subordination, emerging with a charmed authority. And the ability to assess. Did it make sense?

It didn't, and still does not. But how to establish alternatives? From their uneasy seat, it looked a risky job to most lecturers.

Reshaping the social sciences

This was only a start of their difficulties, though. Overlaying this struggle was a second, within the academic disciplines themselves, especially the humanities and social sciences. Psychology, Sociology,

History, Anthropology... and finally, Linguistics, were falling under heavy criticism of the limiting assumptions in their theories of knowledge. Positivism and behaviourism were now on the defensive, and unthinking English empiricism was rudely pushed aside. For a start, knowledge, whatever its genealogies, was seen to be marked by its origins in a given generation within a given society. Without being conscious of it, university subjects were part of history and demonstrably prone to adopt the social assumptions and practices of a given age and social milieu (Bourdieu, trans. 1967).

There had to be better frames, therefore, for analysing the social production of knowledge and the ways it was authorised – for better and worse – by agencies like the universities.

Understandably, a key book of the period was *The Social Construction of Reality* (1967), product of a symptomatic partnership between teachers at the New School for Social Research, New York (Peter Berger) and the University of Frankfurt (Thomas Luckmann). It had the good fortune to be timely in the UK. By 1971 it was not only a set book for the new Open University; it suggested the terms for a primary theme – *Teaching and Learning as the Construction of Reality* (School and Society, OU 1971).

This book and others with it also reinforced a second theme, with direct implications for English and Cultural Studies. The neglect – the relegation – of everyday knowledge had to end, claimed Berger and Luckmann: instead, 'the sociology of knowledge must *first of all* concern itself with what people "know" as "reality" in their everyday, non- or pre-theoretical lives... [the] "knowledge" that constitutes the fabric of meanings without which no society could exist' (1967: 27, my emphasis). Just so: and weren't English and Cultural Studies already engaged with social representations of such actors? – their plans, goals, motives, chances, hopes, fears and actions in a social world. And wouldn't a central form for such investigations inevitably be narrative of some kind?

Links had to be made between everyday constructions and explanatory, 'theoretical' categories. If methods were to be found for such an enterprise, then, surely new relations would be discovered with Literary and Cultural Studies?

There was a ferment of positive ideas for new investigations of 'subjective meanings', and the 'conversations' through which groups in a society 'objectified' their 'social selves', building up forms of 'biographical integration' of significant moments in their experience. At the same time, there was a focus on 'habitualised actions' (stock responses?!), institutional structures and, given the division of labour, 'typified' roles within them – all within a historical setting.

Inevitably perhaps, this transforming interest in personal meaning and action in an everyday social world – this abrupt shift towards the concrete, so far as sociology was concerned – also set up a heavy investment in reconstructing past social and historical theory, with the aim of achieving a new synthesis. Berger and Luckmann, to give one instance, had defined their project through critical reading in the sociology of knowledge (Scheler, Mannheim), classical theories of society (Durkheim, Weber), the social psychology of Mead, Schutz's philosophy of everyday life, and Marx...

They were heady days intellectually, for the young in spirit – and also for the combative, rebellious and iconoclastic: for respected authorities were challenged, of course. And appalling gaps in disciplinary assumptions were revealed – by attending to everyday knowledge, too.

There is space for just one instance, an astonishing – and at the time, rather shocking – one from the 'linguistic sciences'. Throughout the 1960s, they had had a field day, in the USA through Chomsky's transformational and generative approach to grammar; in France through the wider influence of Saussurean structuralism. Both projects abstracted language from social context and use, the goal being to define a set of procedures for producing ideal type sentences, or – more ambitiously – an integrated, multi-level set of relations which constituted an ideal language (or was it the unconscious structures of the mind?). There was great intellectual fascination in this work. Certainly, it put paid to current behaviourist accounts of language in the USA. So the awakening of serious linguistic doubts, around 1970, was a rueful moment.

What finally set those doubts loose was an elementary observation by the philosopher, John Austin. When you asked ordinary people what they were using words to do, they could not only answer; they had anything from 1000 to 9999 expressions available in English to draw on. (Everyday knowledge, we might say, outran the specialists.) Thus, at various times in this book I am 'arguing', 'claiming', 'assuming', 'proposing', 'suggesting', 'conceding'... and so on. Of course, I don't introduce each sentence or paragraph with an expression of that kind; in fact, at times perhaps, I am not sufficiently conscious of these actions. But they are happening, all the time, aren't they? And so are your actions in response, incipiently in inner speech at least (agreeing or disagreeing, for instance, querying, qualifying, countering and so on).

This is a very fundamental kind of significance for any utterance (or response), then. But, if so, how do readers construct it, supposing no introductory characterisation is offered? On analysis, it turned out that in writing at least there was no one-to-one correspondence between a specific speech 'act' and linguistic signs. In other words, here was an obvious, irreducible form of indeterminacy in the reader's construction of meaning. (The mind was not so simple, after all.)

What's more, there had to be severe limitations in any theoretical models that abstracted utterances from context and situation (from spoken or written interaction). These were lessons that have taken a lot of learning.

So, whether constructively or destructively, there were powerful new intellectual movements sweeping through higher education, just at the point where students were making utopian and revolutionary demands on it. Sociology became a boom subject, not surprisingly. But the effects and doubts spread much wider, across into the humanities. Cultural Studies was shaken, and even English began to feel tremors.

Women: a new consciousness of themselves in the world

Finally, cutting across the other two, but taking shape more slowly (in the UK, especially) came a third international movement – women's liberation. As the first groups got in touch with each other, they began to raise fundamental questions:

> How do people come to a new consciousness of themselves in the world? How does a new concept of what it is to be female come about? How are new ideas made social through the practical activities of a movement? How is social transformation communicated to the individual psyche?
> (Rowbotham, in Wandor 1972)

These connections between 'new consciousness', 'practical activity', 'social transformation' and 'individual psyche' (made by Sheila Rowbotham in 1969) indicate that at least one women's group was already into the theoretical issues sketched above. They had an articulate political agenda. In fact, to them the 'so-called women's question is a whole people question': domination of women was simply 'the most complex and the most fundamental of links' in a chain that connected 'parents and children, brothers and sisters, teachers and pupils, managers and workers, citizens of one country and citizens of another' (Wandor 1972: 3).

Nevertheless, groups of women had to start from their personal constructions of reality, they found:

> Sharing oppressive experiences with other women gives them the understanding that many of the situations described are not personal but social. The awareness that revealed problems are common to all women in the group consequently shifts the attention away from one's own inadequacies towards finding the real causes of these problems and gives a

A second phase: rebellions, challenges and liberation

perspective that can lead to action. It also gives strength to go back to those inadequacies and start to change them.

(*Shrew*, March 1971, in Wandor 1972)

This group construction of knowledge had a basis in personal narratives, then, but – in order to be socially relevant – it couldn't stop at everyday categories: it had to make new demands on theory. Again, that became a conscious goal from the early days:

> I think the phrase consciousness-raising is misleading. It doesn't refer to some magical point at which you can say someone's consciousness is raised to a level of political security. What it seems to me is that it raises to the surface discontents and reactions which are there within us – more clearly defined and more politically conscious in some women than others.
>
> The most important thing I've learned [in 24 meetings of the group] is the process of connecting what has happened in my own life to abstract thought, and to a way of seeing society as a series of large and complex structures. I've got much more of an understanding of the meaning of the word 'political', and also of the direction I think we can go to change things more effectively.
>
> ('Judy' in Michelene Wandor's report on 'process' in the London Women's Liberation Workshop, 1972: 112)

In fact, such women had already invented a new form of cultural study. Its bedrock was the sharing of personal experiences in the group. But, even in the narrating and typifying of moments in their lives, they were seeking to escape the structures of domination. They were questioning their social representation in everyday life, breaking the moulds, and exploring alternatives.

That led them further: turning to search for reasons and causes, some groups questioned the theories of society that were alive at the time. Theories about the working class – but what about working-class women? Theories about labour and production – but what about labour in the home? Theories of roles for the oppressed – but what about women's rights?

> It was tremendously exciting, [wrote one of the Tufnell Park group in London, looking back.] We felt like we were breaking through our conditioning and learning new things each week... I used to be exhausted and exhilarated after meetings and used to lie awake thinking – couldn't stop.
>
> We argued a lot with each other. We were mostly political, mostly not marxists because our experience and identification was American new left of the first half of the 60s type... I'm glad it was that way. We all felt Women's Liberation at a gut level and for me at least it led to reading (starting to anyway) Marx and Lenin.
>
> (pp.93–4)

This thrilling direction of energies, with its insistent desire for a change in practices in the home and beyond, meant that established theory had to be questioned, its relevance to their stories and their project tested – and if they had to transform it, what better reason?

It was an enormous challenge to take on. Looking back as early as 1969, Rowbotham felt from past experience that 'the dominated can tell stories, they can fantasise, they can create Utopia, but they cannot devise the means of getting there. They cannot make use of maps, plan out the route and calculate the odds. The dominators continue to hold ideology' (Wandor 1972: 9). If so, using maps, making calculations, had to come out of a dialectic between reconstructing the everyday – its stories, dreams and practices – and uncovering the hidden categories that, day in day out, inculcated these versions of self, the other, and society.

Despite the relatively late start, UK feminism had its advantages, then; here the early groups were in contact with radical students; with working-class women, campaigning for equal pay and equal rights at work; and with early Black Women's committees. So, when the movement really took off, in the summer of 1971, its perspectives were wider than those of its middle-class, 'mildly Left' majority.

Higher education was not a primary target, therefore. Nevertheless, the first steps in History and Cultural Studies had actually been made by 1972.

> Women's history – and therefore people's history – has yet to be written and to write it is part of our present struggle... the history we were taught was the history of the male-dominated class society, written to 'explain' (i.e. justify and maintain) the status quo, to show the past as progress towards the present, and not to suggest what might have happened instead...
>
> Very probably [this version of the past] was developed by dedicated historians with faith in their own objectivity and scholarly standards. But without setting 'standards' in a historical perspective and recognising that historians are formed by their background and society, and so more likely to see certain things as interesting (or irrelevant) than others, no-one, however scholarly, conscientious, diligent, or even lucky, will ever achieve more than partial truth.
>
> (Anna Davin, in Wandor 1972: 215)

A historical placing of standards, judgements and perspectives – this was a fascinating project, not simply for History, but inevitably for subjects like English, too. And the focus on social 'formation' – of individuals, groups, or intellectual traditions – was a vital contrast to the 'developmental' metaphors that had dominated the 1960s.

In fact, a Northern Women's Education group had already opened up that vein, too. In the spirit of Hoggart's appeal for a study of everyday

A second phase: rebellions, challenges and liberation 179

literary production, they had started with a popular school reading scheme – the elementary texts of literacy. What kinds of social world, with what kinds of role, were Ladybirds presenting?

> The reading book children live in a world untouched by any of the harsher realities of life... it is always summer... [Peter and Jane] are nearly always free to play with their huge selection of expensive toys in a garden [of] rolling lawns and deep herbaceous borders... [they] are never cold, hungry, thirsty, cross, bored or angry. They never quarrel. Mummy and Daddy never say No...
>
> [Their] parents portray rigidly defined male/female active/passive roles. Daddy drives the car, goes out all day to some unspecified work, paints the house... Mummy is rarely seen outside the kitchen... the parents lead very separated lives... So 'Peter helps Daddy with the car, and Jane helps Mummy get the tea'... [The children] have very different toys and interests... [In play] Mary and Jane pretend to be nurses... [Bob] pretends to be the Doctor... Time after time Peter plays the active part, Jane the passive...

'All in all, (these books for innocents) form an ideological prison from which the child would be lucky to escape' (Wandor 1972: 146–9). The class basis for its fantasies was as obvious as its sexual bias. So what about the other representations penetrating the home and the school: television, radio, popular songs, news stories... literary texts? What escape or further confinement did they offer, for women's formation – and for ordinary people's construction of their social reality?

Academic bases and divided labours

For English lecturers like Cora Kaplan, say, the 1970s was a period of 'productive optimism' in a 'political movement which sought to "marry" socialism and feminism and, at the very least, to consider a temporary alliance between Marx and Freud' (1986: 1). She 'took it for granted that political transformation was possible. Submission rather than resistance needed to be explained' (p.11). Yet like others in the UK, she felt her feminism was 'extra-institutional and, indeed, deeply illegitimate from the point of view of my own work-place... until seventy-eight or seventy-nine'. Feminist teaching meant a subversive restructuring of courses already on the (university) syllabus – or better, 'teaching men and women (but mostly women) of all ages in adult education', outside the prestige academic structures. 'While the first course on gender at my university was taught in 1973, I myself did not teach such a course until about seventy-six' (p.8).

This brief retrospect tacitly explains a good deal. For anyone with revolutionary hopes, the pull of wider movements outside the academy is to be welcomed, not avoided. If a great transformation is conceivable, then you must work with people well beyond elite institutions, to ensure that their voice is heard and that they participate to the full. So 'alternative schools', 'workshops', 'study groups', conference 'commissions' and 'collectives' with open access all had to be invented. Such informal institutions could often start from people's everyday experience and assume a common commitment to action.

At the same time, though, the interrogation of theory – for Marxists, Freudians, Structuralists or whatever – was intensifying. Paris, for example, was alive with new intellectual movements, thrown up by the students' revolutionary expectations in May 1968 and the subsequent shock of a right-wing triumph. In England and Wales, the current Minister of Education was called Margaret Thatcher. Without a better understanding of historical forces, how could the mind-forged manacles be forced open? How were people – intellectuals included – being socially formed against their own interests; how could that formation be internally resisted and collectively renewed? The need for answers was urgent. If small groups could gather in the universities – or the new, expanding polytechnics – they had a responsibility to work on such things.

Not that their attention was ever simply bookish. After the occupation at Birmingham University in 1968, research students at the Contemporary Cultural Centre were properly drawn into analysis of 'the conflicting ways the situation was understood by the participants' and into discussion with local journalists of the 'controlling but unstated "myths" concerning students and political conflict employed in the press' (CCCS *Report*: 1969: 19). And one of the first graphic and detailed case studies on media production – 'Demonstrations and Communication' (1970) – was pulled off simply because the research team at the Centre for Mass Communication (University of Leicester) was prepared to switch projects, three weeks before the deadline, to document a major demonstration against the Vietnam War and the media reports of it.

Extra grants for MA and Ph.D. work did reinforce the focus on theory, though. The postgraduates attracted to CCCS, for instance, rose from around 20 (1971) to 30 (1973) – though that had its difficulties too, given a typical first degree course.

> Graduates find themselves poorly prepared... for the sort of integrated and sustained theoretical enquiry which [work at the CCCS] entails. We are poorly staffed and funded for such an ambitious project. *Interdisciplinary work, especially, is poorly placed and supported:* paid ritual obeisance... in practice it runs up against the boundaries between disciplines, the division of labour in intellectual work, the awkward *problems of relevance and action which flow from truly critical knowledge...* Alternative modes of work are

A second phase: rebellions, challenges and liberation 181

difficult to define and carry through in a climate that is, largely, inhospitable to them.

(CCCS *Report,* December 1971: 6, my emphasis)

In fact, at that moment, the Centre had no externally funded group project (p.19). And with Richard Hoggart away at UNESCO, the teaching staff was down to one and a half: Stuart Hall and Michael Green (part-time). Here as elsewhere in the British universities, new theoretical directions were being left well alone, to make their own way.

And some of them certainly went headlong into it! In 1969, the CCCS seminars for 'collective work' were on French Structuralism (Saussure, Levi-Strauss, Barthes...); in 1970 on a list that began with Williams and ended with Sartre, Goldmann, Marcuse; in 1971 on Marx (The German Ideology, the 1844 Manuscripts, and Wages, Prices and Profits)... As a later *Report* candidly admitted 'This emphasis on theoretical clarification no doubt reflected a problem – which we cannot in any way claim to have solved – as to what the limits of the field of study are' (Jan. 1976). What indeed! – nothing less than some grand theory could be satisfying, it seemed at the time.

Scope and constraint in teaching experiments

Fortunately, not all the new work was so theoretically oriented. New spaces were being made for interdisciplinary courses with undergraduates, too: especially in the new polytechnics. Here the structures were enabling. Thus, under the guidelines of a national Council for Academic Awards (CNAA), poly degrees were designed and theoretically justified by course teams, who had to face the questions of an external panel, given the job of testing the coherence of their aims, the range and scope of the proposed units, and the appropriateness of the forms of assessment.

It was a searching procedure for new courses – and potentially educational in its own right. As a result, undergraduate courses emerged that were 'not simply an aggregate of competing interests and attitudes', as John Oakley and Elizabeth Owen later pointed out (1982). And every five years there was scope for revision.

As a result, by the mid-1970s, studies in literature could be integrated on several dimensions:

- with the work of other kinds of cultural institution (like BBC Radio or Television),
- and in other modes of communication (dramatic, audio-visual,...);

- with historical studies of cultural production (in literature, the arts and beyond), and
- with critical analysis of the ideological perspectives, conflicts and constraints in a given era (and their broad effects on representations of gender, class, race, religion,...);
- with opportunities for students to write something more than 'essays', and to develop a practitioner's understanding of written forms and functions (at least)...

There is a major work to be done, to collect and assess the results of all those experiments. However, the tensions within such work are well represented in *Experiments in English Teaching* (Craig and Heinemann 1976). David Craig, a university rebel, sets down his four axioms:

- treat the kindred media (theatre, cinema, TV, pop and folk song) on an equal footing with books;
- give people a chance to create for themselves;
- have little or nothing to do with the passive anti-educational forms of study, i.e. lectures, dictated notes, exams and tests;
- ignore received opinion as far as possible

(p.7)

Contributors who sympathised with the first three, at least, included John Broadbent (Professor at East Anglia); Jeremy Hawthorn (Sheffield and later Sunderland Polytechnic); Margot Heinemann, Vera Gottlieb, Nesta Jones, Peter Griffiths, Bob Osgerby and others from teacher education; and Albert Hunt, Bill Parkinson and others from Further or Adult Education.

There is a sharp difference, though, in the case of Peter Widdowson (Thames Poly) and Michael Green (Birmingham CCCS). They certainly agreed with axiom one. Their prime focus, however, was on historical and theoretical thinking – 'experiments' of a different kind. Perhaps as a result, both acknowledged initial problems: 'we increasingly feel that our students are over-taught', says Widdowson self-critically (p.137), and Green, discussing a shorter undergraduate course unit, ruefully notes that 'we have retreated from reading Weber or Sartre or Althusser or other theoretical writers, because to do so quickly can make theory seem severely abstract or oppressive' (p.151).

Nevertheless, within the space of a Humanities degree at Thames Poly, there was 'the excitement of perceiving the complex relationships of literature to life':

> A running debate has developed [in the Making of Modern Society course] about the historicism of literature – about its value as historical evidence, its class base, its social rather than individual engendering; and in counterpoint, about the intensified need to understand and evaluate its formal, verbal and textural structures, about the need for close reading

A second phase: rebellions, challenges and liberation 183

when literature is regarded as a historical document, and most importantly, about the way in which literature achieves a kind of historical simultaneity... a synthesis of the diverse and complex pressures at work in a particular time and place.

(p.129)

The notion of a running argument – involving both the teaching team and students – is not a bad paradigm for historical work (though it is still poorly investigated as a teaching method). And with it can come the excitement of analysing materials with rich social significance. Here the Birmingham course unit too was finding its point of take-off: 'The media is almost always the topic students prefer' – analysing a week's coverage of the press; a television genre (the police series); the current accounts of 'deviants' and scapegoats; the struggle to recreate audiences in *Spare Rib* as against *Nova*...

The lack of an institutional centre

How about the students' questions of History and Theory, though? What had happened to *their* storm of creative thinking? Green tacitly gives the answer: 'politics is itself a further absence from the campus at this time' – in the redbrick university, at least (Craig and Heinemann 1976: 144). Paradoxically, he was now analysing 'student protest in its absence' (p.150). The broad movement, he could have added, had been splitting into sects, often grouped around charismatic figures (Marcuse, Illich, Fanon, Mao and so on). Segregated in smaller groups, students had moved off into factory work, community activism, or sexual politics. Within higher education, collective utopian dreams were on the wane – and the fierce pressure from below to construct new kinds of social knowledge was slackening.

Yet in other ways, spaces for fresh thinking were being kept open. From 1972 the CCCS had been publishing regular *Working Papers* in Cultural Studies and the Society for Education in Film and Television had expanded *Screen Education* and *Screen*. By the mid-1970s, Middlesex Poly was starting *Literature and History*; a collective based at Ruskin College the *History Workshop* journal; Essex University their regular *Sociology of Literature* conference proceedings and the journal *Oral History*. Later the women's movement added *Feminist Review* (1979)... The very existence of such journals indicated an established network working on many shared problems.

Nevertheless, at the time each journal and group was inevitably constrained, partial in its range, and prone to the schematic. Staffing and finance were tight again, after the 1973 'oil crisis'. 'We could imagine Cultural Studies degrees or research based, just as effectively, on visual (rather than literary) texts, on social anthropology (rather than sociology) and with a much stronger input from historical studies... [The Centre] chose to specialise in those areas which the small staff felt *capable of supervising'* (Hall 1980: 15, my emphasis). (And the institutional demands on research theses in new domains could be quite arcane, I should add.) How were the *Working Papers* produced, in fact? By luck and good will, at times: 'the first issue was designed and overseen by Trevor Millum, one of our first successful Ph.D. students, in a period of post-thesis euphoria' (p.16).

The basic difficulty overall was the division of labour, stemming from the absence of major interdisciplinary centres, where groups of teachers might have learnt to integrate work with undergraduates and postgraduates, while engaging a wider range of people through Adult Education. This is the silent message of *Experiments in English Teaching* and its era. Theorising the field of Literature, Culture and History was a job beyond the existing institutions. The work was going to be piecemeal, not systematic; partial syntheses seemed bound to be quickly overtaken (by global intellectual movements). And in the drive towards theoretical answers, the questions and experience of ordinary people stood to be marginalised.

CHAPTER 16

Into dialogue, but against the grain

Theoretical gaps and a shift of focus at CCCS

In 1973, Volosinov's *Philosophy of Language* was finally translated. It was not easy to come by in the UK, admittedly, but the silence that greeted it has to be significant. It was not mentioned in Terry Eagleton's book on *Marxism and Literary Criticism* (1975), perhaps understandably. In the CCCS's working papers it did not appear till 1976, in an article on 'The semiotics of working-class speech'. As this demonstrated, and Andrew Tolson conceded in the same issue, 'the [UK] marxist analysis of discourse is embryonic' (*Working Paper* 9: 202). The following year Raymond Williams used Volosinov much more fully to re-analyse the concept of sign (*Marxism and Literature*, 1977), but omitted the concept of dialogue. By 1980 there was nothing further.

Undoubtedly, a sharp shift of focus helps to account for this lack of interest. For in 1973 the Birmingham Centre took on a major enquiry into 'The transition from school to work'. This was followed by *Resistance through Rituals* (1976); *Learning to Labour* and *Limits of Masculinity* (1977); *Working Class Cultures* and *Policing the Crisis* (1978). Reconceptualising youth cultures and social theories of deviance were among the key interests of the time. The initial interest in discursive forms – in Literature, in the Press, Radio, Television and so forth – was no longer focal. It was, of course, a matter of priorities.

Nevertheless, I believe this gap was critical. Dialogue, studied in context, challenges all previous theories of discourse, I would claim. And, crucially, it exposes the fallacies of literary and cultural studies that supposedly restrict their analytical enquiries to the 'text' – thus, whether consciously or not, privileging a specific reading, that of the theorist.

Similarly, without a dialogic theory, the 'text' itself is not placed as a response, in its turn, to what others have said or written. It is abstracted, to some degree, from its context of production. Equally, any given reader and reading is to some degree abstracted from the personal and social context in which meaning and significance were constructed. When this happens, the work of both production and reception is uprooted from its formative shaping in society and history.

No alternative centre – so far as I know – pursued these interests in the 1970s. Work on dialogue did go forward, and I believe it was of fundamental importance. But though the scattered participants did know something of each other's work, they did not develop a joint tradition with continuity. Investigations of 'readers' went on for much of the decade, largely unnoticed it's true; this too lacked a synthesising movement. Fortunately, however, the historical placing of production and reception did emerge as a major theme, with an interim British synthesis by 1981. In the next two chapters, then, I want to bring this fragmented work together. In doing so, I willingly concede, I will become less of a historian, more of a theorising colleague.

Making meaning, socially constructing, and interacting

The title of this section signals a paradigm shift in language studies. Not 'language' but 'making meaning' – an activity, involving people, in a context. Not just 'text', the array of signs, but also the 'constructing' – the progressive building up of experiences, thoughts and dispositions from incoming and inner signs. Not 'speaking and writing', as if only an isolated 'producer' was having effects, but 'interacting' – recognising that writing itself is in part a response, and acknowledging that readers' responses include a productive contribution.

To reach this model in the 1970s, there had to be a revolutionary break from defining language as reified object, towards observing social processes dependent on signs in use.

Yet something like this frame had emerged, piecemeal I would say, by the end of the decade. It was by no means fully recognised or developed in the UK, and certainly not widely implemented – in fact, I doubt if it is now. As for its fight to 'emerge', institutionally, this will have to wait. Within this book, the best I can do is to propose a gradual gathering of its theoretical components – all of them, significantly, arising from empirical studies. In fact, the key instances I have chosen are drawn from observation, recording and analysis in two associated fields:

- early language development, and especially Michael Halliday's *Learning How to Mean* (1975)
- classroom dialogue, in Douglas Barnes and Frankie Todd's study of *Communication and Learning in Small Groups* (1977).

Into dialogue, but against the grain 187

How about literary and cultural studies, meanwhile? It was a great drawback to both fields, I believe, that in the UK they were not involved in this kind of modelling. Both wings came under pressure during the decade to produce more objective evidence, based on signs and structures. But the (unconscious) resistance to studying readers or viewers was very strong – particularly where structuralist or formalist assumptions about 'semiotics' held sway.

By 1979, though, the paradigmatic break was already striking people as alert as Raymond Williams, for instance: 'if I had one single ambition in literary studies it would be to rejoin them with experimental science... It is so curious that this was an identical ambition of Richards in the 1920s... What is needed is... an introduction of literary practice to the quite different practice of experimental observation' (p.341).

Yet there were major difficulties for contemporary 'observers'. Quite apart from designing experiments that were sophisticated enough to elicit a genuine process, there was limited access in the early 1970s to essential equipment. Thus, cheap and unobtrusive video-recording was not available till the 1980s. Yet everyone working on oral dialogue before that realised that the audiotape on which they depended wasn't enough – it omitted so many other kinds of communicative signs (eye contacts, facial expressions, gestures, stance, sympathetic movements...). Obviously work on television viewing was doubly affected by such constraints: without cheap, reliable VTRs, and fast winding-on or back, the 'visual events' weren't open to re-viewing and close inspection – not to speak of trying to elicit and record viewers' responses on the spot.

These technological drawbacks undoubtedly reinforced the textual focus of so much work in the mid-1970s – for example, in stylistics or on film structures. Such studies, you might say, still pretended that the reader or viewer didn't exist: that the analysis wasn't itself just one form of reading, and dependent on pre-analytic kinds of reading at that. If Saussure took some responsibility in Europe, in the English-speaking world there may well have been a hangover from the New Criticism, too.

What precisely motivated the break, then? First, in the period of academic rebellion and challenge, linguistics was struggling to recover from a major setback – its past omission of speech acts, and all that that implied. It was the kind of moment when a few people have the temerity to acknowledge the obvious. 'People not only speak', said Michael Halliday to Herman Parrett in 1974, 'they speak to each other' (1978: 57). 'I am trying to characterise human interaction' (p.51). 'We're interested in the text, in what people actually do and mean and say, in real situations (p.40). I find little use for the classic dichotomies [langue/parole, competence/performance]... My former teacher, Firth, himself criticised these very cogently' (Halliday in 1978: 51).

Thus 'we see language as what goes on in the head AND what goes on between people – both are taken seriously'. (p.51) People understand language in use 'by looking at what the speaker says against the background of *what he might have said*' (p.52, my emphasis). In fact, as Halliday had recently conceded in 1972, a 'text is meaningful not so much because the hearer does not know what the speaker is going to say, but because he does – abundant evidence, from his knowledge of the linguistic system and his sensitivity to the particular cultural context, enables him to make *informed guesses* about the meanings that are coming his way' (1978:61, my emphasis). It was fighting talk. This must be one of the first occasions, I guess, when a linguistic theoretician conceded a dynamic, participatory role to the listener.

Such a revolution in interests was bound to call for renewed empirical studies. Halliday himself had begun to observe and record his child's 'utterances', as he put it – perhaps in direct response to the groups of teachers he was working with for Schools Council? In doing so, he formulated 'the child's task' as follows: 'to construct the system of meanings that represents his own model of social reality' (1975: 139). But how could a task of that magnitude be tackled by a mere 2-year-old?

> This process takes place inside his own head; it is a cognitive process. But it takes place in contexts of social interaction... the learning of the mother tongue is also an interactive process. It takes the form of the continued exchange of meanings between the self and others. The act of meaning is a social act.
>
> (p.139)

Had he just been reading Volosinov? I wonder.

Learning how to mean

The book of this title, published in 1975, offers an excellent case study of the original theorist struggling with contradictory tendencies in his disciplinary formation.

Are 'cognitive processes' given full scope – including the listener's guesses and prefigurings? Not really. Is the 'interactive process' analysed, the 'continued exchange of meanings' between the child and his parents? No. At no point, so far as I remember, does Halliday *observe* the father's constructions, or his active attempts to prompt and modify the child's 'system of meanings'. As for the parent's 'model of social reality', it is not in the picture either.

Into dialogue, but against the grain 189

Like many people who make intellectual breaks (as we have seen), at that moment Halliday knew better than he practised. He acknowledged processes that he had still no readily available equipment to deal with. (Not that the rest of us were much better off, at the time.) Nevertheless, in doing so, in unconsciously indicating gaps in his own analysis, he valuably provoked further work on this model.

Some of it was only a short step on. Take Nigel's first attempt at narrative, for example. Some hours after returning home, he is recalling an incident at the Zoo:

> *N*: try eat lid
> *F*: What tried to eat the lid?
> *N*: try eat lid
> *F*: What tried to eat the lid?
> *N*: goat... man said no... goat try eat lid... man said no
>
> Then, after an interval, while being put to bed:
>
> *N*: goat try eat lid... man said no
> *M*: Why did the man say no?
> *N*: goat shouldn't eat lid... (shaking head) goodfor it
> *M*: The goat shouldn't eat the lid; it's not good for it.
> *N*: goat try eat lid... man said no... goat shouldn't eat lid... (shaking head) goodfor it
>
> This story is then repeated as a whole, verbatim, at frequent intervals over the next few months.
>
> (p.112)

In retrospect, we could say this: It is the father who constructs the first utterance as a reference to a recent event; but he is not satisfied. He prompts an interest in recalling the actor. His closed question is successfully construed, the second time, and allows N to answer in a single morpheme, reducing his cognitive load, and thus possibly opening the way for N to introduce a second event and another participant. Sure signs that more is going on 'in his head'.

For the mother's benefit, the two events are set side by side (uncoordinated) in a single utterance. But she is not satisfied either. She prompts N to make explicit the relation between the two. So N explains why the event 'man said no' followed 'goat eat lid'. (Whether he does so in a narrator's role, or dramatically in the role of the keeper, is left open in the transcript.) The mother constructs the head-shake as a negative and by her intonation – to judge by the semi-colon – tacitly indicates a further relation, between 'the goat shouldn't eat the lid' and 'it's not good for it'. N then takes it upon himself to back-summarise – and gets the order of events right, a complex cognitive achievement.

What then, though? Surely something about his mother's final responses – her gestures, facial expressions, or more – affected N? How else can we explain his desire to go on repeating this inspired outcome of his parents' promptings and his own willing co-operation? I suspect that his wonderful start to narrative recall of experience – this major step in using linguistic signs to *construct a meaningful past*, which could then be *recalled and shared at will* – must have been celebrated!

To sum up so far: a shared experience has been recalled, we surmise, using a very limited set of linguistic and enactive signs. But how about visual and motor images: weren't they also recalled at the time? In fact, was it the keeper who first shook his head? 'Cognitively', a lot more was going on in Halliday's mind as he noted this story, we can be sure, and 'inside N's own head', as he progressively told his side of it. (For instance, N was actually holding the lid at the time, we are informed elsewhere!) The vocal signs were only elementary cues.

Besides, transcripts like this necessarily omit a mass of 'affective' and 'evaluative' signs. How did the dialogic pairs motivate each other to pursue – and enjoy – this steady elaboration of cues to a shared experience? In 1975 such vital evidence was missing. (Fortunately, within five years Donald Graves and his team in New Hampshire had videotapes available, showing animated – and much more subtle – interaction with 6–8-year-olds, as they too enjoyed learning to elaborate stories, this time for writing.)

Nevertheless, Halliday was on the right track. A 'model of social reality' was being jointly constructed, we could agree, and this implied in some sense a *'system of meanings'*. Though Ogden and Richards would rightly have shaken their heads at the word at the time, Halliday construed 'meanings' in terms of a set of semantic options. Without altogether disagreeing, I would put it differently, with the focus on cognition first. Nigel stood to learn not only how to produce this story, but also in part how stories were produced. An interest in *participants*, in their *actions*, in *relating the events* thus constituted, in *evaluating the action* as a whole... this set of interests was being cued and motivated.

Cognitively, I could put it this way, then: a kind of template was being developed, through dialogue. Linguistic prompts for filling out a *typical* narrative were being explicitly given by the parents. Linguistic reinforcements to N's efforts were being added, too. (Further, as Halliday made clear, N was also picking up generically useful dodges for signalling cohesion and given/new information.) Next – if Vygotsky was right – it was up to N to internalise all these things as a system, in inner dialogue. The final outcome may indicate him doing so, on this occasion. If so, the next stage would be to realise that the same template had many applications for similar occasions.

How to understand conversations – and reading

'The focus of attention [in research on language development] has gone from the phonological system, to the lexicogrammatical system (syntax), to the semantic system, and is now moving to the cognitive system', wrote Halliday in 1975 (p.139), endorsing Lois Bloom and Bill Labov's recent proposals in the USA. With linguists beginning to talk about cognition and social interaction, a radically new approach had been launched.

And fortunately, within Education there was every motivation to take special account of it. By the early 1970s schoolteachers were getting the chance to study 'language and learning', to borrow the title of James Britton's recent book (1970). Centres had been set up in the universities of Birmingham, Leeds and London, and all of us teaching those courses wanted to understand how students at their best could collaborate. Although a joint approach from Leeds and Birmingham Universities was turned down by the SSRC, the Council finally did make a small research grant. Thus, at Leeds, Douglas Barnes and Frankie Todd were able to carry the analysis a step further in their study of 'communication and learning in small groups'.

As observers, the Leeds team moved a step beyond Halliday: they had learnt an important lesson from Garfinkel (1972). Aiming to alert his students to problems of 'understanding', he had asked them to note down a short dialogue with an intimate friend and alongside each utterance to write, as if for an outsider, the meaning it had for the participant. This procedure demonstrated a number of things of great interest to Barnes and Todd:

- that the initial verbal signs were a kind of shorthand, dependent on further tacit knowledge
- that there was generally a degree of indeterminacy in 'the meaning' of what was said
- that participants each put their own construction on what had been said, supplying tacit knowledge of their own that seemed appropriate
- that the observer could only reconstruct a meaning potential 'imaginatively', after careful study of the linguistic signs and the chain of interactions.

(see Barnes and Todd 1977: 98)

Thus, they summed up their end-position as follows:

We take the view that meaning should not be taken to adhere to an isolated utterance, but should be seen to arise from *the tacit knowledge* of participants which *they use to attribute meaning to what is said*. Different participants bring different bodies of knowledge to the discussion, and at different moments treat one or another sub-system of knowledge as relevant to understanding what is being said'.

(p.96, my emphasis)

This further break was going to be vital to literary and cultural studies. 'Making meaning' depended not simply on external signs (in the dialogue) but also on inner signs, and the experience they had already organised: on 'tacit knowledge'. Each participant in a group was working on an active synthesis of new incoming and old organised 'knowledge', I could say. But each personal synthesis depended partly on what had already been organised, partly on internalised judgements of relevance. Certainly this activity depended on sets of signs and their potentials, but these demonstrably remained less fixed and systematic than Halliday had assumed.

The importance of tacit knowledge is clear enough, if you look back at the first dialogue with Nigel. Why did F ask 'what' tried to eat the lid? Why not 'who', knowing the ways of infants? F, it seems, knew that N had just returned from the zoo. Using this tacit knowledge, apparently, he made an 'informed guess' that N might be thinking of an animal. So he used 'what' in order to invite N, in turn, to make explicit this segment of *his* tacit knowledge. And in later framing of the story, Halliday drew on further tacit knowledge, making explicit the fact that it was N who was holding the lid at the time – a 'relevant' fact, in his view (though N had left it tacit).

However, not everyone shares the story-teller's life – and interactive telling – so intimately as parents and infants. Many stories on the News, in History, or in fiction, come out of relatively unknown worlds. And similarly many new general categories in school and college come at the student rather out of the blue. Tacit 'knowledge' – in the form of verbally organised experiences, ideas, dispositions, evaluations and so on – is needed to fill gaps in the text, but it may be thin on the ground. Indeed, the existence of some gaps may not even be suspected! Yet, to Barnes and Todd, it was the *conjunction* of explicit and tacit 'knowledge' that made possible a construction of meaning by each reader, listener, or dialogic participant. (In linguists' terms, I suggest, 'new information' had to be integrated with the already 'given' and stored.)

If so, both 'knowledge' and 'information' had their drawbacks as descriptive categories. They suggested something already determinate. In reality, as Halliday had in effect conceded, an observer could only make an informed guess at the specific signs and experiences called up 'as relevant' by any one participant.

On this model, we could say, Halliday's idea of a cumulative store of meaning potential was transformed. Something is stored: but not simply a set of language options. Rather there is also a stock of

Into dialogue, but against the grain 193

'knowledge', of experiences, thoughts and evaluations that have previously been verbally organised – though not very systematically, perhaps.

To sum up the model at this stage: what was going on in discussion was 'a matrix of utterances and actions bound together by a web of understandings and reactions', as Labov and Fanshel put it the same year (1977: 30). In discussion, what was said was inflected by what was done – the 'multilayered complex of speech acts' (p.71). So that agreements, doubts, questions, challenges and so forth were signalled throughout the interaction, sometimes rather undifferentiated, sometimes not. And these often constituted tacit evaluations of what had been said.

Briefly, then, 'understandings' and 'reactions' turned out to be far from simple. For Barnes and Todd, with classroom learning in mind, the problem of determinate 'meaning' was opened up again:

> [The search for relevant 'knowledge' in order to understand what is said] does not mean that there is a body of knowledge which is in some objective sense relevant to interpreting each utterance: there is no determinate meaning for an observer to look for... there is no way of limiting what is potentially relevant.
>
> (1977: 98).

In other words, you are bringing to this last quotation – and rightly so – whatever tacit knowledge seems to *you* (after reflection) most relevant, in the light of your past experience, your constructions of what has been said so far, and your interactions with it. In a discussion, we could do better, of course: you could prompt me at this point to recall further tacit knowledge that you feel I am neglecting, and I could reciprocate. We would be in a much better position to arrive at social constructions that were partly shared – providing we could set up collaborative roles.

CHAPTER 17

Reading as dialogue in a social context

Readers construct – and texts constrain

In the late 1960s, when NATE set up its first teacher-research project, the theme was 'Children as Readers'. With Douglas Barnes as convener, a leading aim was to experiment with ways of sampling students' informal reading processes – particularly by taping small groups. This gradually led to a critical discussion and revision of Richards's methodology and of his early modelling of the reader. By the early 1970s, North American educational researchers like Kenneth Goodman and Frank Smith were extending experiments to 'reading comprehension' in general (Smith 1973). Readers' active roles were under empirical observation – in the schools and teacher education at least.

In university English, there was much discussion of 'the reader' at the time, but with a difference: quite often, no empirical evidence was adduced. Readers remained an ideal abstraction. It was particularly valuable, therefore, when a teacher who had spent over twenty-five years collecting such evidence from her graduate students at Columbia University intervened in the growing debate. Louise Rosenblatt's *The Reader, the Text, the Poem* (1978) marked a new synthesis – by an intelligent reader of Bradley, Richards and Empson, as well as Ingarden, Jakobson, Barthes and Hirsch.

Rosenblatt's model pointed to three elements: a text, a constructed experience (the 'poem'), and a contemplative savouring and evaluation of that experience (the 'secondary', or dialogic, 'response'). The focus of her analysis was on the relations between these three.

She was able to begin, in effect, from Empson: 'the process of getting to know a poet is precisely that of constructing his poems in one's own mind' (p.85). What went into that constructive process, as students started to read the text of a quatrain by Robert Frost, for example? What had they to go through 'to arrive at an interpretation'?

> *It bids pretty fair*
>
> The play seems set for an almost infinite run.
> Don't mind a little thing like the actors fighting...

Among the first things the students noted were:

- placing the genre, spotting the fact that the lines rhymed and that this literary form called for a special kind of reading
- wondering whether to see the text as integrated, or as a possibly haphazard series of impressions (and voices)
- conjecturing about who was speaking, under what circumstances, and to whom (all of this being tacit in the text, of course)
- questioning the attitude of the speaker to 'the play', its 'almost infinite run' and 'the actors fighting'
- (suddenly) moving from literal to metaphoric readings of 'the stage', 'the actors', 'the sun', 'the lighting'
- accommodating afresh to the sort of speaker who might make such comments on the world...

So, even at this early stage, 'each reader was active' – 'actively involved in building up a poem' (p.12). And for that purpose, a searching attention to the textual signs was obviously necessary. But the construction, equally obviously, had to go beyond the delicate range of 'cues', which readers progressively registered and used.

'It bids pretty fair': when I recently asked a group of New Brunswick teachers for any cues they noticed in those words, some wondered if the speaker was a bit old-fashioned, a dialect speaker perhaps – or maybe British? It reminds me of my grandmother, one of them commented. They were drawing on tacit cultural experience.

This was essential because, the reader, in contrast to the listener, 'finds it necessary to construct the speaker... the voice, the tone, the rhythms and inflections', says Rosenblatt (p.20). So as they read, we see students 'applying first one and then another tentative sense of a subject, a situation, a setting, a persona or voice that might make it possible to develop a consistent and coherent "meaning" for the four lines' (p.57). All of this depends on summoning up tacit knowledge that seems appropriate.

Then, as the underlying metaphor was tapped, 'notions of mankind as a whole, of war, or of astronomical time, were part of the reader's contribution'. So for each reader, the 'poem' as an experience 'to some degree hinges on the assumptions, the expectations, or sense of possible structures, that he brings out of the stream of his life' (p.11). And for current readers, I should add, that life experience is decades later than the published text of the poem: inevitably, the metaphorical 'meanings' are historically shifted. Is it global warming, nuclear annihilation, or something metaphysical that might form an appropriate referent for 'the sun' and 'the lighting'? – the New Brunswickers asked themselves.

'Thus both text and reader are essential aspects or components, one might say, of that which is *manifested in each reading as the poem*' (p.15, my emphasis). 'The text presents limits or controls; the personality and culture brought by the reader constitute another type of limitation on the resultant synthesis, the lived-through work of art' (p.129). Within the States, with its vast range of ethnic cultures, the point was deeply significant.

This is the general case. Yet, in practice, 'the text is seen to serve as *a kind of pattern which the reader must to some extent create* even as he is guided by it' (p.129, my emphasis). The model tries to account for both feed-forward and feed-back effects in any reading. Each of us 'selects out and seeks to organise according to already acquired habits, assumptions, and expectations' (p.17); but readers may discover that they have 'projected on the text elements of [their] experience not relevant to it, and which are not susceptible of coherent incorporation' (p.11). Thus, 'the reader's creation of a poem out of the text must be an active, self-ordering and *self-corrective* process' (p.11, my emphasis). 'This imposes the delicate task of sorting the relevant from the irrelevant in a continuing process of selection, revision, and expansion' (p.53).

A dialogic 'secondary' response

This, briefly, is Rosenblatt's modelling of our construction on the writer's behalf, as I would call it. But that is only half the story: once constructed, 'this experience may be the object of thought, like any other' (1978: 21). Thus the secondary, dialogic response.

> Even as we are generating the work of art, we are reacting to it. A concurrent stream of feelings, attitudes, and ideas is aroused by the very work being summoned up under guidance of the text... The reaction to the emerging work may be felt merely as a general state of mind, an ambience of acceptance, approval, incredulity. Such responses may be momentary, peripheral, almost woven into the texture of what is felt to be the work itself. Or the reaction may at times take more conscious form.
> (p.49)

So there is an inevitable dialogue in the act of reading. The signs in inner speech may be very fragmentary, we could say, but we certainly feel their presence. And this has a concrete frame in social life: 'the aesthetic experience, though distinguishable, is not separable from the ongoing life out of which [a reader] comes to the text, and to which he must return. The literary transaction, like the act of literary creation, has social origins and social effects' (p.157). Thus, 'every reader brings to the transaction not only a specific past life and literary history, not only a repertory of internalized "codes", but also a very active present, with its preoccupations, anxieties, questions and aspirations' (p.144).

For example, how could my own reading of the Frost poem not be lightened, in July 1990, by the winter revolutions in Europe – only to be darkened again by trigger-happy reactions to the invasion of Kuwait? It is this living context, I could say, with its deeper interests, which shapes both the reading and the dialogic evaluation – unless, of course, that is stifled and repressed in the classroom or the professor's study.

For the 'process of reporting on the aesthetic event does not occur in a vacuum but is deeply conditioned by the social context', Rosenblatt continues (p.135). 'Whether there will be any such discussion, what form it will take, what aspects will be articulated, what assumptions and interpretive systems will be brought to bear' – these depend on institutional practices, and power.

So institutions have obligations to readers. And there is a profound difficulty to be acknowledged first. A reading cannot simply be 'externalized' in some magic way. In reporting what happened, and its personal significance, readers are caught in a kind of paradox: interpretation 'involves an effort to indicate the sensed, felt, thought, nature of [the world that was conjured up] while at the same time applying some frame of reference or method of abstracting to characterize it' (p.135). The criteria underlying this frame or method have to be made explicit. And even then, whatever the academic currency of a specific 'abstractive approach', Rosenblatt insists that the reader's 'primary subject matter is the web of feelings, sensations, images, ideas, that he weaves between himself and the text' (p.137). What follows later must be rooted in that event.

So what are the implications for teaching and learning? On this model 'we cannot simply look at a text and predict what a reader will make of it' (p.137), nor talk about 'the poem itself'. The starting point of criticism is a reading. References to 'the informed reader' or 'an ideal reader' simply reflect the elitist view of literature and criticism 'that in recent decades has tended to dominate academic and literary circles' (p.138).

In fact, don't critics and literary scholars tend to represent a rather narrow spectrum of literary response?

> Readers may bring to the text experiences, awareness, and needs that have been ignored in traditional criticism. Women, for example, are finding their own voices as writers and critics, as are the ethnic minorities and

special cultural groups. Workers... are themselves becoming articulate and self-aware.

(p.142)

On this view, it seems to me fair to say, a 'preferred reading' emerges because of experiences that are conditioned by ethnicity, class and gender. Rosenblatt herself explicitly offers an example: her own preferred reading of Housman's poem on the jubilee of Queen Victoria –

>...Look left, look right, the hills are bright,
>   The dales are light between,
> Because 'tis fifty years tonight
>   That God has saved the Queen.
>
> Now, when the flame they watch not towers
>   About the soil they trod,
> Lads, we'll remember friends of ours
>   Who shared the work with God...

Applying the criterion of literary complexity to the readings suggested above, I find that the satiric readings... provide a much more subtle, finely modulated experience... I recognize also that these satisfy my own point of view about the self-complacency of British imperialists. Of the two alternative possible satiric readings, I again find the predilections I bring to the text leading me to prefer [a reading in which] the common man is honored for patiently and efficiently doing his duty as he sees it, while political or even divine power are seen as given the credit and the glory. I sense, too, an overtone of reproach that he lets himself be used in this way.

(p.126)

Both the reading arrived at (after careful attention to potentials in the text) and the satisfactions felt in the constructed experience manifestly arise from a range of criteria, 'formal... ethical, religious, and political', as Rosenblatt notes. What distinguishes her approach is that she is more aware of these and prepared to make them explicit. This seems to be a crucial implication of her model. Equally, it seems to follow that teachers who are not so aware could be a danger to their students, as well as to themselves as readers.

Of course, there will inevitably be motivations for a preferred reading of which we are less conscious. Rosenblatt acknowledges the 'unconscious and subconscious activities' postulated by depth psychology as shaping individual consciousness. But she takes this no further, resisting 'the particular repertory of psychological mechanisms such as Freudians and other schools have produced' (p.151).

Her primary concern is to reinstate the knowledge of ordinary readers, as against a critical establishment; to explain why a 'family resemblance' among readings is likely, not a consensus; and to ground differences in preferred readings (and satisfactions) in the differentiated social experiences of women and men, from more than one social class and from varied ethnic groups.

Social reception and production of art

If texts are read, 'poems' constructed, and responses elaborated by historically formed individuals (or groups), no criticism can be worthwhile without a detailed understanding of the social forces that shape both readings and production. And this will apply equally to viewers and listeners, to producers working more individually (in writing, photography, composing...), and to those engaged in collective production (drama, film, television...).

It seemed an obvious need; but some of the difficulties had been made clear enough in 1961, when Edward Thompson took Raymond Williams to task over his first effort to relate texts of the 1840s to their social and historical context. Richard Hoggart's inaugural lecture had pointed to further gaps in sociological investigation – and early working papers from the Birmingham Centre showed how established patterns of 'audience research', for instance, had to be resisted and somehow subverted before a start could be made. By 1973, however, an issue of *Cultural Studies* on Literature and Society felt able to begin 'mapping the field' – and pointed to some of the enabling factors I have outlined earlier, including the 'shift in the whole intellectual universe of the social sciences' (No. 4: 27). Progress was being made.

Eight years later, Janet Wolff – attached to the Centre as a graduate student in its early years – produced a valuable synthesis of the dispersed work of the 1970s: *The Social Production of Art*. This has often been my guide in the present section.

'I will try to show', she began, 'how practical activity and creativity are in a mutual relationship of interdependence with social structures': 'the existence of these structures and institutions enables any activity on our part, and this applies equally to acts of conformity and acts of rebellion' (p.9).

In this developing model, then, the prime object of study becomes institutionally organised activity. Just as people produce social change, so, we could say, they produce, 'read', and enjoy the arts, 'but they do so as historically located actors, and not under conditions of their own choosing' (p.23). The options are structured within institutional frames.

Thus, as we have seen, in the 1880s branches of the Extension movement aimed to spread the enjoyment of Shakespeare, Greek drama and recent poetry among miners, working men's institutes, and co-op members (women as well as men). The organising committees did not see such works as the preserve of a cultural elite. There were new cultural choices to define; but there were also many tacit constraints. For instance, the institutional forms set up were not adapted to encouraging students to practise poetry themselves. (Not surprisingly, it must be added, for in the new elementary schools 'composition' did not even figure on the timetable. Its place had already been filled, by 'dictation'.)

In 1920, however, the first issue of Ogden's post-war *Cambridge Magazine* carried an illustrated article by Marion Richardson, a pioneer of children's painting: schoolchildren were learning to produce art and it was worth discussing in a university journal – that was the new message. Similarly, during the mid-1960s, printed anthologies of poetry and prose from local schools became almost commonplace, as NATE branches spread. Young students could actually write poetry as well as read it, and it was worth publishing locally.

In all these cases, institutionally organised minorities were promoting change. They were opposing a model of literature and art as the concern of a leisured elite (with a classical education), and increasingly rejecting a notion of the arts as the exclusive products of highly specialised individuals, endowed with creative genius. The conditions of existence for the arts were shifting.

As Janet Wolff summed up: 'In the production of art, social institutions affect, amongst other things, *who* becomes an artist, *how* they become an artist, how they are then able to *practise* their art, and how they can ensure that their work is produced, performed, and *made available* to a public' (p.40, original emphasis). In the same spirit, we might add that institutions affect who do *not* practise the arts, in a given society, and *which segments* of artistic production various social groups or classes are likely to encounter – or enjoy.

The movements I have described were, of course, political: they aimed to transform the cultural powers of working-class people and many others – to change the scope and very nature of popular participation in the arts. And they produced inevitable reactions within established institutions. Thus, after 1965, as some schools and colleges tried to break away from a relatively closed set of canonical texts (in 'A level Literature', for instance) and to take in live drama or film, Black Papers and caucuses on examination boards were organised against them: such innovations wouldn't count as 'education'.

In fact, cultural institutions like schools, colleges of the arts, or universities turned out to be key places in the 1970s for studying conflicts over the potential place of the arts within the lives of ordinary people as well as elites.

During the same period, too, there was an increasingly critical analysis of the schooling of literary reception, of the ways 'individual responses' were structured, for instance, in school and beyond. The assumptions embedded in the typical essay 'questions'; the scope of the 'essay' (and the length of time allowed for it); the type of expected 'references' or 'illustrations' from the original text; the transactional role of the student writer and of the teacher as 'reader' of this peculiar text – these and other institutionalised practices defined an astonishingly uniform type of product for the majority of students, young or old, whatever critical school (or muddle) the teacher adhered to (Dixon 1979).

'Not under conditions of their own choosing': the old quotation from Marx had a particularly ironic ring in this case. But the practices just outlined were not exactly 'chosen' either. They were sets of presuppositions and conventions which the teachers fell in with by virtue of their own institutional formation, without conscious or critical deliberation. As most of us – including the full-time artists – do much of the time.

No one was clearer about this, in the 1970s, than the Women's movement. In the first place, they saw how women were relatively excluded from producing in many of the arts, or relegated to minor roles. But worse in a way, many women were acquiescing in the prevailing social construction of their 'limited artistic capacities'. New institutional foundations had to be built – Women's Studies, for a start. And 'resistant' readings had to be invented to counter the dominant masculine voice of so many texts.

This was not as simple as it looked at first. As a sixth-former of the time, Alison Light can remember arguing in the margins with Kate Millett, but using her – as a 'decidedly eccentric authority on *Sons and Lovers*, my A level text':

> In my own reading at seventeen I identified desperately with Miriam, and contrived to reject Paul even though I was well aware that I was often reading against the grain. My objections, however, [to Millett's insistence on seeing the arrogant Paul Morel as simply Lawrence's mouthpiece] point to my recognition that if Lawrence *is* Paul, he is also Paul's mother and girl-friends, and if, as Millett does, we take their part, we haven't somehow escaped Lawrence but exposed the way in which novels, as constructs of the imagination, might be attempts at 'ungendering', and, however unsuccessful, at dispersing or even at transgressing the gendered experience of an author and its usual constraints. *I suspected that it was these displacements, contradictions, and tensions which I enjoyed in following a narrative.*
>
> (in Mary Eagleton 1986: 178, my emphasis)

Displacements, contradictions and tensions in reading

A new, more discerning way of reading was being registered, authorised and developed, then. Readers no longer had to be innocent: they could be rebels against socially inculcated practices, conventions and assumptions. The practice of reading could be socially 'critical', and this meant a new kind of attention to ambiguous potentials in language – to struggles that might have gone into women's novels, for instance, as well as those of men like Lawrence.

There were many difficulties: even those in the Movement, who had experienced a shift of consciousness, felt that they had continually to work against the grain. In a world dominated by masculinity and patriarchy, it was hard to produce an alternative voice – beyond femininity. The very moulds of discourse seemed set in antagonistic forms.

It was all the more vital, then, to grasp how conscious and unconscious processes were being shaped and distorted by gender in the primary institutions: the family and school.

Not that the analysis could stop with gender. Some children's parents were black, some manual workers, some 'immigrants' holding as fast as they could to their cultural roots. Whose voices did each of them want – and need – to hear in the arts? How were they to read the dominant voices of upper- and middle-class white English masculinity?

We could put it this way. Ethnicity, class and gender are inevitably present in the taken-for-granted 'knowledge' that lies behind the production of every text, and in the answering 'knowledge' that readers for their part call up as relevant. Why is this so? Because literature, television, film and other arts characteristically draw on knowledge in the form of social 'experiences' – remembered events and images that were structured by thoughts, feelings, attitudes, evaluations, dispositions to act... And these are precisely the things that are being verbally constructed, organised and inculcated every day in the family, the school, and other institutional settings.

Admittedly, such everyday accounts were likely to be 'polyphonic' and 'unsystematized' ideologically – two ideas that began to spread in the later 1970s after more of the Bakhtin circle had been translated. Everyday constructions would often incorporate the contested meanings of social events, from the perspectives of both dominant and subordinated groups. This socially formed 'knowledge', then, could indeed be expected to include 'tensions', 'displacements' and 'contradictions', and that fact set a new agenda for theories and investigations of reading or production.

But then the question followed: what selection of texts should students be reading – or producing – in literary and cultural studies?

Selecting 'texts' and studying readings

Authoritative commentary on authorised texts: this is where the universities began in the 12th century. Even in the 1870s, when Tom

Green began to develop a social philosophy of his own, and to elaborate it publicly in Balliol College, Benjamin Jowett – his old ally and one-time tutor – was deeply concerned. 'Philosophy' should mean the analytic discussion of established texts, not inciting people to philosophise. Ironically, by the time Richards was attending Moore's lectures in 1914, this time-hallowed situation had almost been reversed: only philosophising counted – and the work of former philosophers was treated largely as error. There was more than a touch of this attitude in Moore's pupil, I must say.

Thus, it is not surprising to find that in the 1920s, Richards and Forbes produced no critical writing on canonical texts at all, despite the current grip of 'English Language and Literature'. Nor did Tillyard, till he finally capitulated in 1929. Richards's main lectures were on theory of criticism, typically a meta-subject. And the poems his students recall him bringing in were equally typically contemporary and modernist. 'In my first year Yeats's volume *The Tower* came out,' Muriel Bradbrook remembers, 'and Richards lectured on it immediately. This felt like the birth of a new poet' (1973: 64 – see Part II). Before her time the poet had been Eliot or Hopkins (finally published in 1918).

For Richards, the question of an authorised canon did not arise, in effect. On the contrary, he was explicitly calling for the serious study – somewhere or other – of popular writing, best-sellers, the press, the cinema, advertising... And to steer such studies, he was proposing a new meta-subject, the experimental investigation of cultural responses. The focus was to be on signs like 'Your Country' or 'Love', together with the sentiments and dispositions they were used to organise on specific occasions. (I suppose today he would add 'Englishness'.)

Even Forbes, who lectured on historically recognisable periods, was, unconsciously or not, iconoclastic in a different way. When he expected his students to write poems, and submitted his own to them, he was tacitly demonstrating the relevance of a new kind of text to courses on English life, literature and thought. And Q, plugging for 'the English Moralists' in 1925, equally hoped that the young men who attended would learn to write.

So far as I know, however, none of these profound issues surfaced in public at the time. They lay buried for over thirty years, finally being raised in the mid-1960s, and initially in secondary schools.

There, younger students were learning to dramatise texts (and improvise on their themes); to write in emulation of them (and from oral traditions); and to choose, discuss and study them without the expectations of going on to produce a formulaic type of 'essay'. A renaissance in 'children's literature' stimulated and responded to this new tradition, from the 1960s on. By the later 1970s many of its leading writers were women, some black, some working class in origin. And within the schools some teachers were including modern media production alongside print. But post-16 (in the sixth) and on entry to higher education, this situation was normally reversed. Texts were set and were treated as canonical. They were grouped in historical 'periods'. And there the syllabus often ended.

Why? – schoolteachers learned to ask. What gave those texts their privileged position? What social classes had originally given them their focus? What ideological interests and tensions did they articulate then – and now?

There had already been fragmentary attempts to construct historical answers. For example, since the 1950s Ian Watt had analysed the ideological attractions, first of Defoe, later of the 18th century novel in general, for a rising middle class. But it was not until the 1970s that such work began to be incorporated into a tradition.

Thus, as Wolff recalls, by 1978 Raymond Williams had made a new effort to relate social experience, ideology and literary form in the complex period around 1848. At that moment of social crisis, he had showed,

> there is a new recognition in literature of class relations and class conflict; there is a new emphasis on the subjectivity of experience. But the emergent elements co-exist with other, more traditional, elements in the realist novel. In formal terms, this tension is expressed by the relative abandonment of the dominant authorial voice (whether first or third person).
>
> (Wolff 1981: 299)

On this view, I would suggest, new recognitions and polyphonies in middle-class constructions of everyday experience were setting up the conditions for new options in literary form. Moreover, Wolff continues:

> What Williams demonstrates about that particular period is, I think, true to a large extent of all complex cultural products. Unless the rules and conventions of literary and artistic production are very tightly defined and circumscribed, which is not the case in contemporary industrial societies, then texts will be the arena for the play of diverse, and perhaps conflicting, ideologies and voices.
>
> (pp.124–5)

Which ideologies, in the 1970s? First, for women everywhere, forms of patriarchy; for subordinated classes in Europe, the traditional forms of capitalism and the emergent forms of multinational corporatism; for 'immigrant workers' and their 'Third World' homelands, the developing forms of imperialism – economic, social and cultural.

There was one place where these ideologies seemed bound to dominate production: the complex institutions of 20th century media. In fact, as we have seen, by the mid-1960s the US political elite was being offered the prospect of world-wide domination through those media. Culturally, at least, by 1980 that domination was well on its way.

For those interested in power – but not university English departments – the audio-visual media were recognised to be the 'emergent' cultural institutions, to borrow Williams's terms; publishing, the 'residual' form, was increasingly going to follow in their wake (Booker-prized, you might say).

Nevertheless, the people engaged in British television planning, programming and production, say, were rarely the mere ideological agents of power. Their role *vis-à-vis* dominant and subordinated voices was usually much less direct, mediated by further 'professional' structures. So much had been made clear as early as 1970, in the analysis of the 'Grosvenor Square demonstration' and the process of reporting it.

Why was it that 'after relatively few incidents of confrontation between police and demonstrators' five out of the six national dailies in the study fulfilled their own predictions by giving front-page coverage to a photo 'of a policeman apparently being held by one demonstrator and kicked in the face by another'? And why did they not picture or report two demonstrators who immediately went to protect him? The Leicester University team had traced the whole process from the events to the journalistic decisions. 'The selections made are the logical outcome', they summed up, 'of particular ways of working and of a shared set of criteria of what makes material newsworthy' (Murdock 1973).

How about the readers, audiences and viewers, though? What tacit experience were they bringing to bear? Surely some of it would affect what they made of the categories, events, images and reports they were offered? Further, was their 'viewing and listening' being institutionally structured in various ways – and, if so, with what effects? Thus, what role were the audio-visual media playing in the structuring of people's social experience and the taken-for-granted knowledge many of us were drawing on? Unfortunately, for lack of VTRs, there were no comparable investigations, at the time. Worse, many analyses tended to exclude the complex effects of viewers' resistances, of the irony and parody that help keep power at bay, of oppositional ideologies, or of the tensions and sometimes contradictory potentials waiting to be released in audio-visual signs.

Nevertheless, crucial discoveries were made. The unconscious shaping of speaker and listener, of reader and writer, of production teams and audiences: this was on the agenda. Three kinds of structuring – by ethnicity, class and gender – were being actively explored. Exclusion and inclusion in the practices of the arts was being fiercely contested.

Just as the solitary reader was an analytic fiction, so – it turned out – was the solitary 'individual'. For in certain respects, as we have seen, the consciousness of both sides is penetrated, and constituted, by dialogue with others. And the crucial dialogues were taking place in institutional and historical settings: the family, school, workplace... watching television at home, reading for essays...

What we should be studying, in that case, was 'the living socially embedded utterance in context' (Wolff 1981: 64) – and that implied a person engaged in, committed to, social interaction through the medium of 'texts'.

Potentials to develop

The 1960s and 1970s, then, were a period rich in potential, much of which – I feel – is still in danger of being overlooked or relegated in higher education. Drawing together many, varied strands of achievement in the UK, I would want to include the following:

(a) Students became producers in the arts, not simply readers or viewers. In a renewal of democratic confidence, oral traditions of story-telling were recognised and celebrated; scenes were improvised and scripted; poems and stories were written by the academically 'rejected'. The conditions of existence of the arts were shifted and a new 'republic of letters' glimpsed.

(b) Stories and lyric moments in serious conversation were seen as a human propensity, a social foundation for the more crystallised products of the arts. Everyday narratives were potentially reshaping and revising a personal and social world; inner speech added dreams and suppressed, divergent perceptions; both interacted with stories and themes from radio or television, as well as literature in the broadest sense. Empowering students in that process of interaction with dominating cultural institutions was a necessary priority for literary and cultural studies in a democracy.

(c) Thus, Education could institutionally foster the discussion invited by the novel and all its related forms, including some of the stories from News and Documentary. Students could learn to respond, from their social and personal experience, to the possibilities, interests and evaluations offered in a book, a play, a film, a news extract...

(d) As they did so, they had to learn to question the categories and tacit assumptions that framed both the play etc. and their own immediate reactions. How adequate were these to the wider historical and social activity they were progressively engaged in?

What were the limits to their explanatory power, in the construction of social experience?
(e) Thus, both production and response – in its increasingly varied, active forms – were seen as provisional constructions. Models or hypotheses of this kind were principally set up to cope with the complexities of everyday social living and interaction. Through reflection and synthesis, they were organising and steering longer-term paths through life for self and others. Such everyday knowledge began to be studied, especially among women, and related to categories of theory – a crystallised product.
(f) Behind every course in literary and cultural studies, in that case, lay tacit or explicit constructions of learning, studying, teaching and investigating, including the appropriate social relation and context for these activities. Many of them had to be challenged. Thus, teachers and students started to try out, criticise and develop new discursive opportunities, in group discussion, in writing and in response: but these transformations entailed rejecting the dominating role for teachers and the severely constraining context that an archaic exam tradition still sustained.
(g) From this perspective, texts were not authoritative and canonical monuments, but voices in a dialogue. Their plural potential left room for desired readings to be selected, and for critical readings to liberate writer and reader from engrained assumptions – about gender, class and ethnicity, for example. At the same time, the care taken in construction on the writer's behalf opened the reader to new potentials in experience.
(h) Teachers' responses too had to be dialogic, oriented to positive elements in the students' thinking. Teachers and fellow students could suggest scope for further learning and prompt emerging directions for study, but without appearing infallible – leaving the way open for revision, negotiation and choice.
(i) Linguistic, iconic and enactive signs did not serve as bits of information; instead, within rather fuzzy constraints, they were cues for construction by readers and viewers. Readers should properly see themselves as constructing in the first place on the writer's behalf. But a secondary, dialogic form of construction was inevitable as incoming signs were integrated with personal knowledge – experiences, thoughts and dispositions already organised by signs.
(j) These sets of signs, these processes of construction, and the dialogues they served were all structured by specific speech communities; by publishing and broadcasting institutions; by traditions of writing, reading and viewing; and by social

conventions and assumptions that underlay whatever generic strategies were in favour.

So literary and cultural studies had recurrently to bring into the open the conditions of existence for all these practices, and to analyse their organising forces in a given historical era – including the present, the moment when student and teacher are themselves producing texts and readings.

AFTERWORD

Lessons for the future?

Placing the cultural historian

History, said Walter Bagehot in a sceptical review of Gibbon, 'may be generally defined as a view of one age taken by another'. Thus, 'there are two topics of interest – the [historian] as a type of the age in which he lives, – the events and manners of the age he is describing; very often almost all the interest is in the contrast of the two' (1856). It was a very useful reminder.

So how about the manners and interests of the current age: how have they shaped the events described in these three episodes? To begin with, writing as I do in 1990, I have been trying to represent democratic traditions in their struggles with institutions dominated by a powerful elite. This accounts for my choice of three periods when students in higher education longed for something better and different, when there were teachers prepared to respond, and when an institutional break was possible.

This is not the whole story – I am far from pretending that. To begin with, important ideas and practices have been passed over: in the 1930s, 1950s and 1980s especially. But, in their case, the structures and conditions were far less enabling, I would claim; thus the degree of distortion those latent movements have suffered, and are still suffering. Crucially, they lacked the ardent support and challenge of a new body of students.

Of course, the aspirations represented here are also far from fulfilled in 1990; the struggle has a long way to go. That's not surprising: most people in Education have spent the last decade wintering out. Ironically, it was a wave of 'voluntary redundancy' that gave me the chance to write this book, though it did not stop me thinking about the millions who ended up on the dole instead. However, I assume that the current regime will not go on indefinitely. Symptomatically, there is already talk of doubling or tripling the chances of higher education in the UK. But in whose interests? That question has been at the back of my mind throughout this account, shaping my story.

What institutional structures could give the majority the hope and conviction that their education in the 21st century will be lifelong, not cut short at 16 or 17? Something pretty different from the norms we have now, surely? Just imagine what they might expect: a curriculum that has direct meaning to them; ways of learning, investigating and teaching each other that excite their latent interests; teachers capable of questioning and analysing their own elite formation; institutional structures which assign power to students, together with their teachers, as a start. All these things would have to be considered afresh, as I've learned from friends in London and Yorkshire schools, and in teacher education across the English-speaking world.

Traditions still to be drawn on

If change is needed, it may not be easy, then: what experience has the next generation in higher education to draw on? There are relevant traditions of lasting importance, I believe, especially among those sketched here.

Take the first obstacle that faces the 17–18-year-old thinking of higher education: the pre-university exams and especially the standard A Level papers in English Literature. The practices and conditions of this formative system run contrary to almost everything I have recorded in this book. Even to Bradley and Moulton they would surely appear narrow, superficial and oppressive. Why ask students to write about the experience of literature without having the text by them? Why demand generalised argument — about concrete, dramatic experiences? Why keep exclusively to writers from the UK?... An exam system of this type, whether for entry to higher education or as the climax of a degree course, doesn't even live up to our best teachers of the 1890s, to go no further.

Take the next issue, for generations brought up in a culture of television and radio as well as books: where are the places in 'English' beyond 16 for contemporary media? By 1925 Richards already knew that the formative media in a society had to be studied. Within social consciousness, their operations are pervasive, not separable. Thus, Harding had already pointed a generation ago to a continuum in stories – whether printed, listened to, or viewed. What's more, both Richards and Harding had realised that a study of signs in itself was inadequate; there must be investigations of interpreters and their diverse responses. These would reveal the way traditional and innovating media were organising sentiments, dispositions and so forth. So, on behalf of tomorrow's students I must ask: why is this tradition still neglected?

A further issue, of equal importance. Since the 1960s teachers have been able to watch films of young primary children or hardened Borstal boys producing drama and language of indisputable quality. And they have read with their classes writing of similar quality, produced in school. Why are these kinds of productive work excluded in standard A Levels, and in much that follows after them? Can anyone with democratic hopes for education today run the risk of forming consumers – and not producers?

Here are three key places, then, where I believe that voices of the past speak directly to the present. Inevitably their pioneering work will need to be developed and at times transformed. So much the better. But this, in turn, will depend on deepening our disciplinary understanding. Here again, I claim that the same movements have something to offer.

I'll foreground, for the moment, cultural history, social dialogue, and signs in use. I began, you will remember, with the students' need to place any course in literary and cultural studies: to recognise how institutions have shaped the practices they are engaged in. How can students learn to place both production and response – their own today and those of the past? By 1904 Stephen had introduced an explanatory model that showed how thriving production in the arts depended, in specific ways, on the projects of a rising class, and their close relations with writers and readers. This model also accounted for the fact that, at specific times, literary production – and readerships – split and differentiated, perhaps liberating voices from below. It was the 18th century that was in view, but surely there were lessons for the 20th?

Better, by the 1970s women's groups had made it clear that the social context of reception for the arts would be equally important – and that gender and ethnicity, at least, must be integrated into the analysis. I am not claiming that this modelling is somehow finished. There is every reason to encourage a continuing argument, let's agree, about historical framing – and this book is itself just part of such an argument. But where do these interests appear in standard A Level Literature – and how widely and steadily are they explored beyond that stage? (Where are the gaps in A Level still being authorised?)

Finally, social dialogue and signs in use. The challenge is there, still, in the *Cambridge Magazine* of 1920. It was valuably extended, and more subtly theorised, by the Bakhtin circle. By the 1970s, Halliday, Labov, Dell Hymes, Barnes and others were actually reworking these traditions, consciously or not. The results constitute a searching critique not simply of UK practices in reading and criticism, but equally of current analytic frames derived from structuralism and all that followed it.

Without some theory of signs within dialogic constructions, how can literary studies claim a secure foundation, I wonder. And the theory of verbal interaction must affect all other signs. How can audio-visuals – with their enactive and iconic signs – be dealt with adequately without taking account of inner speech?

It has been clear since Forbes and Richards, I would claim, that students whose attention is not drawn to signs in action are not getting to grips with fundamentals. So why is this study still excluded from standard A Level Literature – and much that goes on after it?

Necessary institutional structures

There are two remaining areas where higher education stands to learn from the experience of schools, colleges and polytechnics in the 1960s and 1970s. Both concern the institutional support needed when new curricula are pioneered.

What Bradley, Collins, Moulton and the others conspicuously lacked was a centre for discussion of developing courses and theoretical exchange. There was neither a place nor a journal. Ogden, Richards, Wood and the like had at least a journal, but there was no institutional recognition at Cambridge that their investigations could potentially have far-reaching repercussions on existing syllabuses. Yet in the 1970s many schools had an active role in pilot curricular experiments, and as late as 1975 central teams were set up in an effort to develop alternative programmes for education post-16. (One of those national teams, of which I was a member, encouraged teachers to produce three different types of alternative to A Level Literature, for instance. Why none of these has yet become the mainstream is another story.)

Today, then, it would seem folly to expect individual departments to meet the demands of a new range of students. Joint planning of courses among sufficiently like-minded groups would be a vital preliminary. Discussion and joint evaluation of pilot projects would have to follow, using video and other documentation to study what actually went on. What were students getting out of it – what range of experience, expertise, understanding, and productive abilities...? This would be the key question. And – a question about which current syllabuses are uniformly silent – what developments in their thinking, imagining and discussing would be showing up in the course of three years? What would count as signs of progress?

Such curricular experiments are actually not expensive. The Schools Council rarely if ever had more than ten people seconded full-time to work on the field of English, covering students aged 3–18. (And they were responsible overall to something like 150,000 teachers.) Given the will, literary and cultural studies in higher education would need a similar number – not to produce blueprints, but to inform, co-ordinate and service groups of departmental teams. CNAA already has methods for overviewing the outcomes of such work and the curriculum guides that would need to be produced.

Education post-18 would be a new field for such ventures, it's true, and the cuts and stabs of the 1980s have hardly encouraged such hopes. Nevertheless, like Sir Claus Moser in his recent address to the British Association, I wonder how much longer Britain can afford to sink behind the rest of Europe (not to mention Australasia and North America). Some day soon the real costs of short-term accountancy and draconian management are going to be brought home.

I have mentioned teaching and learning earlier, and perhaps I should end with them. While higher education catered for a select elite, some teachers – like their 19th century predecessors – could live a charmed life. Students well grounded in school could pretty well teach themselves, especially if their essays were generally to be modelled on existing books and articles. If higher education is going to welcome something like the majority, whether at 18+ or better as mature students, this sheltered existence won't continue. And for teachers who are intellectually open, it will be no great loss.

The simplicity of the language of Bradley, Moulton... Rosenblatt, Wolff and many of the rest – taken at their best – speaks of an effort to cut through to fundamentals, to seize the central problems of the day, and to do so by thinking closely about everyday experience. This was their response to students with unprecedented cultural expectations. Women's associations, Rochdale Pioneers, Mechanics' Institutes, colliery village groups... brought people before them who called for fresh thinking. After the havoc of the Great War, Ogden and Richards had similar people in mind – across the world. Will it happen again? It may: but only if readers of books like this are determined, when a chance emerges, to go out and create a new class of students – in dialogue with them.

Bibliography and references

General

Baldick, C. (1983) *The Social Mission of English Criticism 1848–1932*, Oxford: Clarendon Press.
Doyle, B. (1989) *English and Englishness*, London: Routledge.
Eagleton, T. (1983) *Literary Theory*, Oxford: Blackwell.
Graff, G. (1987) *Professing Literature*, Chicago: University of Chicago Press.
Hawkes, T. (1986) *That Shakespeherian Rag*, London: Methuen.
Palmer, D. S. (1965) *The Rise of English Studies*, Oxford: Oxford University Press.
Potter, S. (1937) *The Muse in Chains*, London: Cape.

Part I The University Extension 1867–92

Armitage, W. H. G. (1955) *Civic Universities*, London: Benn.
Arnold, Mary (see Ward, M. H.).
Association for the Education of Women in Oxford (1892–1920) Reports, Bodleian Library GA Oxon 8 1123.
Bradley, A. C. (1868–72) Contributions to *The Miscellany*, Bodleian Library, MSS Don.e.35.
—— (1880) 'Aristotle's conception of the state', in E. Abbott ed. *Hellenica*, London: Rivingtons.
—— (1881) Testimonials in favour of A.C.B.... for Liverpool, Bodleian Library, Gough Adds.
—— (1884) The Study of Poetry... a lecture, Bodleian Library 3966 e.5.
—— (1889) Poetry and Life: an inaugural lecture, Bodleian Library 3966 e.13.
—— (1889) The Nature of Tragedy, British Library.
—— (n.d.) Lectures on English Literature, Bodleian Library, MS Eng. Misc. e.860.
—— (1891) The Teaching of English Literature, Balliol College Library.
—— (1901) *A Commentary on Tennyson's 'In Memoriam'*, London: Macmillan.
—— (1904) *Shakespearean Tragedy*, London: Macmillan.
—— (1909) *Oxford Lectures on Poetry*, London: Macmillan.

Brown, J. C. (1892) *First Page of the History of University College, Liverpool*, Liverpool.
Butler, J. E. (ed.) (1868) *Women's Work and Women's Culture*, London: Macmillan.
—— (1892) *Recollections of George Butler*, Bristol: Arrowsmith.
—— (1928) *An Autobiographical Memoir*, ed. G. W. and L. A. Johnson, 3rd edn, London: Arrowsmith.
Caton, R. (ed.) (1907) *The Making of the University*, Liverpool: Liverpool University.
Clarendon Report (1864) *Revenues and Management of [Nine Public Schools]*, Royal Commission Report.
Clough, B. A. (1897) *Memoir of Anne J. Clough*, London: Arnold.
Cole, G. D. H. (1944) *A Century of Co-operation*, Manchester: Co-op Union Ltd.
Collins, J. C. (1888) *Hints for the Systematic Study of Elizabethan Literature*, Boldeian Lib. 2693 e. [1].
—— (1891) *The Study of English Literature*, London: Macmillan.
—— (1891) *Illustrations of Tennyson*, London: Chatto.
—— (1895) *Essays and Studies*, London: Macmillan.
—— (1903) *Studies in Shakespeare*, London: Constable.
Collins, L. C. (1912) *Life and Memoirs of J. C. Collins*, London: John Lane.
Cooke, K. (1972) *A. C. Bradley and his Influence*, Oxford: Oxford University Press.
Courthope, W. J. (1895) *A History of English Poetry* Vol.1, London: Macmillan.
Creighton, L. (ed.) (1902) *Mandell Creighton: Thoughts on Education*, London: Longmans.
—— (1904) *Life and Letters of Mandell Creighton*, London: Longmans.
Cunningham, A. (1950) *William Cunningham*, London: SPCK.
Davie, G. E. (1961) *The Democratic Intellect*, Edinburgh; Edinburgh University Press.
Dixon, J. (1989) 'If it's narrative, why do nothing but generalise?', in R. Andrews (ed.) *Narrative and Argument*, Milton Keynes: Open University Press.
Dixon, J. and Freedman, A. *Levels of Abstracting*, Ottawa: Carleton University Occasional Papers.
Dobson, H. A. (ed. W. H. Griffin) (1897) *Civil Service Handbook of English Literature*, London: Crosby Lockwood.
Elton, O. (1906) *Frederick York Powell*, Oxford: Clarendon Press.
Farnell, L. R. (1934) *An Oxonian Looks Back*, London: Martin Hopkinson.
Firth, C. H. (1909) *The School of English Language and Literature*, Oxford: Blackwell.
Gardner, P. (1903) *Oxford at the Crossroads*, London: A. & C. Black.
Garvin, J. L. (1932) *The Life of Joseph Chamberlain*, London: Macmillan.
Gissing, G. (1892) *Born in Exile*, London, A. & C. Black.
—— (1898) *Charles Dickens: a Critical Study*, London; Blackie.
Green, T. H. (ed. A. C. Bradley) (1883) *Prolegomena to Ethics*, Oxford; Oxford University Press.
Gross, J. (1969) *The Rise and Fall of the Man of Letters*, London: Weidenfeld.
Herdman, W. (1907) in Caton, R. (ed.) *The Making of the University*, Liverpool: Liverpool University.
Hodgson, S. (ed.) (1943) *Ramsay Muir*, London: Lund Humphries.

Holyoake, G. J. (1875–7) *History of Co-operation*, Manchester.
—— (1893) *Self-help by the People*, London: Swan Sonnenschein.
Jepson, N. A. (1973) *The Beginnings of English University Adult Education*, London: Joseph.
Johnson, B. J. (1923) 'First Beginnings 1873–90', in G. Bailey (ed.) *Lady Margaret Hall: a Short History*, Oxford: Oxford University Press.
—— (1938) in R. F. Butler and M. H. Pritchard (eds) *The Society of Oxford Home Students*, Oxford: Oxonian Press.
Jones, D. R. (1988) *The Beginning of the Civic Universities*, London: Routledge.
Kelly, T. (1960) *Adult Education in Liverpool*, Liverpool: Liverpool University Press.
—— (1981) *The University of Liverpool 1881–1981*, Liverpool: Liverpool University Press.
Lodge, O. (1881) Introductory Address, Liverpool University, British Library.
—— (1882–1930) A collection of articles, British Library.
—— (1931) *Past Years*, London: Hodder and Stoughton.
Luce, M. E. (1908) *Memories* [of J. C. Collins], Eton College: Spottiswoode.
MacCunn, J. (1907) *Six Radical Thinkers*, London: Arnold.
—— (1911) *Liverpool Addresses on Ethics*, London: Constable.
Mackail, J. W. (1936) 'A. C. Bradley', *Proc. British Academy* XXI.
Mackay, J. M. (1914) *A Miscellany Presented to J. M. Mackay*, Liverpool: Constable.
Mackinder, H. and Sadler, M. (1891) *University Extension, Past, Present and Future*, London: Cassell.
Marriot, S. (1984) *Extra-mural Empires 1875–1983*, Nottingham: Nottingham University Press.
Moulton, R. G. (1884) Illustrations to Lectures, British Library.
—— (1885) *Shakespeare as a Dramatic Artist*, Oxford: Clarendon Press.
—— (1887) *The University Extension Movement*, London: Bemrose.
—— (1890) *The Ancient Classical Drama*, Oxford: Clarendon Press.
—— (1891) Syllabus: A Literary Study of the Bible, British Library.
—— (1891) Oxford Extension Fourth Summer meeting: Interpretative Recital, Oxford.
—— (1895) *Years of Novel Reading*, London and Boston: Heath.
—— (1903) *The Moral System of Shakespeare*, London and New York: Macmillan.
—— (1911) *World Literature and its Place in General Culture* (2nd edn 1915) New York: Macmillan.
Moulton, W. F. (1926) *R. G. Moulton: A Memoir*, London: Epworth.
Nettleship, R. N. (ed. A. C. Bradley) (1897) *Philosophical Lectures and Remains*, London: Macmillan.
Oxford University Calendar 1896–7 (Exam results).
Oxford University Gazette 1895–6 (Schedules of Lectures).
Oxford University Honour School of English Language and Literature (1896–) Schools' Examination papers, Bodleian Library 2626 e. 267.
Pattison, M. (1868) *Suggestions on Academical Organisation*, Edinburgh: Edmonston and Douglas.
Powell, F. Y. (1889) Syllabus for the Home Study of Shakespeare, Bodleian Library, M. adds. 35.e.15.
Rathbone, E. (1905) *William Rathbone*, London: Macmillan.
Rendall, G. H. (1882) Inaugural Address, Liverpool University College, British Library.

Richter, M. (1964) *The Politics of Conscience: T. H. Green and his Age*, London: Weidenfeld.
Roberts, R. D. (1893) 'University extension, its past and its future', Cambridge: Cambridge University Press.
Sadleir, M. (1949) *Michael Ernest Sadler*, London: Constable.
Saintsbury, G. (1896) *A History of Nineteenth Century Literature*, London: Macmillan.
Sheavyn, P. (1909) *The Literary Profession in the Elizabethan Age*, Manchester: Manchester University Press.
Sidgwick, A. and Sidgwick, E. M. (1906) *Henry Sidgwick*, London: Macmillan.
Slee, P. R. H. (1986) *Learning and a Liberal Education*, Manchester: Manchester University Press.
Stephen, L. (1904) *English Literature and Society in the Eighteenth Century*, London: Duckworth (see 1927 edn for refs.).
Stuart, J. (1868) *Six Lectures to Workmen of Crewe*, Cambridge (private, British Library).
—— (1889) 'An inaugural address' in *Reminiscences* (1912) below.
—— (1912) *Reminiscences*, London (private, British Library).
Taunton Report (1868) *The [Endowed] School Enquiry*, Royal Commission Report.
Toynbee, A. (1884) *Lectures on the Industrial Revolution in England*, London: Rivingtons.
Tropp, A. (1957) *The School Teachers*, London: Heinemann.
Ward, M. H. (1873–6) Notebook of Oxford Lectures for Ladies, Committee Minutes, Bodleian Lib., Oxon e. 537.
—— (1888) *Robert Elsmere*, London: Smith and Elder.
—— (1918) *A Writer's Recollections*, London and New York: Harper.
Ward, W. R. (1965) *Victorian Oxford*, London: Frank Cass.

Part II Cambridge 1919–29

Ayer, A. J. (ed.) (1968) *The Humanist Outlook*, London: Barrie and Rockliff.
Bennett, J. (1973) in Brower, R., et al. (eds) *I. A. Richards*, New York: Oxford University Press.
Benson, A. C. (1917) *Cambridge Essays in Education*, Cambridge: Cambridge University Press.
Bradbrook, M. (1973) in Brower, R., et al. (eds) *I. A. Richards*, New York: Oxford University Press.
Brittain, F. (1947) *A. Quiller-Couch*, Cambridge: Cambridge University Press.
Brower, R., Vendler, H. and Hollander, J. (eds) (1973) *I. A. Richards*, New York: Oxford University Press.
Cambridge Review 1916–21.
Carey, H. (1984) *Mansfield Forbes*, Cambridge: Cambridge University Press.
Empson, W. (1930) *Seven Types of Ambiguity*, London: Chatto (revised: see Penguin edn 1961 for page refs).
—— (1952) *The Structure of Complex Words*, London: Chatto.
—— (1988) *Argufying: Essays on Literature and Culture*, London: Hogarth.
Florence, P. S. (1968) 'The Cambridge Heretics 1909–1932', in Ayer, A. J. (ed.) *The Humanist Outlook*, London: Barrie and Rockliff.

Florence, P. S. and Anderson, J. R. L. (eds) (1977) *CKO*, London: Elek.
Ford, F. M. (1925) *No More Parades*, London (Penguin edn 1948).
Gill, R. (1974) *William Empson*, London: Routledge.
Gordon, G. S. (1943) *The Letters of G. S. Gordon*, Oxford: Oxford University Press.
Graves, R. (1922) *On English Poetry*, London: Heinemann.
—— (1929) *Good-bye to All That*, London: Cape.
Graves, R. and Hodge, A. (1940) *The Long Weekend*, London: Hutchinson.
Harding, D. W. (1933) 'I. A. Richards', *Scrutiny*, Vol. I.
Hayman, R. (1976) *Leavis*, London: Heinemann.
Homberger, E., Janeway, W. and Schama, S. (eds) (1970) *The Cambridge Mind*, Boston: Little, Brown.
Hotopf, W. H. N. (1965) *Language, Thought and Comprehension*, London: Routledge.
Howarth, T. E. B. (1978) *Cambridge between Two Wars*, London: Collins.
Jackson, G. H. (1932) *Selected Writings* Vol. 2, London: Hodder.
Knights, L. C. (1937) *Drama and Society in the Age of Jonson*, London: Chatto.
Leavis, F. R. (1943) *Education and the University*, London: Chatto.
Leavis, F. R. and Thompson, D. (1933) *Culture and Environment*, London: Chatto.
Leavis, Q. D. (1932) *Fiction and the Reading Public*, London: Chatto.
—— (1943) 'The discipline of letters', *Scrutiny*, Vol. XII.
—— (1947) 'Professor Chadwick and English Studies', *Scrutiny*, Vol. XIV.
Lekachman, R. (1967) *The Age of Keynes*, London: Penguin.
Levy, P. (1980) *Moore: G. E. Moore and the Cambridge Apostles*, Oxford: Oxford University Press.
Lucas, F. L. (1926) *Authors Dead and Living*, London: Chatto.
—— (1933) Criticism of Poetry, Warton Lecture, British Library.
Malinowski, B. (1923) 'The problem of meaning', in Ogden and Richards (1923).
Marwick, A. (1965) *The Deluge*, London: Bodley Head.
Mulhern, F. (1979) *The Moment of Scrutiny*, London: Verso.
Ogden, C. K. (1915) *Militarism versus Feminism* (1987 edn), London: Virago.
—— (ed.) (1913–19) *The Cambridge Magazine* (weekly).
—— (ed.) (1920–3) *The Cambridge Magazine* (quarterly).
—— (1921–9) *Psyche*: a quarterly review.
Ogden, C. K. and Richards, I. A. (1920) 'Symbolism', *Cambridge Magazine* 10: 1.
—— (1921) 'The art of conversation', *Cambridge Magazine* 10: 2.
—— (1921) 'On talking', *Cambridge Magazine* 11: 1.
—— (1923) *The Meaning of Meaning*, London: Kegan Paul.
Ogden, C. K., Richards, I. A. and Wood, J. (1922) *The Foundations of Aesthetics*, London: Allen and Unwin.
O'Malley, R. (1984) in Thompson, D. (ed.) *The Leavises*, Cambridge: Cambridge University Press.
Peirce, C. S. and Welby-Gregory, V. (1977) *Semiotics and Significs*, Bloomington: Indiana University Press.
Phillips, A. (ed.) (1979) *A Newnham Anthology*, Cambridge: Cambridge University Press.
Quiller-Couch, A. (1944) *Memories and Opinions*, Cambridge: Cambridge University Press.
Richards, I. A. (1919) 'Art and science', *Atheneum*, 27 June.

—— (1919) 'Emotion and art', *Atheneum*, 18 July, (collected in *Complementaries* 1976).
—— (1924) *Principles of Literary Criticism*, London: Kegan Paul.
—— (1926) *Science and Poetry*, London: Kegan Paul.
—— (1929) *Practical Criticism*, London: Kegan Paul.
—— (1932) *Mencius on the Mind: Experiments in Multiple Definition*, London: Kegan Paul.
—— (1976) *Complementaries: Uncollected Essays*, Cambridge, Mass.: Harvard University Press.
Riding, L. and Graves, R. (1927) *A Survey of Modernist Poetry*, London: Heinemann.
Russell, B. (1968) *The Autobiography of Bertrand Russell*, London: Allen and Unwin.
Russell, D. (1975) *The Tamarisk Tree* Vol. 1, London: Virago.
Russo, J. P. (1989) *I. A. Richards: his Life and Work*, London: Routledge.
Rylands, G. (1928) *Words and Poetry*, London: Hogarth.
Thompson, D. (ed.) (1984) *The Leavises*, Cambridge: Cambridge University Press.
Tillyard, E. M. W. (ed.) (1929) *The Poetry of Sir Thomas Wyat*, London: Scholartis.
—— (1958) *The Muse Unchained*, London: Bowes and Bowes.
Volosinov, V. N. (1929, trans. 1973) *Marxism and the Philosophy of Language*, New York: Seminar.
Vygotsky, L. S. (1934, trans. 1962) *Thought and Language*, Cambridge, Mass.: Massachusetts Institute of Technology.
Willey, B. (1968) *Cambridge and Other Memories 1920–53*, London: Chatto.

Part III Restructuring an elite system, 1960–79 (more selective)

Anderson, P. (1968) 'Components of the National Culture', London: New Left Review 50.
Association of Teachers in Colleges and Departments of Education (ATCDE) and Education Department, BFI (1960) Film and Television in Education.
Atkinson, J. (1969) in Nagel, J. (ed.) *Student Power*, London: Merlin Press.
Austin, J. (1962) *How to Do Things with Words*, Oxford: Oxford University Press.
Bagehot, W. (1856) 'Edward Gibbon' in (1911) *Literary Studies* Vol. 2., London: Everyman.
Barnes, D. (1976) *From Communication to Curriculum*, London: Penguin.
Barnes, D. and Todd, F. (1977) *Communication and Learning in Small Groups*, London: Routledge.
Barnes, D., Britton, J. and Rosen, H. (1969) *Language, the Learner, and the School*, London: Penguin.
Berger, J. and Mohr, J. (1967) *A Fortunate Man*, London: Penguin.
Berger, P. L., and Luckmann, T. (1967) *The Social Construction of Reality*, London: Penguin.
Bloom, L. (1970) *Language Development*, Cambridge, Mass.: Massachusetts Institute of Technology.
Blythe, R. (1969) *Akenfield*, London: Penguin.

Bourdieu, P. (1967) 'Systems of education and systems of thought', in Young, M. D. F. (ed.)(1971) *Knowledge and Control,* London: Collier Macmillan.
Britton, J. N. (1963) *Literature,* in *Studies in Education,* Evans for London Institute of Education.
—— (1970) *Language and Learning,* London: Penguin.
Britton, J., Burgess, T., Martin, N., McLeod, A. and Rosen, H. (1975) *The Development of Writing Abilities 11–18,* London: Macmillan.
Centre for Contemporary Cultural Studies (1968–79) *Annual Reports.*
—— (1971–7) *Working Papers in Cultural Studies,* 1–10.
Clements, S., Dixon, J. and Stratta, L. (1963) *Reflections,* Oxford: Oxford University Press.
Cockburn, A. and Blackburn, R. (1969) *Student Power,* London: Penguin.
Cox, C. B. and Dyson, A. E. (eds) (1969) Fight for Education: a Black Paper, *Critical Quarterly.*
Craig, D. and Heinemann, M. (1976) *Experiments in English Teaching,* London: Arnold.
D'Arcy, P. (1973) *Reading for Meaning,* Vol 2, London: Hutchinson.
Department of Education and Science (1979) *Aspects of Secondary Education,* HMSO.
Dixon, J. (1967) *Growth through English,* Oxford: Oxford University Press.
—— (1979) *Education 16–19: the Role of English and Communication,* London: Macmillan.
Dixon, J. and Brown, J. (1984/5) *Responses to Literature – What Is Being Assessed?* Schools Council Publications.
Eagleton, M. (ed.) (1986) *Feminist Literary Theory,* Oxford: Blackwell.
English in Education (Journal of the NATE) 1967–.
Flower, F. D. (1966) *Language and Education,* London: Longmans.
Friere, P. (1972) *Pedagogy of the Oppressed,* London: Penguin.
Garfinkel, H. (1967) *Studies in Ethnomethodology,* Englewood Cliffs, NJ: Prentice-Hall.
—— (1972) 'Remarks on ethnomethodology', in J. Gumperz and D. Hymes (eds) *Directions in Psycholinguistics,* New York: Holt, Rinehart.
Goodman, K. S. (1967) 'Reading: a psycholinguistic guessing game', *Journal of the Reading Specialist,* May.
Groombridge, B. (1961) *Popular Culture and Personal Responsibility,* London: National Union of Teachers.
Grugeon, E. and Walden, P. (eds) (1978) *Literature and Learning,* London: Ward Lock.
Hall, S. (1973) 'The world at one with itself', in S. Cohen and J. Young (eds) *The Manufacture of News,* London: Constable.
—— (1975) 'Introduction' to A. C. H. Smith, *Paper Voices,* London: Chatto (from the original report of 1970).
—— (ed.) (1980) *Culture, Media, Language,* London: Hutchinson.
Hall, S. and Whannel, P. (1964) *The Popular Arts,* London: Hutchinson.
Halliday, M. K. (1972) Chapter in (1978) *Language as a Social Semiotic,* London: Arnold.
—— (1974) Chapter in (1978) *Language as a Social Semiotic,* London: Arnold.
—— (1975) *Learning How to Mean,* London: Arnold.
—— (1978) *Language as Social Semiotic,* London: Arnold.

Halloran, J. D., Elliott, P. and Murdock, G. (1970) *Demonstrations and Communication*, London: Penguin.
Hanson, A. H. (1970) 'Some literature on student revolt', in B. Crick and W. A. Robson (eds) *Protest and Discontent*, London: Penguin.
Harding, D. W. (1967) 'Considered experience', *English in Education* 1: 2.
—— (1967) 'Raids on the inarticulate', *Use of English* 19: 2.
Hardy, B. (1968) 'Narrative', *Novel*, Vol. 2. 1, Providence, Rhode Island: Brown University.
—— (1976) *Tellers and Listeners*, London: Athlone.
Hoggart, R. (1957) *The Uses of Literacy*, London: Chatto.
—— (1961) 'Mass communications in Britain', in B. Ford (ed.) *Pelican Guide to English Literature* Vol. 7, London: Penguin.
—— (1963) 'Schools of English and contemporary society', in (1970) *Speaking to Each Other* Vol. 2, London: Chatto.
Jakobson, R. (1960) 'Linguistics and Poetics', in T. A. Sebeok (ed.) *Style in Language*, New York: Wiley.
Kaplan, C. (1986) *Sea Changes: Culture and Feminism*, London: Verso.
Labov, W. and Fanshel, D. (1977) *Therapeutic Discourse*, London: Academic.
Light, A. (1986) 'Feminism and the literary critic', in Eagleton, M. (ed.) *Feminist Literary Theory*, Oxford: Blackwell.
Lockwood Report (1964) *The Examining of English Language*, HMSO.
Luria, A. and Yudovich, L. (1972) *Speech and the Development of Mental Processes*, London: Penguin (reissue with preface by James Britton).
McGregor, L., Tate, M. and Robinson, K. (1977) *Learning through Drama*, London: Ward Lock.
Mead, G. H. (1934) *Mind, Self, and Society*, Chicago: University of Chicago.
Moffett, J. (1968) *Teaching the Universe of Discourse*, Boston: Houghton Mifflin.
Murdock, G. (1973) 'Political Deviance' in S. Cohen and J. Young (eds) *The Manufacture of News*, London: Constable.
Nagel, J. (ed.) (1969) *Student Power*, London: Merlin Press.
New Left Review (ed. S. Hall) (1961–2).
Norwood Report (1941) *Curriculum and Examinations in Secondary Schools*, HMSO.
Oakley, J. and Owen, E. (1982) '"English" and the CNAA', in P. Widdowson (ed.) *Re-Reading English*, London: Methuen.
Open University (1971) *School and Society*, London: Routledge.
Plumb, J. H. (ed.) (1964) *Crisis in the Humanities*, London: Penguin.
Robbins Report (1963) *Report of the Committee on Higher Education*, HMSO.
Rosenblatt, L. (1978) *The Reader, the Text, and the Poem*, Carbondale: Southern Illinois University Press.
Ruthrof, H. (1981) *The Reader's Construction of Narrative*, London: Routledge.
Schiller, H. I. (1969) *Mass Communications and American Empire*, New York: Kelley.
Schools Council (1979) *English in the 1980s*, WP 62, London: Evans/Methuen.
Shuttleworth, A. (1965) 'A humane centre', CCCS Occasional Paper.
Sinclair, J. and Coulthard, M. (1975) *Towards an Analysis of Discourse*, Oxford: Oxford University Press.
Smith, A. C. H. (1975) *Paper Voices*, London: Chatto.

Smith, F. (1973) *Psycholinguistics and Reading*, New York: Holt, Rinehart.
Spriggs, S. J. (1972) 'Doing Eng. Lit.', in T. Pateman (ed.) *Counter Course*, London: Penguin.
Squire, J. (ed.) (1968) *Response to Literature*, Urbana, Illinois: NCTE.
Steiner, G. (1965) 'To civilize our gentlemen', in (1967) *Language and Silence*, London: Penguin.
Terkel, S. (1967) *Division Street, America*, London: Penguin.
Thompson, E. P. (1963) *The Making of the English Working Class*, London: Gollancz.
Universities and Left Review (1957–9).
Wandor, M. (ed.) (1972) *The Body Politic*, London: Stage One.
Watt, I. (1951) 'Robinson Crusoe as a myth', *Essays in Criticism* (quarterly).
—— (1957) *The Rise of the Novel*, London: Chatto.
Williams, R. (1958) *Culture and Society*, London: Chatto.
—— (1961) *The Long Revolution*, London: Chatto.
—— (1962) *Communications*, London: Penguin.
—— (1974) *Television: Technology and Cultural Form*, Glasgow: Fontana.
—— (1976) *Keywords*, Glasgow: Fontana.
—— (1977) *Marxism and Literature*, Oxford: Oxford University Press.
—— (1978) 'Forms of English fiction in 1848', in Barker, F., *et al.* (eds) *Literature, Society, and the Society of Literature*, Colchester: Essex University.
—— (1979) *Politics and Letters: Interviews with N.L.R.*, London: Verso.
—— (n.d.) *Writing in Society*, London: Verso.
Wolff, J. (1981) *The Social Production of Art*, London: Macmillan.
Young, M. D. F. (ed.) (1971) *Knowledge and Control*, London: Collier Macmillan.

Name index

Acland, A., 17
Arnold, Mary (*see* Ward, M.H.)
Arnold, M., 4, 7
Atkinson, J., 172
Austin, J., 175

Bagehot, W., 209
Bakhtin, M., 135 ff, 202
Baldick, C., 2–4, 34, 57, 91, 97, 104
Barnes, D., 156, 191–3, 194, 211
Barrow, J., 48
Beard, C., 22
Bennett, J., 122
Berger, J., 161
Berger, P.L., 174–5
Black, D., (*see* Russell, D.)
Bloom, L., 191
Blythe, R., 162
Bourdieu, P., 174
Bradbrook, M., 122–3, 203
Bradley, A.C., 6, 22, 24–5, 29–31, 33–4, 39 ff, 49 ff, 57, 138, 141
Bréal, M., 93
Britton, J.N., 156, 160, 164, 191
Brower, R., 88
Brown, J., 165
Brown, J.C., 22
Bryce, J., 15
Butler, J.E., 15, 20

Carey, H., 84, 110, 121–2
Chadwick, H., 83, 91, 129–30
Clements, S., 152
Clough, B.A., 14, 20
Collins, J. C., 17, 29–31, 34, 39, 69
Coulthard, M., 156

Courthope, W.J., 63–4
Craig, D., 182
Creighton, L., 5
Creighton, M., 5
Cunningham, W., 21

Davin, A., 178
Dickens, C., 28, 57
Dickinson, G. Lowes, 82
Dixon, J., 49, 139, 165, 166, 201
Dobson, H.A., 67
Doyle, B., 3–4, 34, 36, 91, 97

Eagleton, T., 1–2, 4, 8, 33, 97, 185
Earle, J., 63
Eliot, G., 57
Eliot, T.S., 119, 125, 137
Empson, W., 124, 126–8, 194

Firth, C.H., 62–3
Fitch, J., 15
Forbes, M., 83–6, 88, 104–5, 107, 120–2, 125, 129 ff, 203, 212

Garfinkel, H., 191
Gissing, G., 57
Glehn, L. von (*see* Creighton, L.)
Goodman, K.S., 194
Gordon, G.S., 131
Graff, G., 7, 104
Graves, D., 190
Graves, R., 80, 117, 124
Green, C., 6
Green, M., 181–3
Green, T.H., 6, 16, 39, 47, 51, 61, 203
Gross, J., 131

Hall, S., 151, 152, 159–60, 167 ff, 181, 184
Halliday, M.K., 186 ff, 211
Harding, D.W., 160–1, 164, 210
Hardy, B., 161
Hawkes, T., 39
Heinemann, M., 182
Herdman, W., 24
Hoggart, R., 151, 156, 158–60
Hough, G., 153–4

Jackson, G. Hughlings, 121
Jakubinskii, L., 140
Jepson, N.A., 16
Johnson, B.J., 6
Jowett, B., 5, 61, 203

Kaplan, C., 179
Kelly, T., 22
Keynes, J.M., 82
Knights, L.C., 106, 125, 133–4

Labov, W., 191
Lasalle, F., 35, 58
Leavis, F.R., 104–5, 109, 120, 125, 128, 130, 131, 133, 153
Leavis, Q.D., 105, 122, 125, 131, 133
Light, A., 201
Littlewood, J., 152
Lodge, O., 23–5
Luckmann, T., 174–5

MacColl, E., 152
MacCunn, J., 24, 25–6
Mackay, J.M., 25
Mackinder, H., 18
Markby, T., 15
Martin, N.C., 156
Marx, K., 35, 58, 134, 136, 143, 201
Mead, G.H., 163
Medvedev, P.N., 135
Moffett, J., 162
Mohr, J., 161
Moore, G.E., 81, 91
Morley, J., 28
Moser, C., 213
Moulton, R.G., 2, 17–19, 28–31, 34–9, 46, 49, 56–7, 59
Muir, J. Ramsay, 42
Murdock, G., 205

Napier, A.S., 63
Neil, S., 19
Nettleship, R.N., 30, 46, 53

Oakley, J., 181
Ogden, C.K., 80–3, 87, 88 ff, 104, 120, 128, 137, 142 ff, 212
O'Malley, R., 104, 105, 106
Owen, E., 181

Pace, J., 104
Palmer, D.S., 62
Parker, C., 152, 161
Pater, C., 5, 6
Pater, W., 5
Pattison, F., 6
Pattison, M., 6, 27, 30, 61
Peirce, C.S., 93–4
Piaget, J., 104, 165
Plumb, J.H., 153
Powell, F. York, 33, 41

Quiller-Couch, A., [Q], 80, 82–6, 91, 203

Rathbone, W., 20–2
Reisz, K., 151
Rendall, G., 23–5
Richards, I.A., 83–7, 88 ff, 104 ff, 125, 129 ff, 135, 137, 138, 141 ff, 164, 203, 210, 212
Richardson, M., 200
Riding, L., 124
Roberts, R.D., 18–19
Rosenblatt, L., 41, 194 ff
Roth, Q.D., (see Leavis, Q.D.)
Rowbotham, S., 176 ff
Russell, B., 81
Russell, D., 89
Russo, J.P., 84, 85
Ruthrof, H., 50
Rylands, G., 128

Sadler, M., 18
Saintsbury, G., 33
Sapir, E., 96
Sassoon, S., 80–1, 109
Saussure, F. de, 93, 136
Schiller, H.I., 148
Seeger, P., 152
Selincourt, E. de, 63
Shaw, H., 19
Sheavyn, P., 70
Sinclair, J., 156
Slee, P.R.H., 64
Smith, A.C.H., 167
Smith, F., 194
Spriggs, J., 173

Squire, J., 160
Steiner, G., 153
Stephen, L., 28, 70 ff
Stewart, J. (*see* Pace, J.)
Stuart, J., 3, 14–18
Stubbs, W., 7, 62

Taine, H., 70
Teall, J., 21
Terkel, S., 162
Thompson, D., 133
Thompson, E.P., 151, 199
Thompson, P., 162
Tillyard, E.M.W., 82–5, 104, 129 ff
Todd, F., 191–3
Toynbee, A., 58

Volosinov, V.N., 135 ff, 185
Vossler, K., 136
Vygotsky, L.S., 139 ff, 163, 190

Ward, M. Humphry, 6, 58
Watt, I., 204
Wandor, M., 176 ff
Whannel, P., 152
Widdowson, P., 182
Willey, B., 82–6, 130
Williams, R., 151, 154, 155, 157, 158, 185, 187, 204
Wittgenstein, L., 87
Wood, J., 90, 92, 104
Wolff, J., 199 ff
Wyatt, A.J., 82–3

Subject index

achievements in 'English' (in summary), 58–9, 75–6, 132–3, 206–8
Association of Teachers in Colleges and Departments of Education, 158

Beerbohm's *Zuleika Dobson*, 126–8
Blake's *Songs*, 84, 86, 121
British Association for
    Advancement of Science, 28, 213
    Social Science, 28
British Film Institute, 155, 183

Cambridge
    English Tripos (1926), 124, 129–30
    ex-service students, 79–80
    Extension syndicate, 17
    Girton College, 20
    Heretics Club, 80, 120
    Local Exams Syndicate, 23
    Magdalene College, 82, 90
    Modern Languages degree, 82, 129
    Moral Sciences Club, 116
    Section A English (1917), 82 ff
Cambridge Magazine, 80–2
    and network, 88
    quarterly version, 88–9, 95
Clarendon Commission, 27
classical education, 7, 27, 30, 32, 40, 42, 82–3
comprehensive schools, 150, 151
consciousness and signs, 94, 140–1
    and experience, 93, 142
    crystallised ideologies, 143
    'unsystematized' dialogue, 142
Contemporary Cultural Studies
    Birmingham Centre, 158–9
    graduate studies, 180
    limited funding, 181, 184
    shift of focus, 185
    Working Papers, 183
Co-operative movement, 3, 17, 18, 26
    Congress, 21
    Co-operative News, 18
    reading rooms, 56
cultural histories, 1 ff, 209 ff, 211
    breaks, 9
    conflict and difference, 4
    institutional structures, 7–9, 210, 212
    modern media, 9, 210, 212
    networks, 6, 8

democratic agitation (1866–), 13
    radical proposals, 13, 25
    reform of Commons, 5
dialogue and language, 7, 136 ff, 185 ff
    and consciousness, 140–1
    constructing meaning, 191
    dependence on tacit knowledge, 192
    indeterminate meanings, 193
    inner speech as dialogue, 139
    monologue an abstraction, 137
    polyphonic, 202
    re-evaluating new elements, 142–3
    responsive signs, 138
    in science or literary life, 137
    all utterance as response, 137
discourse strategies
    analytical function, 98, 127–8
    appreciative function, 126
    in classroom discussion, 156
    and collaboration, 123
    enumerating types, 68

Subject index

exploratory thinking, 121–2
  in Extension lectures, 48 ff
  and imagery, 53 ff
  and interaction, 53
  levels of abstraction, 162, 165
  'new now organising' speech, 121
  in reading character parts, 41, 49 ff, 57
  signs in oral readings, 120–1
  social constraints, 56 ff

'elite system' in UK (1960)
  class and gender bias, 150
  fee-paying schools, 149, 151
  proportions selected, 149–50
  with selection at 11+, 149
  with 16+ selection, 150
  see higher education

'English'
  see Cambridge, Section A and English Tripos
  see modern subjects
  see Oxford, Language and Literature

English (beyond Language and Literature), 1, 151–2, 167
  and class, ethnicity and religion, 202
  fiction as discussion, 160
  in integrated degrees, 181
  live presentations, 152
  modern media, 152, 154, 156, 182
  narrative as a primary act, 161–2
  and radio news, 168–9
  representations of gender, 179, 201, 202
  and social class, 151
  writing and discussion, 151, 156, 182, 203

English studies and Englishness, 4, 34, 64
  literary internationalism, 153
  see world literature

examinations and 'English'
  alternatives at 16+, 157
  Cambridge Magazine opposition, 89, 124
  Civil Service entry, 4, 61
  early criticisms, 5, 21
  effects on abstraction, 162
  essay questions, 200–1
  London University degrees, 30
  officially condemned, 150
  Oxford honours papers, 64–8
  and practical criticism, 130
  in schools from 1860s, 30
  unreformed at A level, 203–4, 210–12
  including unseen poems, 85

Frost's *It bids pretty fair*, 195

German scholarship, 25, 69

higher education
  advanced technology colleges, 150, 151
  associations to promote, 15, 20, 22, 25, 33
  degrees in education, 150, 154
  early specialisation, 149
  lifelong opportunities, 210
  and a new class, 213
  new universities, 150, 153
  Open University, 150
  polytechnics, 150, 174
  restricted access (1960), 149
  sudden expansion (1960s), 147
Housman's *1887*, 198

International Library, 87, 104

journals, 212
  Cambridge Magazine, 89, 92, 200
  English in Education, 160
  Psyche, 91, 128
  reading and memorising, 31
  Review of English Studies, 131
  short life in 1920s, 131
  specialist journals of 1970s, 183
  Use of English, 159
  Victorian periodicals, 28

language and learning, 156, 191
  and collaboration, 164, 180
  teachers' roles, 156, 164
Lawrence's *Piano*, 115
linguistics
  cognitive processes, 188
  contexts of interaction, 176 ff
  limits to evidence, 190
  Schools Council project, 165
  speech acts, 175
  study of dialogue, 176
  see dialogue and language
literary criticism
  analytical function, 127–8
  appreciative function, 126
  assumptions and categories, 202
  its communication, 98
  concrete not theoretical, 44–5
  distracting influences, 38
  and dynamic experience, 40
  and evaluation, 98–100
  experience of art, 98
  investigative, 29
  new model, 108

of 'poem' not 'text', 40
reflective products, 43
as scientific hypothesis, 38
spectator's response, 37, 46, 160
stock responses, 99, 112–13
see reading investigations
literature and society, 69 ff, 133, 182
    advertising and education, 133
    dominant class interests, 70–1, 73–4
    institutional base, 70 ff
    markets and supply, 74, 133
    mass production, 133
    social attitudes and appeals, 133–4
    under Elizabeth and James, 73
    under Queen Anne, 70–3
    under Walpole, 73–5
    see social production of art
Liverpool University College, 22
    inception, 22–3
    part-time students, 24–5, 41
    University Court, 22, 25
    women's admission, 22
London Society for University Extension, 17
London University
    exam questions, 30
    external degrees, 36
    matriculation, 30

Macbeth: lectures by Bradley, 49 ff
Mass Communications, Leicester Centre, 180, 205
modern subjects, 22
    Applied Sciences, 24
    Experimental Physics, 22, 23
    Geology, 19
    Modern Languages, 23
    Modern Literature, 3, 22, 33, 58
    Modern History, 22, 30, 67–8
    Political Economy, 21, 22, 58
    Production and Distribution of Wealth, 21

narrative
    and evaluations, 190
    inviting discussion, 160
    parents' roles, 190
    as personal and social history 161, 190
    in radio news, 168–9
    tensions within, 201–2
    transforming sense of self, 177
National Association for the Teaching of English, 152, 156, 160
English in Education, 160
    and international seminar, 160
    local anthologies, 200
    London branch (LATE), 155
    teacher-research, 194

Oxbridge in 1867
    annotated literary texts, 29–30
    catechetical teaching, 7
    coaching, 60
    higher degrees and research, 62
    inter-collegiate lecturing, 6
    Local exams, 5, 30
    married fellows, 5
    Pass and Honours degrees, 27, 32, 61
    professor's role, 7
    students, 27, 33
    terms, 16
    tutorial system, 6
Oxford University (1867–96)
    Balliol College, 6, 61
    English Language and Literature degree, 1, 62 ff
    exam papers and questions, 64 ff
    Extension Lectures' Committee, 17
    lectures provided, 63
    results (1896), 63

Perse School, 84
philosophy teaching, 203
public libraries, 21
'public' schools, 27, 60, 149

reading investigations, 103 ff, 144, 187
    active expectancies, 101
    as collaborative exercise, 123
    communication problems, 107–8
    critical readings, 202
    developing discrimination, 117
    a dynamic process, 100 ff
    ideological fieldwork, 111
    institutional shaping, 197, 210
    and interests, 114, 117, 198
    mental goings-on, 109
    preferred readings, 198
    readers' constructions, 195
    referential and emotive signs, 92 ff
    resistant readings, 201
    secondary responses, 196–8
    and self-corrections, 196
    and sentiments, 116
    stress, tempo and pitch, 84
    stressing selected signs, 102
religion in decline, 4, 5, 8
    Bible as Literature, 34

Bradley's unorthodoxy, 33
the Christian myth, 46
the Clapham sect, 46, 53
ideological conflicts, 58, 69
Unitarian Church, Liverpool, 22
see Cambridge, Heretics Club
Robbins Report (1963), 149
Rossetti's 'Gone were but the Winter', 110

Schools Council, England and Wales, 152
curriculum development, 152, 160, 165, 212–13
semiotics and text, 187
signs and interpreters, 92 ff
attitudes and beliefs, 99
context of situation, 94
interpreting experience, 94
provisional models, 95–6
referential and emotive, 94, 96
signs as hints, 140
signs as lower limit, 140
verbal, enactive and iconic, 212
in writing systems, 97
social construction of knowledge, 174
in everyday life, 174
subjective meanings, 174
theoretical categories, 174–5
in university subjects, 4, 174
see dialogue and language
social production of art, 159, 171, 199
access and exclusion, 200
forms and ideologies, 204
institutional frames, 199 ff
schooling in segments, 200
and social experiences, 204
Society for Education in Film and Television, 155, 183
Soviet Union
foreign intervention, 135
revolutionary circles, 135–6
shift to despotic power, 135
the Space Race, 147
structuring of meanings in news
assumptions about society, 169
categories of news, 168
categorising witnesses, 169
institutional structuring, 171
omitting social context, 169–70
student protest of 1960s, 172 ff
against Vietnam War, 172
counter-courses, 173
hidden curriculum, 173
LSE model in UK, 172

media myths, 180
teachers and power, 172

Taunton Commission, 14, 21
television
Centre for Mass Communication, 180
constraints on study, 155, 187
cultural institution, 205
and imperialist penetration, 148
Pilkington Report (1962), 158
UK commercial channel, 158
working practices, 205
texts
as canon, 119, 199, 200, 203
as exam textbooks, 30, 65–7
selected for study, 33
Trades Unions, 6, 26
Congress, 6, 21

Union of Democratic Control, 81
United States in 1960s
and Britain, 147
Civil Rights movement, 148
military-industrial complex, 147
New Math and Science, 147
penetration by media, 148
Project English, 147, 159
Space Race, 147
student resistance, 148–9
Universities and Left Review
clubs and forums, 151
leading speakers from WEA, 151
teachers' network, 151
university colleges, 20
University Extension movement, 2, 3, 7, 15–17
'classes', 2, 40, 48
Co-operative Societies, 15
courses, 5, 15–17, 32–4
expenses, 19, 32
lecture and recital, 31
Leeds, 2, 20, 21
Literature texts, 31, 33–5
Liverpool, 2, 14, 20 ff, 25
local committees, 3, 19
Manchester, 2, 20
Mechanics' Institutes, 2, 15, 17, 56
Midlands, 18, 20
Newcastle, 15, 20
Northeast coalfield, 19, 48
Northern Council, 15, 20
resident lecturers, 20–1
Sheffield, 2, 19, 20
and social class, 16, 18, 19, 21

    syllabus outlines, 37, 41
    in the USA, 31
    Working Men's College, 17
    written work, 15, 21

War Propaganda Bureau, 79, 91
women's movement
    alternative to Oxford, 6
    elementary teachers, 5
    excluded from degrees, 85
    Extension committees, 5
    Extension lectures, 14 ff
    and 'formation', 179
    Girton College, 20
    liberation movements, 176
    new consciousness, 176
    questioning theories, 177
    resident lecturers, 20
    schoolmistress societies, 14
    secondary teachers, 14
    with vote from 1917, 91
    women dons recognised, 129
    women's history, 178
    women's studies, 179, 201
world literature
    evolutionary study, 35
    fixed and floating, 36
    and national cultures, 36
writing theory
    abstraction levels, 165
    assumed interests, 167
    CCCS research on Press, 166 ff
    London Writing Research, 162 ff
    provisional thinking, 164
    reciprocal interaction, 167
    sense of audience, 163–4
    and significant others, 167
    and social relations, 165, 167
    social transaction, 167–8
    teachers' roles, 164–5